DEVELOPMENT CENTRE SEMINARS

D1332714

INVESTING IN ASIA

Edited by
Charles P. Oman, Douglas H. Brooks
and
Colm Foy

DEVELOPMENT CENTRE
OF THE ORGANISATION FOR ECONOMIC CO-OPERATION AND DEVELOPMENT

ORGANISATION FOR ECONOMIC CO-OPERATION AND DEVELOPMENT

Publié en français sous le titre :

INVESTIR EN ASIE

Sous la direction de Charles P. Oman, Douglas H. Brooks et Colm Foy

*

* *

Foreword

This volume contains contributions from participants in the second conference of the International Forum on Asian Perspectives. The conference, entitled "Investing in Asia", was held in Paris on 3 and 4 June 1996, in the context of the Development Centre's research programme on Global Interdependence and as part of its External Co-operation activities. It was jointly organised by the Forum's co-sponsors, the Asian Development Bank and the OECD Development Centre.

Table of Contents

PART TWO:
DYNAMICS AND OPPORTUNITIES

Preface

A remarkable feature of the sustained rapid growth of the dynamic Asian economies is the extent to which it has been financed by domestic savings. Recently, however, foreign investment has increased. This trend can be expected to continue: countries from India to Vietnam are implementing market reforms, and economies throughout the region are turning to foreign investment to help satisfy their growing needs in different areas, ranging from infrastructure to advanced technology.

Investment from within Asia accounts for a growing share of FDI in the region. Nevertheless, the bulk of investment still comes from Japan and the United States. Europe's absolute investment has also grown, but its share has declined.

It is against this background that the OECD Development Centre and the Asian Development Bank decided to focus their joint, annual International Forum on Asian Perspectives on the issue of "Investing in Asia," with particular reference to European investment in the region. This volume presents the results of a two-day meeting on the subject in Paris. It comprised an experts' seminar at OECD Headquarters on 3 June and an open panel discussion on 4 June 1996 at the Pierre Mendès France Conference Centre, graciously placed at our disposal by the French Ministry of Economy and Finance.

The topic was not intended to be restrictive. Indeed, as became clear throughout the 1996 Forum, investment flows are two-way streams. European investment in Asia generates Asian investment in Europe, with benefits accruing to both regions. Discussions centred on this commonality of interest which is not always obvious. For instance, one difficulty for policy makers is to convince their populations that overseas investment is good for the national economy, and can even assist in maintaining employment at home.

Another element is the institutional and regulatory environment for foreign investment. Reform of this environment opens up new opportunities for investment in both directions. Asian economies are currently undertaking reform and creating institutional and legal environments that are more investor-friendly. The proposed Multilateral Agreement on Investment also seeks to promote such an environment, but is looked upon with suspicion by Asian businesses and policy makers.

Consequently, besides new rules, strengthening Europe-Asia relations requires new attitudes conducive to better mutual understanding. Thus, European and Asian businesses must revise the views that they hold of each other. Similarly, analysis does not substantiate the claim of a fundamental cultural divide between Europe and Asia in the sphere of corporate governance.

These are some of the main conclusions from the 1996 Forum on Asian Perspectives brought together in this volume and which European and Asian investors can no longer afford to ignore. We can therefore claim that this publication represents a significant contribution to understanding how ties between Asia and Europe might be strengthened for the benefit of the peoples of both regions.

Jean Bonvin   Mitsuo Sato
President   President
OECD Development Centre   Asian Development Bank

November 1996

Opening Address

*Jean Lemierre**

Co-chairmen, ladies and gentlemen, I am delighted to welcome you on behalf of Mr Arthuis, Minister of the Economy and Finance. Today you will be dealing with an important, difficult and entirely strategic theme, the relationship between Asia and Europe in the sphere of investment. During the recent Bangkok summit, Mr Jacques Chirac, President of France, stressed the need for strengthening the ties of France in particular and Europe in general with Asia. This was an important meeting which emphasized the need for strengthening economic and human links between Europe and Asia. In the domain of investment, the summit of business people which will be held in Paris in October 1996 will surely encourage direct investment between the two economic areas. These remarks are simply to show the great importance and timeliness of the theme being dealt with today.

Why do we consider the theme being dealt with today so important? First, because there is currently high growth in the investment flows of the OECD countries to the countries of Asia and undoubtedly these flows will continue to grow in the medium and long term, but probably they will also tend to balance out and reach an equilibrium. The second reason for assigning importance to today's work is because we think that the growth of mutual direct investment between the two areas should be based on common interests of Asian and OECD countries.

Economic globalisation is a common, convenient and widely used theme with respect to investment flows. It is true that today companies must increasingly deal with markets which are not simply international but global. To do that they cannot just export, but more and more must set up production facilities outside their home territory. Direct investment flows from OECD countries to the rest of the world have

---

*   Opening speech on behalf of the French Minister of the Economy and Finance to the second International Forum on Asian Perspectives.

regularly increased since the beginning of the 1980s. In 1995 they were greater than $250 billion. Annual sales of the OECD countries' companies' subsidiaries located in the rest of the world are greater than the value of total exports of the OECD countries.

There are some developments not widely known in France. During the past ten years, France became the world's fourth ranking destination for foreign direct investment. Conversely, France became the world's fourth largest source of foreign investment. Such facts show that these subjects are much more important to France than 15 years ago.

Asia has of course become an area of high growth and is obviously especially attractive to foreign investors. Two-thirds of the foreign investment in developing countries went to Asia in 1994. China, the leading destination or area of investment, received almost $100 billion in foreign investment during the three last years. The ASEAN countries are attracting more and more investment, and other countries, India in particular, are becoming associated with this trend.

Growth of foreign direct investment involves a long-term process. Of course, it is a cyclical movement extending over some years and its character changes in the course of time. Today this cycle has been completed in some Asian countries and a new equilibrium is developing in countries like Singapore and Korea, whose direct investment in Europe, and especially in France, have greatly increased in recent years.

This highly developed movement of direct investment between Europe and Asia, which should increase in the coming years, can only properly exist if it is based on mutual interest. Direct investment is important for the development of the recipient country for various reasons. It not only is a matter of financial flows, but of technology transfers and also of advances in research and commerce. The outlook of countries concerned by this phenomenon has changed. Some countries are relatively selective about the type of investment, only authorising foreign investment in some sectors. Other countries, whose numbers are increasing, have fairly liberally and openly encouraged the presence of foreign enterprises. This is the trend of the future.

In some countries, this process requires the creation of a clear, unquestionable legal framework to facilitate the establishment of foreign enterprises and investment. It is clear that legal uncertainties lead to uncertainties about taxation. Taxation agreements are decisive for a harmonious investment policy. It is necessary to have reliable laws, strict courts and a correct implementation of laws and taxes that remain stable over time. Of course, the essential idea is that direct investment is based on mutual confidence, not only in economic development but in the development of the institutional and legal framework.

The OECD countries have considerable interest in direct investment. The world is more and more open after several decades of growth in Asia, and Asian markets have become important. We have to learn the specificities of the Asian markets, the technology and how to deal with new difficulties. The development of foreign investment, whether in France or in Asian countries, is a major symbol of a new form of economic co-operation. We consider this economic co-operation a key factor for the development of the world economy.

As foreign investment increases in the world, it is increasingly evident that a framework for common multilateral rules is needed. Such a framework will permit more transparent regulations for multinational enterprises, open national markets to them under better conditions and harmonize the conditions of competition in this domain.

Let us not be mistaken. France is a county that is completely open, entirely subject to the rules of competition for a simple reason which provides a guarantee for everyone, because we belong to the European Union and the development of the European Union is based on the free movement of capital, people and goods, and that will be the basis of our growth and future. As we greatly wish, all these rules and approaches should apply to international trading and financial arrangements, and in this respect a multilateral agreement on investment is being negotiated at the OECD. With the goal of defining ambitious rules by 1997, the agreement will be open to OECD non-Member countries. This is important to us, and France supports the opening of this investment agreement to countries which are OECD non-Members, among which Asian countries are pre-eminent.

The OECD Members decided at their May 1996 ministerial meeting to undertake a closer dialogue with OECD non-Member countries through these negotiations. We hope that Asian countries will confirm their interest in these negotiations and that these negotiations can then be extended to the other countries of the world under the WTO. We attach great importance to the signing of the multilateral agreements, which are indispensable for rapidly growing investment flows. This is one of the great challenges we have to resolve in the coming years. We believe that this development will bring economic and social benefits.

We believe in the development of dialogue on investment, we believe in competition as long as it is harmonious and balanced, and each participant profits. That has been the case in recent years in particular for OECD Members, thanks to the OECD. I believe that one of the great merits of the OECD is that it has been able to promote and oversee balanced relations among OECD Members, even during difficulties. Today we will deal with new stakes and examine new questions.

PART ONE

COMMON INTERESTS

Introduction

Colm Foy

When economists speak of investments, their costs and their benefits, they may sometimes seem to lose sight of the reality on the ground, of the business people who must make strategic investment decisions and of the politicians who must justify investment policies to their populations.

This book is, therefore, in two parts, indicating the desire of the Asian Development Bank and the OECD Development Centre to take into account both technical analyses of the situation and the national political and business contexts.

While overseas investment may have a positive effect on the macroeconomy as a whole, it may be perceived by some sections of the community in the sending countries as having a negative effect on employment and on investment at home. At the same time, reactions in the receiving country to foreign investment also need to be understood and practices adapted accordingly in order to avoid, for example, impressions of interference in national economic policies from abroad.

Europe has participated less in Asian economic development than it might have otherwise done. The concern now is to reverse this trend, to seek the reasons for the decline and to give a new impetus to economic and financial relations between the two regions. Some steps are already under way, particularly at the senior political level, such as the 1996 Bangkok Summit. Business leaders, however, may need their own "summits" through which they, too, might learn to understand each other and to appreciate the complimentarities which exist for them in inter-regional investment.

The primary observation in these pages is, therefore, the perceived communality of interest in European investment in Asia, and Asian investment in Europe. Experience does show that there are mutual benefits. Trade flows between countries and regions do increase in line with investment flows. Willy de Clercq tames the demon concept of relocation, the shifting of employment opportunities from the investor to the receiving countries. He points out that foreign investment is actually a way of producing jobs at home through strengthening local companies and entering into business partnerships with Asian entrepreneurs. Nicolas Imboden reaches much the same conclusion from the point of view of his own country, Switzerland. While the truly multinational companies may be "national" in name only, since their head offices must be geographically located somewhere, Imboden makes a distinction with the smaller and medium-sized enterprises. These national companies are seeking markets and overseas partners which would be difficult to find without investing overseas. Unlike the great multinationals, smaller enterprises require assistance from governments to find partners. What the European Union is doing on a large scale to help European investors extract the best benefits from their investment strategies, as described by Pierre Defraigne and Willy de Clercq, national governments should do to help to create a positive foreign investment climate at home.

French experience bears testimony to the value of such a strategy. The progressive opening up of the French economy has led to large inflows of job-creating foreign investment, but it has also led to outflows of French investment overseas and to the rest of Europe. In the last decade of the 20th century, France has become not only the world's fourth largest recipient of foreign investment, but also the fourth largest source. This evolution has been produced by providing legal guarantees for foreign investors and policies creating the right climate for investor confidence in both directions. Both Jean Lemierre, representing the French Minister of Economy and Finance, and Xavier Musca make this point strongly. The lesson, therefore, again, is the mutuality of interest enjoyed by both sides. Economies which do not welcome foreign investment will not benefit from the job creation which accompanies it.

National imperatives, however, can have an impact on the type of outside investment which can be allowed into a country. While it is true that the world economy is becoming increasingly "globalised", this cannot be an excuse for a planetary economic free-for-all, where national sovereignty and priorities are ignored. This is particularly the case for investment in infrastructure and sensitive economic areas, such as national security and regional development policies. In France, for example, some areas are still not perfectly open for foreign funding. In China, India and Viet Nam, the most potential for large-scale foreign direct investment is probably in infrastructure, where the whole range of political interests — international, national regional and local — must be considered. This point is made by Hugh Barras, who emphasizes the need to take such political considerations into account when making the kind of business calculations necessary for profitability. Yet the extension, renovation and introduction of infrastructure, such as telecommunications, roads and air transport systems, is vital to the development process. Without such facilities, other initiatives in the economy, whether they involve foreign investment or not, will be reduced in their overall effect.

Countries in Asia are recognising this and opening up their strategic economic sectors to foreign capital, providing the legal and institutional framework to make their economies attractive to foreign investors in this area. Thus, China has opened up new sectors of its economy, liberalising formerly restrictive legislation and allowing foreign investors secure access through reform of banking laws, profits-repatriation regulations and administrative structures. At the same time, points out Zhang Xiaoqiang, China is seeking to widen its base of foreign investment to include more diverse sources, including from Europe. Viet Nam shares many of the same concerns as China and is undertaking a thorough restructuring of its economy, as described in the contribution to this book by Tran Xuan Gia. In this case, the increase in the non-agricultural share of the GDP and the acceleration of the divestment process will also require substantial inflows of foreign investment, not all of which can be expected to come from Asian sources. The opportunities for Europe are, thus, quite clear.

The other giant of Asia, India, is slowly undergoing a radical restructuring of its economy, including its opening up to foreign investment. Narayanan Vaghul makes the point explicitly that his country needs so much foreign investment to stimulate reform that sources will be sought all over the world. This is particularly so because domestic sources are stretched. Reform of the financial sector has already permitted access to foreign firms and these will naturally be expected to seek external sources for funding. Like China, India is introducing a regulatory structure to encourage and reassure foreign investors. European investors, therefore, should increasingly find in India the kinds of guarantees which will enable them to participate in that country's accelerated growth and to contribute to it.

Several contributions in the pages that follow refer to the need for infrastructure investment and to its social impact. This social aspect is one which should not be ignored. It is, however, an area in which, as we have seen, profit considerations need to be placed alongside political and social realities. The role of the Asian Development Bank in fostering investment in social-impact projects has been primordial in the region, particularly in the developing countries. Pierre Uhel brings this commitment into relief by stressing the catalyst role of the ADB in identifying projects and acting as an intermediary between financial suppliers and users. It should be remembered that, though growth rates and savings rates in Asia are among the highest in the world, many countries in the region are struggling to emerge from economic stagnation, bringing with it poverty, backwardness and inadequate services for the majority of the people.

If the reasons for investing in Asia from the European point of view and welcoming such investment from the Asian perspective can be clearly identified, a framework of international investment still remains to be defined. This is, essentially, the aim of the Multilateral Agreement on Investment Initiative, launched by the OECD Council of Ministers in May 1995. The aim of the MAI, explains William Witherell's contribution, is not to exclude OECD non-Member economies from international rules on investment. It is, rather, to provide a framework to embrace all investment flows to the benefit of all. The MAI is intended to harmonize the currently diverse investment regimes obtaining in the different countries of the world and thereby to "level the playing field". How this is to be done remains to be defined in the "final free-standing international treaty" which will embody the principles of the MAI. This process is not intended to exclude the World Trade Organisation's forums, but will be carried on in concert with the WTO.

It is important to note that the MAI will not be a substitute for regional initiatives towards free trade and investment flows, and the co-operation within APEC, described by Ippei Yamazawa, will retain its importance. Indeed, regional understandings, such as that embodied within APEC are the building blocks of wider international concertation. The specificities of APEC to the region and its function as a focal point for consultation with other parts of the world, including Europe, are likely to ensure its continued central role.

The possibility thus exists for the first time that an internationally accepted and defined set of rules will apply to foreign investment. The effect of this will be to stimulate investment flows and to contribute to the liberalisation of the world economy in general. In this climate, the opportunities for European investment in Asia and for Asian investment in Europe will naturally tend to grow. Whether these opportunities are taken up, however, depends in part on a reform of European attitudes towards Asia.

For many investors, cultural differences between Europe and Asia are perplexing. Many of the views which Europeans have of Asia, however, are outdated. Supachai Panitchpakdi points out that business in Asia is now less regulated by informal relationships than in the past and that these relationships are being replaced by legal structures which would be recognisable to any European firm. On the other hand, Asians may see Europe as a continent closing in on itself through greater integration within the European Union. A consequence of this, says Jean Bonvin, is that Asian investors may imagine that their investment in Europe will be limited by European Union protectionist rules. In reality, the legal situation is just the opposite.

The habit European companies have of concentrating on exports to and imports from Asia, rather than on the opportunities due to proximity through foreign investment in the region, hampers European penetration into Asian markets. The problem is largely one of perception; European investment in Asia lags behind that of other regions, notably the United States, because the misconceptions have taken longer on the "Old Continent" to dissipate. In the same way, public concerns about market saturation from cheap Asian goods and job losses due to relocation are just as real as they are ill-founded. It behoves Europe's leaders on both the Union and national levels to contribute to a better understanding of the realities.

The contributions in this volume from specialists in so many different fields, countries and organisations describe the challenges in particularly potent ways. They demonstrate that the "Asian challenge" is not to resist Asian economic growth and development, but to contribute to it. The peoples of both sides stand to benefit from participation in the mutual rewards.

The Context for Investment in Asia

Jean Bonvin

The subject of this year's Forum, "Investing in Asia" may appear commonplace because everyone is familiar with the extraordinary dynamism of the Asian economies, and at the OECD we often consider how to strengthen the relationships between enterprises of Member countries and those of other countries.

However, this subject is far from being banal, for this Forum is concerned with business relationships between Asia and Europe, which are not as close as they could or should be. We are meeting today to understand why this is so and to try to find a remedy.

Of course, the primary actors are executives of enterprises whose daily decisions determine the business relationships between Asia and Europe. However, we cannot assign to them the entire responsibility for developing ties between our two regions, because it is clear that governments and the European Union in Brussels also play a role and their decisions are fundamental for European-Asian relations.

These governments are subject to the influence of pressure groups and they have to take into account the fears and wishes of the peoples they lead. Thus public opinion on this subject, which is particularly sensitive in Europe, cannot be neglected. Although governments have to take this into account, they are also the only actors who are able to change public opinion and make people understand that we can all benefit from more rapid development of relations between Asia and Europe.

This is a political challenge for our leaders, because they alone, and not technocrats, can influence public opinion by showing everyone the advantages for the two regions of closer economic and financial ties, and by the same token, all the advantages they will lose if these ties are not strengthened in the coming years.

This may appear to be easy to say, since history has proven that the strengthening of ties between Europe and North America has contributed to growth on both sides of the Atlantic. For the past 30 years, the same process involving Southeast Asia and the United States, especially California, has had the same effects. However, in reality Europe's present problems make this discourse difficult. High unemployment rates have persisted for some years and major structural changes have led to the virtual disappearance of some occupations. These developments have given rise to a deep sense of insecurity and, consequently, to fear, and even to a total rejection of any change.

In such a context, many Europeans consider the dynamism and increasing competitiveness of Asian enterprises and economies as a threat to employment and their standard of living, rather than as a means for developing some sectors and helping them solve their problems. Of course, European exporters know what their companies owe to the conquest of new markets in Asia, and statisticians can try to allay the pessimism by drawing attention to the small share of imported Asian products on many of our markets, but that will not be enough to reassure public opinion destabilized by unemployment.

Asians, for their part, may misunderstand European integration, seeing it as having a protectionist orientation, and therefore conclude that the possibilities of developing closer relationships with Europe are rather limited. To be sure, the growth of Asian exports to Europe, or the customs policy of the European Union, makes such scepticism groundless, but such unjustified fears can hamper the development of closer relations.

As can be seen, there are real problems of perception, or misperceptions, in the relationship between our two regions and it will be useful to consider together how to help our leaders understand these problems better, for making their public opinion understand the advantages of developing relationships between European and Asian enterprises.

Why did we choose the theme of investment? For two reasons, one technical and the other political, namely the lag of European investment in Asia.

The technical reason is the key role increasing played by investment. Of course, trade still retains its importance, but by investing in an Asian country an enterprise makes a long-term commitment and really strengthens the economic ties between our two regions. Moreover, experience shows that such investment tends to increase trade between our two regions, not reduce it.

On the other hand, in the present context of globalisation, a firm's proximity to its customers, that is, to the local, national or regional market, and proximity to its suppliers, are increasingly important. That means that if European firms and economies want to contribute to and benefit from Asian economic growth, they must invest more there and strengthen their presence and economic weight.

The European lag in Asia is self-evident. Indeed, the developing Asian countries became the leading destination for foreign direct investment (FDI) flows to developing countries after having overtaken Latin America in the 1980s.

Since then the growth of these flows has accelerated. The stock of FDI in Asia doubled in the seven years from 1988 to 1995 and the value of FDI flows increased from $32 billion in 1992 to $60 billion in 1994, and to an estimated $104 billion in 1995. This amount represents more than half the total investment flows to developing countries.

Half of these investment flows come from the OECD countries. Europe has the smallest share, and its share has decreased in recent years in China and the ASEAN countries. So there is a real problem of European underinvestment in Asia.

A study on "The European Union's Direct Investment in Asia", (*Investing in Asia's Dynamism: European Union Direct Investment in Asia*) prepared by the European Commission and the UN Conference on Trade and Development, suggested several reasons which could explain the lag of European investment in Asia.

The first reason is that the construction of a single market — the deepening of European integration — has attracted foreign investment into Europe both from within and outside the Union, in particular during the second half of the 1980s. The same reasoning applies to the expansion of the Union and also the vast changes in Central and Eastern Europe.

All these changes diverted attention from the opportunities for European investment in Asia, even though the opportunities have grown with the creation of new free trade zones in China, and especially by liberalisation policies towards foreign direct investment in Asia. There has also been considerable deregulation and an increase in privatisations.

Moreover, according to the study, it appears that many European companies underestimated the growth potential of the dynamic Asian economies, especially in the first stages of growth. That error is explained in part by the exceptional performance of these economies.

Furthermore, it also appears that many European companies retained an outmoded view of the situation in Asia. They did not perceive, or at least had not registered, that apart from Hong Kong and Singapore, many countries had relaxed the traditional restrictive practices which formerly had been in effect.

Finally, the study concluded that the lag of European investment in Asia stems from the fact that "In general, European enterprises are more concerned with their direct exports than with opening trade offices and developing large sales networks. This has often handicapped them in investment and trade".

Today, however, there are many reasons why things will change. As we have heard from Mr Lemierre, at the March 1996 Bangkok conference of European and Asian heads of state, governments expressed their determination at the highest level to do everything possible to strengthen relations between the two regions.

In Europe, there are efforts to make it better known that increased trade with Asia and investment in Asia can be mutually beneficial, and an ambitious project has been launched to resolve the problems that can hamper investment.

In Asia, the regulatory framework is becoming more and more liberal and thus increasingly favourable to private activity, while governments are doing more and more to promote foreign direct investment.

The purpose of our conference is to indicate what can and should be done. Since this Forum is entitled "Investing in Asia", it is expected that most remarks deal with problems and prospects of European investment in Asia. However, some papers raise the question of Asian investment in Europe. For we should never forget that strengthening relationships between our two regions is a two-way street for the benefit of everyone concerned.

The Asian Development Bank and Investment in Asia

Pierre Uhel

Last year the OECD Development Centre and the Asian Development Bank organised the first International Forum on Asian Perspectives. This forum helped to enhance economic integration between developing countries and members of the OECD. We chose today's topic, "Investing in Asia", to increase economic integration and our understanding of factors that affect it. As a financing and technical assistance institution, the Asian Development Bank is actively involved in investing in Asia. The Bank finances and co-finances investment, and increasingly helps to develop financial institutions and capital markets. The Bank also increasingly helps private enterprises invest in developing member countries, through its co-financing window. Thus the Bank is playing a catalytic role in encouraging investment in Asia.

Asia and the Pacific constitute the most dynamic economic region in the world. From this point of view it is probably the centre of the world, not in absolute terms, but with respect to trends. The rapid development in Asia in recent decades has created enormous trade and investment. The figures are impressive: Asian exports to the European Union amounted to $92 billion in 1994. Conversely, imports from Europe amounted to $97 billion. Both figures are roughly four times their 1985 levels. Moreover, from 1987 to 1994 the net inflow of capital into Asia grew from $17 billion to $109 billion, more than a six-fold increase.

As we have seen, however, these impressive figures conceal disparities in investment flows to Asia and we find that Europe is lagging behind. As a rule, European investment in Asia should and could increase further.

Despite the general improvement in the Asian economies, problems still persist. Asia contains more than half of the world's poor. Disease, impure water, poor sanitation, persistent malnutrition and illiteracy remain common. Urban congestion and pollution are growing. The Central Asian Republics are just beginning to recover from the economic shock caused by the collapse of the former Soviet Union. Economic stagnation persists in many of the Pacific island countries. To overcome these problems and secure sustainable growth into the next century, the region will have to address its huge capital requirements. Growth is impressive, but its sustainability is not at this stage assured. Investment in physical and social infrastructure are essential for sustainable development. It is estimated that the region will require an investment of about one trillion US dollars for physical infrastructure alone during the rest of this decade.

Asia is in some ways unique compared to other continents; it is characterised by a higher level of savings and, as a consequence, by higher levels of domestic investment. Thus Asians have been able to finance much of these huge investment needs. However, it is obvious that Asia alone, in spite of all its dynamism, for the time being, is unable to satisfy all of its needs. Consequently, the mobilisation of capital and technology will be crucial.

Europe has much to offer Asia in capital growth, financial services and technology, and Europe could expect to benefit from Asian prosperity and trade. Europe has everything to gain from a healthy, prosperous, peaceful Asia.

The Asian Development Bank was founded in 1966 to promote economic and social development in Asia. Most European countries were founding members of the Bank. The ADB now has 58 members of which 14 are European countries. As the attractiveness of Asia is becoming clear, more and more countries want to join from other continents, from Latin America, for example, but also from the former Soviet Union. Since its inception, the Bank has provided more than $50 billion in project and technical assistance to its developing member countries. Much of this assistance is financing for infrastructure projects. More recently we have increased the amounts for social-sector projects. These projects are directly aimed at reducing poverty, improving the status of women, accelerating human development and sustaining environmental management: they are the prerequirements for sustainable growth in Asia.

As an intermediary between suppliers and users of financial services, the Asian Development Bank's strength lies in its knowledge of the region. The Bank relies on its financial and human resources, its extensive development experience and its credibility within the region. The Bank is eager to expand and improve its role as a catalyst for investment in Asia. Asia is changing so rapidly that Asian economies have changed more in one or two decades than in other centuries. It is probably an exceptional phenomenon in history. The industrial revolution in Europe was probably less rapid. Perhaps the only case which could compare to Asia is that of Germany in the 19th century, but even in Germany the period of growth, of take-off, took longer than in Asia.

There are still enormous challenges in Asia. Asia needs resources, technology and knowledge to invest in business, infrastructure and civil society. From this point of view, the OECD countries, especially European countries, have a lot to offer. At the same time, Europe can benefit from high growth and rapid expansion of business in Asia.

Perspectives for European Investment in Asia

Supachai Panitchpakdi

What are the real perspectives for European investment in Asia? Is it already too late because Asian markets are now being flooded with all kinds of investment from the United States, Japan, or Korea? Is it too late for European firms to enter Asian markets? Considering the ongoing sustainable high rate of economic growth in Asia, some 6 to 8 per cent per annum, compared with 2 to 3 per cent in Europe, the possibility that profits that could be earned from participation in Asian markets could be highly significant in the future.

It is therefore quite ironic that there seem to be difficulties in strengthening economic relationships between Europe and Asia. To cite some statistics for information: between 1985 and 1994, a ten-year span of time, intra-Asian trade, trade within Asia, surprisingly increased from 25.6 per cent to 40 per cent of total Asian trade. Thus Asian nations are trading much more with one another, and, of course investment goes with trade. Statistics for trade with the OECD countries show a significant drop during the same period from 53.5 to 44.26 per cent, so, while trade among Asian countries has been increasing, trade between Asia and the OECD countries to the contrary has been declining. Around 12 per cent of total Asian trade is with Europe, about the same level as for the past decade. How can this trend be explained?

There are three major reasons for this. The first reason could be the economic slowdown in Europe, leading to preoccupations with parochial issues: the single European market, the EMU, eastern Europe and so on. There could be a reduction in the net surplus of funds that Europe could invest elsewhere. The remedy is to find an alternative use of funds that would create larger, higher returns. Instead of allocating them to places where the returns are smaller and lower, they could be invested in Asia where the returns could be guaranteed at a high level. Evidence for this is the recent emergence of trust funds, investment funds and country funds that are managed by European financial institutions. Moreover, expansion of the European presence in Asia could be a remedy for the recessionary trend in Europe.

Secondly, the deep perceived differences in the pattern of corporate governance between European systems — more legalistic, more based on a logical framework — and Asian ones based on informal relationships may be dissuasive to Europeans. This, however, would be a misunderstanding of the crux of the issue. The various patterns of corporate governance in both Europe and Asia are in transition and are changing. The world is changing because of trends towards globalisation and the new trading regime fostered by the World Trade Organisation. Thus patterns of corporate governance will tend to converge. Though it is sometimes said that corporate governance in Asia is predominately influenced by personal relationships and connections, the reality is not very much different from the modern Western concepts of networking and strategic alliances. These business-school concepts are in fact what Asians have always practised.

The third reason why European corporations might hesitate to do business in Asia is that investment in Asia tends to be overregulated and is sometimes burdened with many types of restrictions. However, in spite of the fact that joint ventures have been preferred in Asia, wholly owned foreign enterprises are quickly becoming an acceptable alternative for various Asian governments. As for the Thai government, we have set our sights on the full liberalisation of foreign investment in Thailand, eliminating all sorts of preconditions and restrictions on foreign investment. This is also the case in other Asian contexts. Biases against foreign enterprises are being eliminated as more businesses formerly deemed suitable only for indigenous corporations are being opened up. For example, electricity generation and power — which is a high growth area in Asia — telecommunications, shipping, insurance and water supply are just a few areas opening up to foreign investment. Rapid relaxation of controls on inward foreign direct investment have several dimensions, for example, greater rights of establishment for foreign investors through relaxation of approval procedures. Everything has been simplified and even the time frame has been reduced.

We are witnessing more complete application of national treatment through removal of performance requirements on foreign corporations. This used to be highly burdensome for foreign investors who were required to export a large proportion of their products, but all these performance requirements have now been eliminated. Reductions in administrative controls on capital and factor income movement are being implemented so that capital movements which had to be registered, controlled and reported in the past, are now being liberalised. Regulatory reform in Asia not only means deregulation and liberalisation of investment practices, but it also sometimes means that new regulations are needed, in particular concerning the protection of intellectual property rights.

All these points make it clear that European investors should not feel at a disadvantage when investing in Asia. Indeed, perspectives for investing in Asia are getting brighter and brighter. First, Asian countries are seeking ways to climb up the product cycle ladder, for which they need and have to encourage high technology-based investment. Encouraging investment that brings advanced technology is crucial for Asia. Secondly, there will be no deceleration of investment in infrastructure in Asia, in particular because of the privatisation of the power and communications sectors.

Thirdly, liberalisation in trade and investment is being pursued not only at the national level but also at the regional and also at the international levels. At the national level, various countries in Asia are doing more than they have committed themselves to in the Uruguay Round. For example, the ASEAN countries have set their sights on accelerating the speed of tariff reduction. At the regional level, the ASEAN free trade area is proceeding at a faster rate than in the past. At the international level, the Asia-Pacific Economic Co-operation is trying to accelerate implementation of the Uruguay Round commitments and to go ahead with full trade liberalisation without being committed to the World Trade Organisation negotiations at all.

Fourthly, the Asia-Europe meeting, the ASEM, is taking on a life of its own. In 1998, Britain will play host to this summit between Europe and Asia, which is fine on the political level, but what is more important is that a business council, the Asia-Europe Business Council, is being established. This will mean that at the corporate level, there will be exchanges of ideas, issues and complaints on a more regular basis for relay to the national level. This represents a great improvement.

Fifthly, ASEAN will soon increase its membership so that, in three years time, the ASEAN seven will become ten with the addition of Lao PDR, Cambodia and Myanmar. Political questions about Myanmar are for the political leaders, but that country has been urged to consider serious democratisation before being accepted as a member of ASEAN.

Finally, there is no reason to believe that stability and growth will not be sustainable in the ASEAN group. Of course, some economies in Asia are subject to a tendency to overheat, but the level of overheating is now under control and, considering the substantial level of international reserves in most Asian countries, particularly the most advanced ones, where there are high saving ratios and strong export performances, a Mexican-type crisis is highly unlikely in Asia.

If all is so well in Asia, why are we asking for investment from Europe? The answer is that Asia and Europe need each other and, because of their complementarities, can create more added value and more benefits for one another.

Asia: A Challenge Europe Can Win

Willy de Clercq

A few points need to be taken into consideration in a discussion of the relationship between European investment and Asia. First, Asia is a challenge which should not give rise to fears but to encouragement and incentive for winning it. Second, we have been completely overtaken in Asia by our immediate competitors, Japan and the United States. Third, despite all the uncertainties, fear is a poor advisor, and despite these fears, hesitations and even opposition due to relocations which, it is said, automatically causes the disappearance of production units and growth of unemployment — as we have already have 20 million, that is enough — despite all that, our direct investment should be promoted and not halted or decreased. The European Union, as such, has adopted some measures for that. If these measures are not enough, what should be done in addition?

First point. Today, we in Europe too often consider Asia as a continent flooding our countries with cheap toys, cheap electronic goods and cheap cars. This attitude is wrong. Asia should not be considered by the European Union and our industrialists as a threat. On the contrary, we must consider the Asian continent and its market as a challenge, a challenge we can win. We all know that the domestic Asian market is enormous. More than half the world's population lives in Asia which is thus an enormous pool of consumers. According to the World Bank, by the year 2000, one billion Asian people will have considerable purchasing power and, of that billion, 400 million of them, which is more than the total population of the whole European Union, will have incomes which are as high as, if not higher than, their contemporaries in Europe or the United States. These are the facts. Thus the huge Asian market presents the European Union, with its 20 million unemployed people with enormous prospects, not least for new jobs, but the harsh reality is that at present the European Union is being overtaken, overtaken in the fastest growing part of the world by Japan and the United States. Not only is the Union's share of exports in East and Southeast Asia lower than that of Japan and the United States, even more important in the long run, the EU's share in foreign direct investment has fallen sharply. Between 1960 and 1992, only 10 per cent of the FDI came from Europe. FDI must not necessarily be regarded as relocating from high-wage countries to low-wage countries, with higher unemployment rates in our countries as a result, though this is a powerful political argument used against investment outside the European community.

First of all, relocating is a highly complex concept which covers several situations. There are different types of relocations. There is a brutal relocation, in the strict sense of the word, the relocation which simply results in the disappearance of factories or of services in Europe with a decline in employment opportunities. We find that mainly in the textile sector where, of course, labour costs are 20 per cent of total costs. However, fortunately, that is only 8 per cent of foreign direct investment. On the other hand, to simplify, there are two other forms of relocation. There is a relocation with expansion, retaining what exists at home while adding new production units abroad. These units are sometimes indispensable for maintaining current facilities in the EU, in Asia, Latin America, or in Eastern and Central Europe, the third major region in full expansion. Finally, there is a relocation with diversification where new products, production units or services are created, complementing what exists in the countries of the European Union. While the first type of relocation naturally is negative and prejudicial, it is fortunately very limited, something which is always forgotten by the naysayers. The two other forms of relocation, make penetration of foreign markets more efficient and constant, and are positive and contribute to growth for the future of employment in Europe.

Thus the importance of FDI in Asia is not threatened by the relocation effects if we consider the real significance and importance of those phenomena. FDI should be promoted and not restrained. Most European politicians and entrepreneurs still do not sufficiently understand the economic importance of European FDI in Asia, just as they have underestimated Asia as a whole. The European Union has already adopted some measures, concluding a number of commercial and co-operation agreements with various countries in Asia, and on 14 July 1994 the European Commission submitted an excellent document, *Towards a New Asia Strategy* to the European Council. Furthermore, as we all know, for the first time a Europe-Asia meeting of heads of governments took place on 1 and 2 March 1996 in Bangkok to strengthen the overall relationship between the two regions. Many people feel that those are good intentions, good meetings and good works but would like to see more action.

Now the European Union is acting, and here are only two examples of many. First, there is the European Community Investment Partners (ECIP), whose objective is to encourage FDI by small and medium-sized European Union firms not only in countries throughout Asia, but also in Latin America, in the Mediterranean area and in South Africa. The European Community Investment Partners promotes the establishment of joint ventures. It is an important and relatively successful initiative. Second, the European Union is involved in a number of managerial training programmes in Asia. It has helped to establish and continues to sponsor the China-Europe International Business School in Shanghai. It has also links with the ASEAN Institute of Technology in Thailand, and the European-Asia Invest programme is planning information seminars for business people in Asia. So there are two examples out of many. We can only approve of them, while also admitting that they are absolutely insufficient. European FDI is still lagging behind in Asia compared to that from Japan and the United States.

What can be done? First, let us be clear with our European entrepreneurs. While government policies can contribute to gaining a significant European Union investment and trade presence in Asia, it is evident that the main thrust must come from business itself. The government cannot act on behalf of the European entrepreneurs. A government is not a trader or an industrialist, nor should it be. Second, there should be greater co-ordination between measures undertaken by the European Union and by individual member states, given the resource constraints at both levels. Third, one of the most important, if not the most important, aspects of the transformation taking place in Asia is that, for the first time, a major world region outside Europe or an area of European settlement is reaching sustainable growth. This is a new phenomenon in recent world history. This implies that a major problem for very many European businesses, in particular small businesses, is ignorance of, and hence the fear of Asian culture and Asian ways. Here, precisely, an extremely important role exists for the European Union. It should be noted in this context that the European Union has achieved considerable success with its Executive Training Programme(ETP) in Japan, whereby young businessmen can spend 18 months in that country in order to learn the language and acquire business experience on the spot, while obtaining an introduction to the Japanese way of life.

In 1994, the European Union's trade deficit with Japan fell by 17 per cent while during the same period the deficit with the United States increased by almost 45 per cent. Furthermore in 1991, the EU trade deficit with Japan was 85 per cent of the US deficit with Japan. Two years later, in 1993, the figure had been cut back to barely 49 per cent, which is still tremendous but nonetheless an improvement. Of course, this improvement is not due uniquely to the European training programme but nevertheless at least a major part of the relatively favourable figures are due to the success of such a programme which makes people aware of the real situation, helps them to understand what is happening, and helps them to speak and understand the language of the people with whom we want to deal, which for some Europeans seems still almost an impossible challenge.

With the successful outcome of our programme in Japan, this sort of programme should be expanded throughout the whole Asian continent. Our young people, too, should have greater opportunities to learn Asian languages and to learn about Asian culture. This should be done, if possible, from the secondary level onwards. We have to abandon our feelings of supremacy, thinking that the rest of the world has to speak our language, accept our culture and accept our ways.

The Minister of Finance of Thailand is a kind man, for he says we need Europe. Yes, everyone needs everyone, but which of us knows the other best? The Asians, whose internal trade has grown tremendously into a tremendous market for consumer goods and infrastructure, or the Europeans? Who needs the other more? Of course, we all need each other. Consider the following fact concerning the presence of Asian students in European and American universities: there are 60 000 Chinese students in the United States and, 6 000 Chinese students in Europe. Those figures need to be improved on our side. We all know that there are difficulties, that doing business in Asia is more difficult than doing business in the United States or in Central and Eastern Europe. The difficulties are there for politicians to solve, not for them to complain about. We should not be afraid of Asia. We should regard Asian markets as a great challenge that we can win. In order to do so, however, we best set our own house in order, and today rather than tomorrow.

Financing Reform in Viet Nam

Tran Xuan Gia

Over the past decade, Viet Nam has pursued a policy of economic reform. During that time our country has made important achievements that have been recognised both in my own country and worldwide. During the next five years, Viet Nam will continue with its open-door policy to industrialise and to modernise the country, and step by step to narrow the development gap between Viet Nam and other countries in Southeast Asia and the rest of the world.

According to our forecasts, for the period 1996-2000, Viet Nam will continue to develop agriculture, forestry and fisheries at an annual growth rate of between 4.5 and 5 per cent. In doing this, we will ensure sufficient food for our people and increase our capacity for providing the raw materials needed for processing industries and for exports. We will also pay a great deal of attention to reforming the economic structure of rural areas where 80 per cent of our people live with a rather low standard of living.

In the industrial sector, we will develop small and medium-sized industries to create employment. These industries will also contribute more and more to the national economy. We will also develop certain heavy industries, such as oil and gas, manufacturing and electronics so that one day they can expand overseas. It is estimated that the average annual industrial growth rate during the 1996-2000 period will be 14 to 15 per cent. Service and newly established industries such as tourism, banking, and insurance will grow with the rest of the economy. With this economic development policy, Viet Nam could have an average annual GDP growth rate of 9 to 10 per cent. Per capita GDP by the year 2000 could be double that of 1990. So by the end of the century, Viet Nam will still be a poor country but the general living conditions of its people will be greatly improved.

In order to achieve our goals, the Government of Viet Nam intends to develop the economy at the same time as changing the general economic structure. The agricultural sector's contribution to the GDP, for example, will account for less than 20 per cent by the year 2000. Together with the development of the economic triangles in the North, the Centre and the South of the country, the government will also give much attention to general socio-economic development programmes in order to minimise uneven development between different regions. The government will continue to speed up the implementation of its reform policy in order to increase the wealth of our people, increase the strength of our nation and achieve greater equality within our society.

Thanks to the high economic growth rate, the domestic savings rate has grown from zero during the 1980s to 20 per cent of GDP in 1995. This has helped to meet the need for domestic investment, and has provided the necessary conditions for attracting foreign investment, including ODA, FDI and commercial loans. This has also created conditions for developing and diversifying the local economy with different forms of ownership. Viet Nam highly appreciates the ODA that we have received from foreign countries and international organisations, particularly from OECD Member countries, and international financial institutions such as the Asian Development Bank and the World Bank. The reform process has allowed Viet Nam to attract more ODA funds and to use them more effectively, helping us to improve our socio-economic infrastructure, to develop science and technology, and to make better use of our labour resources in order to speed the country through the industrialisation and modernisation process. At the same time, Viet Nam has increased its capacity to repay debts to other countries and international organisations. Approved private foreign direct investment in Viet Nam so far stands at more than $20 billion, of which $6 billion has been realised. This is a very important capital source that has contributed greatly to the economy's development and the country's export capacity. Foreign investment has also helped bring advanced and high technology into the country.

Viet Nam is now a member of ASEAN and is participating in AFTA — the ASEAN Free Trade Area — all in an effort to improve the investment environment and increase our export capability — a very urgent task for us. The Government of Viet Nam is currently streamlining the Foreign Investment Law and related legal instruments in order to make the investment environment more attractive to foreign investors. The government will be implementing a number of measures to encourage investment from all domestic and foreign economic sources.

The private and co-operative sectors have been encouraged strongly, enjoying equal conditions to participate actively in the economy. The Domestic Investment Law has been promulgated to encourage investment from all economic sectors. The non-state sector currently contributes 60 per cent of the national GDP. In agriculture, the non-state sector accounts for 98 per cent. In commercial and service industries, the non-state sector also plays a very important role. In the industrial sector, even though its share of the GDP is smaller, the non-state sector accounts for a large share of small and medium-sized industries, creating many jobs.

State-owned enterprises contribute 40 per cent of GDP. The Government of Viet Nam is in the process of reforming this sector to make it work more efficiently. The number of state-owned enterprises has been reduced from 12 000 a few years ago to 6 000 today. Of these, some 2 000 are under the management of the central government. Twenty general corporations, state-managed companies that control the resources of a number of enterprises in key industries, such as oil and steel, have been established to co-operate with local and foreign private investors. These general corporations control important sectors of the economy to ensure the stable development of essential public utilities, the socio-economic infrastructure and some key industrial sectors.

Our government is implementing different forms of equitisation of state-owned enterprises to increase their efficiency. During the implementation of its renovation policy Viet Nam has paid much attention to developing a complete legal system based on the 1992 Constitution. Since then, we have promulgated a great number of laws including the Civil Law, Company Law, Foreign Investment Law, Land Law, Labour Law, Environmental Protection Law, etc.

We are also conducting general administrative reforms and developing personnel training. We have implemented a number of measures to increase the people's cultural standards and to develop our human resources.

During the implementation of our reform policies, we have received considerable assistance from many countries and international organisations, including the Asian Development Bank and OECD Member countries. I would like to take this opportunity to thank them all for their support, and we hope that our future co-operation will be strengthened and further developed for the mutual benefit of all sides.

The Benefits of Outward Investment

Xavier Musca

In the aftermath of World War II, Keynesian ideas and the war economy were deeply imprinted in the reigning economic philosophy in our country, as in most other western countries. That was the context for understanding the French planning experience, which was based on two original ideas that are still retained: first, flexible, nonconstraining planning for the private sector, and, second, a dialogue and consensus between social partners is the basis for this planning. The government then tried to influence productive investment in our country in part through the financial market which was formerly highly segmented, and also by investments of the large public enterprises. These nationalised firms weighed heavily in the French economy until the end of the 1970s through large investment and infrastructure programmes, which obviously had a macroeconomic significance, especially in the nuclear domain and in telecommunications. It is clear that under those circumstances foreign investment was not a central concern of the government and, again, this was not a unique situation but one common to most European countries, even most western countries, despite the specific French characteristics, its preoccupation with national independence, which at times gave the French experience its own particular accent.

The building of the European Community worked deep changes in this outlook and practice by liberalising trade and capital movements between member states. In 1990, investment from countries of the European Union was completely liberalised. In 1992, this was extended to investment from the European Economic Area. The European Union Treaty provided for completely free movement of capital within the European Union and between the European Union other states as of 1 January 1994. It should be noted that France recognises that a European treaty takes precedence over domestic law. Thus we accepted free movement of capital as a quasi-constitutional principle. That is a major point, namely that Europe, and therefore France, is open to capital from other countries. This is at the apex of our legal framework. Of course, free movement of capital and freedom to invest are not exactly the same, but nonetheless they are closely linked.

The last stage of this liberalisation in a way recognised a former de facto situation. In April 1996, the government definitively abolished the system of prior autorisations for all investment coming from other countries, that is to say, from all states outside the European Economic Area. Thus prior administrative authorisation is no longer required. There are a few exceptions to this general rule applying to national defence, public security and public health, which are clearly defined. Moreover, the procedures retained in these domains are very liberal, since authorisation is considered granted if the French administration does not express its disapproval by the end of a month.

The effects of the liberalisation of our foreign investment have been highly positive. The contribution of foreign direct investment to the gross domestic product doubled from 1985 to 1994, increasing from 0.4 to 0.8 per cent. The contribution of foreign direct investment to gross fixed capital formation quadrupled during the same period, from 2 to 8 per cent. The outstanding debt in France of foreign-controlled enterprises was 20 billion francs at the end of 1995. France is fourth largest host of foreign direct investment after the United States, Britain and China. Thus among the OECD countries we rank third, a rather good performance. Finally, a third of the capitalisation of the Paris Bourse is held by non-residents. France wants to continue to increase this economic internationalisation, and the officials of the Bourse are making major efforts to promote French stocks abroad. You also know that under the privatisation programme now being carried out by France a large proportion of the shares are offered to foreign investors, and especially in some privatisations such as that of Pechiney, de facto an extremely high percentage of the shares are held by non-residents, unfortunately not enough by residents of Asian countries, but more frequently by non-resident Europeans and US residents.

What are the lessons of this experience? Caution is necessary. It is clear that the French example cannot be transposed, as such, to emerging countries. It is also clear that the situation of different Asian countries varies considerably, and it not possible to draw conclusions that are too precise or definitive from the French experience alone. However, when this experience is studied carefully and considered at the same time as the experience of Asian countries, and examples elsewhere like in Latin America which have also liberalised foreign investment, some broad general conclusions emerge.

The first lesson is that liberalisation of capital movements and investment is the logicical consequence liberalisation of trade in goods and services. It is clear that as soon as customs barriers and obstacles to trade are removed, it is in a country's interest to try to get the manufacturer who produces for the area to be located on its territory. In this respect, the development of the European Union is very instructive. We have just experienced at the global level an extremely important cycle of trade liberalisation with the successful conclusion of the Uruguay Round. It is necessary to follow that up and extend liberalisation by taking investment into account and treating it at the same global level. The OECD ministerial conference, called for discussions under the WTO on the links between trade and investment. France fully supports that idea and hopes that such discussions lead rapidly to real negotiations under the WTO and to a WTO agreement on investment.

The second lesson is that liberalisation of investment is an important factor for regional integration. It is clear that investment by European countries in other European countries has greatly contributed to the development of a European identity. The experience of Airbus and GEC Alsthom, show that these bi- or multinational firms make a large contribution to the emergence of a European unity and political will. Similar, but perhaps less sweeping conclusions can be drawn from Southeast Asia. A non-negligible share of the investment in China, Indonesia or Malaysia comes from neighbouring countries, and there, too, contributes to the emergence of a strong regional identity. The European and French examples could be considered by Asian countries, especially the Southeast Asian countries which are seeking new forms of regional co-operation.

The third lesson is that foreign investment brings growth and employment, and permits the transfer of technology, and even more than simple trade liberalisation, it is a major factor in wealth creation and economic progress.

The fourth lesson is not drawn from the French example, in any case not from recent experience. It is that foreign investment is a sound way to finance the balance of payments. When one looks at developments in Asia and Latin America in recent years, it can be seen that direct investment is an important factor in economic security. In this respect, it useful to recall that in France and some other countries there were fears that foreign investment threatened national independence. To the contrary, because foreign investment is a sound way of financing the balance of payments, it is fundamentally a factor of stability and consequently enables independent policies to be followed.

Look at what happened in Asia and Latin America. In Latin America foreign flows increased from $10 billion to $15 billion between 1990 and 1995. During the same period, there was a five-fold increase in FDI flows to Asia, from $10 billion in 1990 to $50 billion in 1995. That was a successful strategy for financing the balance of payments. Direct investment in Asia complemented market financing and was not a substitute. Direct investment's share in capital movements remained stable, going from 54 to 50 per cent between 1990 and 1995, while in Latin America there was a sharp decline from 63 to 44 per cent. This was one of the explanations for Asia's higher growth of 7 to 8 per cent on average against 2 to 5 per cent in Latin America. Finally, this foreign direct investment carries less risk, less short-term financing of the balance of payments, less risk of a liquidity crisis like that which some Latin American countries experienced.

What are the prospects today? The first is the prospect for discussions under the WTO for a multilateral framework for all countries to liberalise investment, whatever their level of development. The second possibility is more immediate. We hope that a multilateral agreement on investment will be reached in the OECD by

1997, as was decided during the last OECD ministerial meeting. We also hope that countries which are OECD non-Members can participate in this agreement, especially in Asia, a wish also expressed during the last OECD ministerial meeting.

Europe and Asia now trying to advance their dialogue. The Bangkok summit was a significant step, even if it was not the only opportunity for communication between the two regions which are being drawn together by their economic dynamism. Evidently, the progress that we can achieve in liberalisation will be an element of this *rapprochement*. The participation of Asian countries in the Multilateral Agreement on Investment and an early start of negotiations under the World Trade Organisation will not only have a simple economic effect, but would also represent major progress in the dialogue between Europe and Asia. France will be participating in that.

Investment in China's Future

Zhang Xiaoqiang

During the last 17 years, under the government's economic opening and reforms, foreign direct investment in China has reached 260 000 enterprises, overall FDI commitments were worth around $400 billion, while the real inflow of FDI reached $135 billion. In 1995, China received about $38 billion in FDI, which made China number one in the developing world.

In fact, FDI already plays a very important role in China's economic and social development. For example, about 50 per cent of the country's industrial output value is due to FDI and enterprises with foreign investment earned about one-third of the country's foreign exchange, employing about 17 million workers. That shows the important contribution of FDI to China.

We have to recognise, however, that there are some issues we still need to tackle. For example, the sectoral distribution of FDI needs improvement: about 50 per cent is concentrated in processing industries and 30 per cent in real estate and hotels. Less than 10 per cent of FDI inflows contributed to infrastructure and basic industries, including 1.4 per cent for agricultural development and only 1.8 per cent for communications.

We are also concerned that even though we received FDI from about 150 countries, the major proportion of this FDI came from Hong Kong, Macao and Chinese Taipei which are, in fact, a part of China. Only 30 per cent of FDI came from other countries of the world. The United States accounted for about 8 per cent and Japan 7.8 per cent. By comparison, European countries are really left behind, accounting for less than 10 per cent. The United Kingdom, Germany, France and Italy, these four great European countries, together only accounted for 4 per cent of total FDI flows to China, only half of the US level. Why are there still problems such as less FDI for infrastructure and relatively little FDI from European countries? There may be several reasons.

First, China's opening policy has been one of gradualism, which means we opened sectors for private foreign capital relatively slowly. For example, we only opened the railway sector in 1992, the electric power sector very progressively in 1993 and the aviation sector in 1994.

The second reason is that the reform of our foreign-exchange management system has also been a gradual process. We only harmonized the two-tier foreign-exchange system that often created confusion for foreign private investors in 1994.

The third reason is that even though there are already new types of private foreign investment in developing countries, such as BOT or project financing, in China we have only recently adopted such procedures. For example, the first BOT project was launched only in 1995 in the thermal power sector and the relevant legislation is still under consideration. Finally, mutual understanding between the European countries and China still needs to be improved, compared with the economic co-operation between China and the United States, and between China and Japan. We recognise that we lack experience in strengthening this kind of co-operation between European countries and China.

The Chinese government is trying to accelerate its reform effort and opening further. In 1996, the Chinese government and the People's Congress approved the next five-year development strategy, to the year 2000. According to the strategy, annual GDP growth will be 8 to 9 per cent and exports should grow by at least 10 per cent. We will also be more and more open to private foreign investors and will try to optimise the sectoral distribution of FDI. That means we want to attract more FDI into infrastructure sectors. The Chinese market is so large, there is such potential that, for example, its electric power sector alone created about 50 million kilowatts of power generating capacity in 1995. In the same year, China created 70 million new telephone lines, the highest number in the whole world. So in the next five years the demand for infrastructure will continue to rise. For example, according to the strategy we want to create an extra 18 million kilowatts of electricity power generation capacity and add an additional 19 million telephone lines. Of course, we will continue to rely on domestic savings and investment but we also should try to attract more foreign private investment.

China will also be introducing some important measures to improve the government's management capability in order to attract more foreign direct investment. Last year the Chinese government published a new document entitled *Interim Provisions on Tightening FDI* and a catalogue for the guidance of foreign investors. According to that document, the sectors opened to FDI have been enlarged to include insurance, retailing, accounting and consulting. In the future, the Chinese government will frequently introduce a project list, to which good conditions are attached, for European countries and other potential investors as we try to attract foreign direct investment. We will give priority to certain sectors, such as agricultural development, and especially electric power generation. Similarly, main roads and highways, important raw material sectors including the petrochemical industry, chemical industry, iron and steel industry, and, of course, high tech industry and the export sector will warmly welcome FDI. The government will try to simplify its screening procedures, increase support for corporations and, of course, provide foreign exchange support. In the future, more and more sectors will be opened to FDI such as civil aviation, foreign trade, and the banking system.

With the assistance of the IFC and ADB we are preparing to publish a new decree concerning BOT and project financing in the second half of 1996. In the meantime we will try to push ahead with national treatment for FDI. For example, in 1996 FDI will be combined into our foreign exchange management system involving banking, saving and purchasing. Previously FDI was treated separately. Before the end of the century our currency will be fully convertible under the current account, and the import duty rate will be reduced continuously. The government has already announced its intention to remove about 30 per cent of the average import duties.

China will actively promote BOT and project financing. The pilot BOT project was opened for bidding in May1996 and the second BOT package whose scope will be enlarged to include thermal power plants, bridges, expressways and water treatment plants will be opened very soon. Many big foreign companies are already involved very actively in China's infrastructure development. For example, in the first quarter of 1996, the Chinese government approved eight big power plants which have investment from private foreign companies including Siemens from Germany, National Power from Britain, ES from the United States and EDF from France. The total power generating capacity of these eight power projects will be about 10 million kilowatts for an investment commitment of about $6 billion.

In principle, the Chinese government will never limit the rate of return for FDI. Some enterprises with foreign investment already obtain very high rates of return, such as Motorola of the United States and Volkswagen from Germany, while other companies earned rates of return above 20 per cent. Some processing-industry projects can earn rates of return even higher than 100 per cent, but in certain sectors, such as the power sector, anti-monopoly, inflation, consumer-rights concerns require the government to negotiate tariffs with investors. This is established international practice. In the commercial market, the Government of China cannot guarantee the rate of return, but if investors can reduce costs and increase productivity, they will get much higher rates of return and we will be very happy.

Another issue is the convertibility of foreign exchange. We fully understand for many of the infrastructure projects, the government or the banking system in the host countries must solve this problem. In fact, China has given firm commitments for the projects approved by the central government that guarantee the convertibility or availability of foreign exchange for debt servicing and for the remittance of the dividends. At lower levels, however, because this is a macroeconomic issue, difficulties have arisen. Some foreign investors have been confused about this. The point is that only the central government can guarantee the availability of foreign exchange.

Co-operation between China and European countries has a bright future because we have very good diplomatic relations and our economies have a high degree of complementarity. European companies are very strong in many industries such as electric power, electronics, the petrochemical and chemical industries, machine tools, automobiles and some construction work. It is also true that European countries have very strong management and financial capabilities. Many European companies have already achieved great success. For example, Volkswagen of Germany already dominates about half of the domestic car market and the French Alcatel company's switch equipment already accounts for about one third of the whole domestic switch equipment supply. Similarly, ABB of Switzerland has had great success in the Chinese electric power market. Through the continuing co-operation, we hope that the European companies will be more and more successful in the Chinese market. In 1995, FDI commitments from some European countries increased dramatically: UK commitments increased by 30 per cent compared with 1994, and German investment increased by 34 per cent in the same period. European countries can do a great deal in the domain of FDI in China. From this kind of co-operation, China will obtain the technology, management capability and the scarce financial resources it needs while Europe will get the contracts and, of course, the profits it seeks. This will benefit the peoples of both sides.

Foreign Investment
from a Small-Country Perspective

Nicolas Imboden

Switzerland is a small country that traditionally has been a large investor in foreign countries. With $84 billion of foreign investment, Switzerland ranks eighth in the world after the United States, Japan, Britain, France, Germany, the Netherlands and Canada. It even ranks fourth in the world in the formation of fixed capital. We adore per capita statistics because in that respect we are a great power: we are the leading investor per capita in the world! Switzerland's investments are closely linked to trade. We are a trading nation with a small market, so our enterprises had to go abroad. Moreover, Switzerland lacks primary materials and often has to obtain them abroad and invest.

The distribution of Switzerland's investment is both similar to and different from the foreign investment of the average OECD country. Like the average OECD country, three-fourths of Swiss investments are in OECD countries: 50 per cent in Europe, 25 per cent in the United States and 25 per cent in developing countries.

The distribution of Switzerland's investments in the developing countries, however, is the just the opposite of that of the average OECD country. Three-fourths of these investments are in Latin America and only a quarter are in Asia. This phenomenon may be surprising, but is easily explained. During the 1960s, it was necessary to invest in Latin America to be able to export there because of the import-substitution policies of the period. On the other hand, it was not possible to export to or invest in Asia. The situation has greatly changed and Switzerland's investment flows have also changed. In 1994, there was disinvestment from Latin America and Swiss investment in Asia increased by 50 per cent. Swiss entrepreneurs have understood the importance of Asia.

Switzerland is represented in Asia by well-established international trading companies. A comparison of Switzerland's share of Asian markets 20 years ago and now near the end of the century, reveals a degree of stability.

Switzerland is also one of the largest investors even in Asia, and there are almost no countries — Indonesia and Malaysia being the exceptions — where it is not among the ten leading foreign investors. At the enterprise level too, Switzerland is not in a bad position for the 21st century. The economy is more internationalised than many others. Switzerland has a relatively large number of globalised multinational enterprises: Nestlé, ABB, Siba, Sandoz and Roche. Ninety-eight per cent of the sales of these enterprises are made abroad. Nestlé and ABB are two of the 18 firms among the 100 largest companies which hold a majority of their assets abroad. Swiss enterprises employ 1.6 million people abroad, a third of total employment in Switzerland. Thus Switzerland appears to be well equipped for the gobalisation of the 21st century. Unfortunately, that is far from being true.

While it true that Switzerland has a significant number of internationalised flagship enterprises, what does that mean? What does it mean that ABB and Nestlé are Swiss, for example, especially when the president of Nestlé tells us every day that he will leave Switzerland the moment that it becomes interesting for Nestlé no longer to be Swiss? What is the meaning of having banks in Switzerland if they buy Warburg and use the London financial centre more than that of Zurich? Of course, foreign investment leads to revenue flows, but does mean that Switzerland will become a nation of *rentiers*, a nation which manages wealth?

Today Switzerland is confronted with a somewhat dual economy. On the one hand, some large globalised enterprises create enterprises abroad, but not in Switzerland. In 1995, the internationalised Swiss enterprises created thousands of jobs throughout the world, but in Switzerland they restructured and in reality decreased employment. On the other hand, the small and medium-sized enterprises which account for 90 per cent of Swiss employment have partly lost their traditional comparative advantages.

Today we are confronted with the second generation of globalisation. It is no longer a question of globalising the internationalised enterprises, but of globalising the small and medium-sized enterprises. Today we are confronting the challenge of relocating part of the activities of small and medium-sized enterprises, to maintain and increase employment, not to decrease it. The globalisation of the economy now enables small and medium-sized enterprises to be present throughout the world. They can finally manage their enterprises from Switzerland even through they must relocate part of their production to maintain their competitiveness. Thus, some factories must be closed to be able to open and enlarge those which are really competitive.

The challenge for a government like Switzerland's, and many others, is to retain some production to conserve research and development activities. The second challenge is to demonstrate that there can be important production in small countries.

That is why Switzerland supports foreign investment. We do not invest abroad to help others but to help ourselves. We must invest to remain competitive at home, to increase specialisation, to seize opportunities and above all to show that investing and exporting are not contradictory but go together. We have made an analysis showing that there is a very close correlation between Swiss investment and growth of our exports.

In promoting investment, the Swiss government does not consider itself a promoter but an arbiter. When speaking of an active policy of promoting investment abroad, it is necessary to differentiate between multinationals and the small and medium-sized enterprises. For the former, a government like Switzerland's cannot do anything with respect to direct support. First of all, multinationals often have better access to the host government where they invest than the Swiss government itself. (It took three weeks for the president of the Swiss Confederation to obtain a meeting with the king of Thailand, while the President of ABB obtained a meeting in three days.) More important, multinational enterprises like ABB or Nestlé do not want to appear Swiss in these countries. They would rather be seen as Chinese or Thai enterprises, rather than flagships of the Swiss economy.

If we can do something for foreign investment in these countries, it is in the macroeconomic framework. To invest abroad it is first necessary to save, and the two countries which still have positive net savings are Japan and Switzerland. All policies favouring the rate of saving favour foreign investment at the same time.

There is nothing better than having a strong currency for assuring an economy's competitiveness and thus to encourage foreign investment. A strong currency enables more to be purchased abroad to encourage investment, and it compels restructuring. If at present Switzerland and Japan are perhaps having a deeper recession than the rest of the OECD countries, their difficulties are preparing them better for the 21st century.

What can we do to promote investment by the small and medium-sized enterprises? Switzerland's experience shows that incentives and administrative protection have very little effect at that level.

What is important, on the other hand, is not so much in the legal framework, but in the opportunities which exist. Confidence in the future, the economy's dynamism and the return on investment are the indispensable elements.

Information and creating contacts are very important, especially to small and medium-sized enterprises.

Finally, a government should assure that small and medium-sized enterprises have access to risk capital, and Switzerland is now establishing a financing corporation to permit this access. However, these are secondary instruments for promoting co-operation with Southeast Asia. What really counts is favouring the opening to the interior of the country. Asia is not a threat but a great opportunity. Finally, protection and nationalism must be opposed in all their forms. The nationality of companies is unimportant today. What counts is job creation, improved competitiveness in the work place and the added value. In other words, investment abroad is not only done abroad but also domestically by domestic policy.

Opening Markets in Asia for Europe

Pierre Defraigne

The European Commission's primary aim with respect to Asia is opening markets. "Fortress Europe" is now an outmoded idea. Trade statistics on the penetration of Asian exports in Europe reveal clearly that Europe's market is very open. That is good because, just as investment creates trade, the links established by trade in turn can become the occasion for co-operation at the level of production and investment.

The European Commission's second concern is obviously to promote an environment as favourable as possible for foreign direct investment. That was the aim of recent steps concerning the investment regime by the Commission, which has recently published a major document on the subject and works within the framework of the OECD and WTO to promote the multilateral rules which accompany the opening of markets for goods and services.

Finally, the third element of the European Union's Asian strategy is economic co-operation in the mutual interest of the two partners, Asia and Europe. Under this economic co-operation we have developed a fairly broad concept called "Asia Invest" which consists of steps for helping Europeans and Asians to become better acquainted through training projects, exchanges of researchers and meetings of managerial personnel in Europe and Asia. Mr de Clerq mentioned some examples: organising meetings of business people and economic actors, and establishing a series of European Business Information Centres (EBICs) across Asia, of which a branch is already open in Bangkok. These centres are going to help local Asian enterprises to obtain information on European markets and European enterprises which come to Asia to obtain information on all aspects of the local markets, since the EBICs will form a network for both European investment in Asia and Asian investment in Europe.

This networking and improvement of mutual understanding encompasses the European Community Investment Partners (ECIP). This group of financial facilities is for helping economic actors, mainly individual enterprises, to surmount all the steps of the process of investing in a joint venture. The first facility helps chambers of commerce and business organisations locate partners who want to establish joint ventures.

A second facility provides enterprises with funds for making feasibility studies of their joint ventures. When necessary, the ECIP even participates in the financing of the joint venture with risk capital. The aim is promote projects that can be financed by the market alone, but when necessary we participate as shareholders. Finally, we provide funds to newly established joint ventures for improving the skills of their workers in order to absorb a possible transfer of technology.

Thus the ECIP is a comprehensive instrument which covers all phases of the investment in a highly decentralised way. Actually we do not provide services to enterprises directly, but use a global network of some one hundred banks, including all the large European banks. In most of the beneficiary countries, local banks also provide the ECIP services to their customers. This system was launched in 1988 with our first partner Sofin-Asia, which was followed by the Banque Nationale de Paris, the Crédit Lyonnais, the Deutsche Bank, and Morgan Grenfell, to mention only a few.

Since then, some 1 600 projects have been started up with about $200 million. The corresponding investment during the 1988-96 period has been about $30 billion. The arrangement works so well that the 1996 budget — 50 million ecus — was almost used up by the middle of the year.

A new ECIP facility for governments provides for a subsidy of 250 000 ecus for the undertaking of build-operate-transfer (BOT) projects. The subsidy supports the preparation of documentation for an international tender. It has two conditions: the agent who prepares the these documents must be European, and the international tender must be open to everyone, including Europeans, under the terms of WTO rules in this domain. This new EC-BOT facility was adopted by the EU Council of Ministers in January 1996.

What have been the lessons for Asia of the ECIP? The first lesson is that countries with the least need have profited the most from it.

The second lesson is that Europe has an asset which can make a positive contribution to establishing ties with Asia. This is the large number of European medium-sized enterprises with up to 5 000 or 10 000 employees. These European enterprises are accustomed to working in an international environment. However, they are often discouraged from investing in Asia because most of the investment policies of the host countries are oriented towards the multinationals. Our scheme's purpose is to provide these enterprises with some advantages.

The last lesson is that the ECIP works well when the actors play their role. It is not a question of states but of chambers of commerce and industry, either European or local. One of the main characteristics of the ECIP is that it treats projects initiated in Europe, Thailand, Vietnam or China in the same way. The agents concerned have to be dynamic and be able to exploit the scheme.

Likewise, the banks play a highly critical role for the operation of this system. They are the agents who deliver its services. A major difficulty is creating projects in Asia that will enable Asians to take the initiative to attract European partners. In this respect, local banks are often lacking or absent.

These are three lessons from actual experience. The ECIP is doing well in Asia, where there have been a large number of projects, but our aim is not only having projects and helping European enterprises set up an operation in Asia. We also want to promote the development of these countries because the other dimension of co-operation is reciprocal interest. If a country is small its interest is doing the right thing; it should rely more on small and medium-sized enterprises which are an asset for its development. That is insufficiently understood. The ECIP is of course "market driven" but nonetheless there should be greater efforts. Intermediaries such as chambers of commerce, trade associations and banks, especially local banks, should get organised to take advantage of this instrument.

APEC and Investment

Ippei Yamazawa

Asia-Pacific Economic Co-operation (APEC) welcomes European firms. Four points will illustrate this.

First of all, three terms characterise APEC in comparison with the European Union. They are diversity, high growth and informal structure, which are interrelated. First, there is a high degree of diversity among APEC members, which is much greater than in the European Union. APEC members are scattered over a huge area. They differ in the size of their economies, natural resources and stage of development, resulting in a wide range of wage differentials among members. Until a decade ago, we were divided into market economies and centrally planned economies, and we are still divided into several groups with different religious and cultural heritages.

Diversity has positive and negative aspects. On the positive side, diversity results in economic complementarity, stimulating trade and investment, and leading to high growth in almost all members which are developing countries. APEC's main purpose is to sustain high growth in the region for the good of all members and the world economy as a whole.

However, diversity also has negative aspects. Mutual understanding is not sufficient. It takes time to build consensus and make decisions. For this reason, APEC has an informal structure and is not based on a treaty like that of Rome or Maastricht. This informal structure leads to APEC's potential often being underestimated, especially given our diverse membership, but nonetheless APEC has an important role in the global economy together with the European Union. The second point is that APEC is an arrangement for open regional co-operation. Open regional co-operation is a fourth keyword characterising the modalities of APEC's action programme. It means promoting regional co-operation in a manner consistent with multilateral rules. All members support this policy because each member has close economic relationships with partners outside APEC, and none of us wishes to limit co-operation to members alone. In November 1994, President Suharto of Indonesia hosted the APEC Leaders meeting in Bogor and announced an ambitious commitment "to achieving free and open trade in the region by 2010 and 2020": 2010 is the deadline for developed countries and 2020 for member developing countries. This liberalisation will be complemented by participation in development co-operation programmes. In November 1995, Japan hosted the Osaka APEC Summit and co-ordinated discussions between members with different economic interests to encourage the adoption of the Osaka Action Agenda for helping individual members move towards the goals set by the Bogor declaration. Individual member governments are preparing their action plans during 1996 and on 1 January 1997 they will begin implementing them.

Open regional co-operation will be the watchword of all action plans. The Osaka Action Agenda is comprehensive. It includes accelerated implementation of the Uruguay Round commitment, so that it is quite likely that APEC will discuss joint promotion of the next round for globalisation with the European Union. The first WTO Ministerial Meeting in Asia, to be held in Singapore in December 1996, will be significant in this regard. Guidelines have already been adopted for liberalising and deregulating foreign direct investment that will be applied to Asia-Pacific firms and European firms alike. These firms will be invited to contribute to the development of new industries and to expand production and employment.

The third point concerns the private sector's relationship to APEC. APEC plans are on schedule. However, the real test of APEC is whether private firms can be convinced that the Asia-Pacific region is attractive for trade and investment. This includes, of course, both Asia-Pacific and European firms. A potentially comparable phenomenon occurred in Europe in the latter part of the 1980s in the form of active cross-border activity by firms, the so-called European fever, after the announcement of the single market. Japanese firms joined their European counterparts in this enthusiasm. Similarly, European firms are quite welcome to take advantage of liberalisation and deregulation within APEC.

There is already a consensus among APEC members to avoid having a large secretariat with an oversized budget. Instead, the aim is to involve the private sector in the APEC process. APEC leaders and ministers meet only once a year but senior officials and working groups meet almost weekly. There are additional ministerial meetings on individual co-operation matters.

At each level, private-sector participation is encouraged. At the apex, the Asia-Pacific Business Council has become the permanent advisory group. It consists of three businessmen from each of the 18 individual member countries, including one from small and medium-sized enterprises. Its job is to advise APEC leaders and ministers on priority areas for liberalisation, deregulation and related matters. Of course, this does not imply that APEC is necessarily well known to all Asia-Pacific firms. A survey by Manila business school Professor Imanira found that less than a third of Philippine businessmen have ever heard of APEC. Very few European firms could survive in Europe without knowledge of the business environment created by the European Union. Eventually there will be a similar situation in the Asia-Pacific region. Knowledge of the APEC programme will certainly be necessary for outsiders interested in doing business in Asia-Pacific as well.

Our final point concerns the Asia-Europe Summit Meeting (ASEM) and Japan's role in it. Economic relations between the Asia-Pacific region and Europe already have a long history. Nevertheless, the March1996 ASEM in Bangkok was symbolic of the effort to strengthen links between Asia and Europe. Asian participants in ASEM 1996 did not include all APEC members but they talked to European leaders on the basis of the APEC position and proposed a joint initiative for global liberalisation. This closer link between Asia and Europe through ASEM is quite consistent with Japan's strategy for APEC, and Japan is very supportive of taking the ASEM process further. Japan, together with Singapore, is co-ordinating the Asian ASEM participants and is the organiser of the 1997 follow-up meeting to be held in Japan prior to the second meeting in Britain in 1998.

ASEM aims to increase the two-way investment flows between Asia and Europe which are much less than those between Asia and North America, and between Europe and North America. Japan has been a pioneer among Asian economies in investing in Europe and in receiving European investment. Tokyo wishes to see an expansion of investment flows between its Asian neighbours and Europe. However, private investment flows are determined by private actors; governments can only encourage them by providing a favourable environment. At the ASEM in Bangkok, Prime Minister Hashimoto of Japan proposed encouraging dialogue and exchanges of views at various levels among businessmen, researchers, other interested parties. Some of the people participating in the International Forum on Asian Perspectives will doubtless be invited to take part.

Information Investment in Asia: A Private-Sector View

Hugh P. Barras

Alcatel Alsthom is in the infrastructure business. Its activities fall into the following main sectors: telecoms, cables, energy, transportation systems and batteries.

In all these sectors we are among the world's leaders. In many, we are the leader. We have local partnerships in over 20 countries worldwide and business dealings in over 130. While two-thirds of our business is in Europe, we see major expansion in the countries of Asia. Already 15 per cent of our sales are in this region (over $5 billion per annum). Alcatel Alsthom has very active local companies in India, China, Thailand, Malaysia, Philippines, Vietnam, Australia, Indonesia, and we are involved in all the economies of the region. We assist in many of the key infrastructure areas which are critical for overall expansion — telecoms, power and transportation.

These comments will centre on several trends that are of particular importance for those infrastructure sectors where Alcatel Alsthom is present:

— First, the correlation between rates of economic development and the availability of infrastructure within a economy;

— Second, global trends that are affecting infrastructure industries; and

— Third, local forces that impact on the growth rate and level of infrastructure development.

Beforehand, two points of reference:

It is important to stress that providing infrastructure is a long-term business. While the pace of changes in the environment is constantly increasing (especially in Asia), the equipment delivered must provide high quality service for many years, even decades. This is not a short-term "ship and forget" relationship between supplier and client.

57

Alcatel Alsthom provides the equipment and systems which enable others to provide services; we do not deliver services to the end-users, be they the person making a telephone call, switching on a light or riding a train. Other institutions, public and private, are service providers to the end users.

Rate of Economic Development

There have been enormous advances in Asia in terms of the quality and availability of infrastructure. In addition, there is no doubt in the minds of many decision makers that infrastructure development is a key element in promoting greater rates of economic growth.

For example, there is a high correlation between the level of economic development and the availability of telephone service. This can be seen by examining the level of telephone penetration, which is the number of telephone lines available per capita. Singapore, Hong Kong, Japan have levels of penetration of 45 per cent, 51 per cent and 47 per cent, respectively — very similar to those of the United States (59 per cent), West Germany (52 per cent), and France (54 per cent).

In other countries of Asia, the network's rate of expansion is high, but starts from a low base. In India, China, Vietnam, and Indonesia the levels are between 1 per cent and 4 per cent. All have ambitious plans underway to raise their levels to those of their neighbours. Korea, Thailand, and Malaysia have achieved levels of 40 per cent, 8 per cent and 20 per cent, respectively, and continue to expand rapidly.

Similar indices can be developed for power and water consumption, completed journeys and so forth. What is clear in all cases is that the plans for the coming decades are extremely ambitious. Let us see in more detail what this means for telecommunications.

Given the size of the population, the targets set for telephone penetration translate into hundreds of millions of new connections over the next ten years. These targets can only be achieved if three aspects are clearly addressed:

— the technology is available;

— the technology can be absorbed; and

— the financial, legal and regulatory environment is favourable.

Telecommunications services can be provided by a range of technologies. Additionally, it is all too clear that the options continue to change rapidly over time. Once, the only economic way to connect subscribers was by copper cables from the exchange to the room in the house or office where the telephone was located. Radio and cable provided the connections between exchanges. Today, there is almost no copper cable between exchanges — it is all fibre-optics; and an increasing amount of fibre-optic cable now extends from the exchange towards the subscriber(if not yet all

58

the way). In parallel, rapid advances in radio technologies (especially cellular and mobile phones) have meant that these can be used to an increasing extent to replace cable, perhaps forever.

The belief that these technologies are more expensive than cable connections is no longer justified, given the regularly decreasing price of cellular systems and the extremely high fixed costs of installing cables.

For policy makers and service providers, radio and cellular systems can be installed very rapidly, and can start to provide service and payback much faster than fixed wire networks. The political requirement to extend coverage to the deprived urban townships of South Africa is a typical example of how the speed of deployment offered by one type of technical response means that it is used first, with expansion of the "traditional" network coming later. This "traditional" expansion can then be more effective because it can be designed to cater for needs that have been demonstrated by actual usage, rather than based on extrapolation of previous experience or models, most of which anyway would have questionable relevance to a situation such as South Africa's. The presence of real telephone subscribers provides evidence to assist planning for other infrastructure — power, water, roads.

The second point relates to the ability of the economy to absorb technology. Infrastructure is like a network. The full benefit is only achieved if there is an efficient network. Telephones, power and transportation all require that someone or something passes from A to B. It is hardly possible to have "half a bridge"; the connection must go all the way. This implies first, that considerable planning and analysis is required to make full use of the allocated services and, second, that programmes, once undertaken, have to be pursued over time. Given ever-changing political, social and economic priorities, such long-term commitments and programmes are difficult to sustain.

A policy decision to permit private enterprise to deliver many of these services means that the financial, legal and regulatory environment assumes an increasing importance for infrastructure projects. Generally, the benefits of increased efficiency and access to new sources of funding are among the primary "forces" behind privatisation and deregulation. The time involved and the complexity of financial arrangements for such investments and the risk appetites of investors are all factors relevant to the attractiveness of a project from the point of view of new investors. On the other side, political and social considerations related to public service obligations, security concerns and views on the role of the state in the economy, all influence the way in which such projects are undertaken.

These variables mean that solutions, costs and infrastructure projects will vary for different economies. The players from one to another infrastructure project will also differ.

Global Trends

These specific considerations are in contrast with the far-reaching effects of global trends.

The privatisation of public enterprises, already referred to, is one such trend. Also implicit in what has been said about different technologies is the fact that products are developed for worldwide applications. This is a second trend.

Continuing with the example of telephony to be concrete, consider privatisation and deregulation. New entrants to the business should be encouraged in order to expand the network with non-public funds, to increase efficiency through the competition of old and new service providers, and to encourage the introduction of new services and equipment. Privatisation also enables government revenue to be increased by the sale of licenses or concessions.

In practice, detailed cost-evaluations are made by the new entrants. These calculations of potential returns probably dominate their thinking and mean that the driving forces are financial, rather than, say, the public-service objectives of a universal provider.

To increase or guarantee the rate of return, these new investors look for both professional and financial assistance. Professional, in terms of entities that have experience in successfully operating such services. Often, these new investor companies are not already present in an economy — though they may be the established North American, European and, increasingly, Asian operators. To guarantee their commitment, these operators are often required to take an equity participation and to receive part of their compensation via this investment.

Financial assistance is sought from both specialised financial institutions (banks, pension funds) and suppliers. For the supplier, which is the case of Alcatel Alsthom (we are not an operator), there are two financial pressures: financing the supply of the equipment and lowest possible prices.

Considering prices first, in many industries there is talk of globalisation of products. In telecoms this is a reality, with the high cost of product development exerting very strong internal pressures towards global products, even though different technical standards still exist today. The external pressure on prices from clients reinforces this process, leading to attempts to achieve economies of scale with fewer production facilities. The introduction of digital technologies and automated production have stimulated these trends. This impacts on the amount of technology transfer, with priority given to those markets offering sufficient yearly and long-term growth to be able to achieve world price levels. The private investors will not pay above these levels because of the financial basis of their calculations.

However, technology development in telecoms can be compared to that of computers, in that there is an ever-increasing emphasis on the software that can be used on standard hardware platforms. Private investors are not only trying to provide a service equal to their competitors, but a better, or, at least, a different one. This can be achieved by offering different facilities to their subscribers by continuously updating software. To be able to evaluate, design and introduce such upgrades, local software engineering centres staffed by local specialists are often established in the markets being served. Their work in their own markets has to be available for other countries and, here, the attitude towards legal protection of intellectual property rights becomes important in determining the location of such centres of worldwide excellence.

What applies to telecoms also applies to other infrastructure projects. Privatisation of energy, water, transportation, and health care, all have implicit knock-on effects in terms of the relative weight given to considerations such as the local integration of local manufacturers and the level of efficiency of the existing service providers — both impacting on the type and the number of local employees.

The Local Environment

Infrastructure projects require a long-term commitment between suppliers and clients. This is not only true between the vendors of equipment and the operators but also between the operators and the end-users. All parties have to take a long-term view to justify their investment and to establish relationships of trust and mutual understanding.

As we have seen, Alcatel Alsthom has partnerships in many countries of Asia. For us, these are really partnerships. The early history of our company was multicultural at different locations throughout Europe. In the last 25 years, we have gradually expanded our non-European presence to a level of over 35 per cent of the Group's sales in 1995. This trend will accelerate as we increase our participation in the development of infrastructure in Asia.

The ability to achieve the ambitious targets that we have set as a company fundamentally depends upon satisfying the requirements of our clients in the context of their local needs. These needs are translated into programmes for procurement, installation and implementation.

This process raises key factors that impact on the critical path of programme implementation. Some are immediately apparent, such as the price and availability of resources domestically and internationally. Also, the costs of social disruption caused by major construction work in city centres for metro or sewer projects are very apparent. However, accurately planning for future population distribution is more difficult.

Investment in infrastructure is expensive and its realisation is relatively slow. All economies are short of resources, so none can be wasted. Flexibility in the planning, provision and distribution of infrastructure services becomes increasingly important.

Additionally, programmes to provide enhanced or expanded services for existing centres of population are probably less risky and financially more attractive to private investors. Does this imply that the state will have to bear the cost of providing services to a declining, relatively less advantaged segment of the population?

Returning to the elements figuring prominently on a critical path, education and skill availability have to be considered. While there are considerable low-skill tasks associated with construction, the maintenance of infrastructure is an increasingly high-skilled occupation. As the products and systems involved become increasingly standardised worldwide, it becomes more feasible for individuals to market their skills beyond their home economy. As these people represent a scarce resource worldwide, they will expect to be compensated accordingly.

For the industrialist, this presents a series of problems beyond the normal managerial tasks of motivating and rewarding employees. Already, Alcatel Alsthom looks to local nationals to be the senior managers in our companies in other countries. We already integrate local software developments into our global research and development programme. We seek to obtain benefits from the experience and training given to all our employees for our company as a whole. If employees leave us to join a local competitor, then there may be little loss for the economy concerned from a macroeconomic standpoint, but if they emigrate to a competitor then both our company and the local economy are worse off. These losses are very difficult to sustain, both for our company and the economy.

The obvious considerations relating to property protection (physical and intellectual), repatriation of profits, tariff protection, local integration requirements, and other environmental factors that impact on local operations are well known and must also be considered.

Finally, a word on corporate governance is perhaps relevant. Alcatel Alsthom has partnerships in many countries in Asia. In some, we hold the majority of the equity; in others, we have a minority position. It is not possible to generalise about the way each relationship should be developed, beyond saying that to be successful, the relationship has to be meaningful to both partners. This requires that each partner have clearly defined objectives and these are understood by the other. Over time, objectives and markets change. Thus the relationship needs to adapt constantly to recognise the new realities. In this dynamic situation, the transparency of company activity and the accurate recording of results are key tools for maintaining mutual trust.

Conclusion

The worldwide drive towards privatisation and deregulation is intended to increase the rate of development of infrastructure. This process has far-reaching consequences affecting the parties concerned as well as legal and social ramifications.

Changes in technology that are driven by worldwide trends, not limited to any single market, also affect the rate of infrastructure growth. It is more efficient to incorporate these trends into the development process of infrastructure networks than to resist change.

Consequently, networks are best designed in ways that will permit future changes to be integrated rather than having a rigid system based on obsolete equipment. Concretely, suppliers and operators of the networks share a long-term commitment to the individual country and have a mutual interest in success. They must share a mutual confidence in a favourable business environment. Ideally, this can translate itself into a virtuous circle of increased investment in economies, leading to an increased growth and a further increase in investment.

Indian Specificities

Narayanan Vaghul

Industrial growth in the Indian economy in 1994 and 1995 averaged around 10 per cent. This has not been due to new investment, but to better productivity using existing investment. If the new investments that are being made as a result of the boom in the industrial sector are taken into account, growth is going to be around 15 per cent for 1996.

A country of 920 million people today, India's annual production of cars is projected to be one million units by the turn of the century. When purchasing power really improves, there will be immense business opportunities in India. This is also true of the power sector, and it is going to be true of roads, ports, airports and other infrastructure.

What does this mean? It means that India is going to provide great economic opportunities for the rest of the world. Beyond the year 2000, when the developed economies are likely to experience a growth plateau, the stimulus for growth in the world economy is going to come only from certain regions. India and China are the two large countries which will offer part of this stimulus. Thus we really have to take these countries very seriously. During the next five to 10 years India will be transformed into a country that is quite different. This is a first observation.

The second point is that though Asia may not need Europe, because Asia is already getting much of its investment from the region's own domestic resources and is able to attract investment from the rest of world, the story in India is somewhat different. India is not like Thailand. India needs everyone, India needs Europe, India needs the United States. There are differences between South Asia and Southeast Asia and East Asia. In East and Southeast Asia, savings rates of upwards of 30 per cent are common. In India, the savings rate is around 24 per cent, but even if this seems to be quite thrifty from the point of view of the rest of the world, from the point of view of India's own development needs, it is rather modest and insufficient for the country's investment requirements. With such a level of savings, India is lucky to enjoy growth of 6 per cent. For growth of 9 or 10 per cent, however, outside investment is a necessity. India's reforms therefore will be dictated by requirements for cross-border investment, which is critical for economic development.

A serious and intense debate has emerged in India on various issues relating to corporate governance following the liberalisation of the economy and its globalisation. The issue is of great relevance to foreign investors in Indian companies and for foreign corporations seeking to establish projects in India or strategic alliances with Indian companies.

Until the mid 1980s, the Indian economy looked inward and functioned behind a protective wall of high tariffs and quantitative restrictions on imports. Self-reliance was the catch phrase and this was supposed to be achieved through the public sector, which was intended to run the commanding heights of the economy. This approach was combined with a strict regimentation of the private corporate sector. Restrictions were placed on growth and almost all industrial activity was subjected to licensing by the government. The financial sector was brought under government control and the capital markets, though theoretically free, were also closely controlled by the government.

In the mid-1980s a beginning was made towards a reform process. However, this was short-lived for a variety of reasons and the economy went back into a shell, resulting in a deep financial crisis in 1991.

The new economic reform, triggered by this crisis, brought about a significant turnaround of the economy. Tariffs were lowered, all import restrictions were removed, the licensing system was abolished and a large part of the economy and markets were freed from government control. The government still retained the public sector, not so much out of any ideological considerations, but because of the problems arising from a redundant labour force.

The development of the Indian corporate sector can be divided into three distinct phases. In the first phase, which lasted from the beginning of independence to the late 1960s, the corporate sector was dominated by 20 family groups who had their beginnings as traders in the pre-independence era and who took a pioneering interest in the industrialisation of the country in the post-independence era. These family groups developed strong political connections and took full advantage of the licensing system to control a large portion of the industrial activity. Each group controlled several corporations, each with different groups of shareholders and significant public shareholdings. In quite a few cases the family groups held even less than ten per cent of the shares. Notwithstanding the diverse shareholding pattern, companies were managed by the same family group with all senior management positions being occupied by the family.

During the second phase of development from the early 1970s to the mid 1980s, which can be called the socialist phase, these traditional family groups came under intense pressure. During this period a Monopolies Commission was established and restrictions were imposed on the expansion of the family groups, ostensibly with a view to broadening the entrepreneurial base in the country. This phase saw the emergence of a new breed of entrepreneurs who quickly seized the advantage and competed for power with the traditional family groups. The pattern of growth, however, remained unchanged except that the new groups were gradually supplanting the old. The pattern of corporate governance by the new industrial groups was in no way different from that of the traditional groups. The second phase also saw the emergence of the financial institutions as shareholders in large companies. Access to credit from the financial institutions was based on an important conditionality of converting loans into equity, and this gradually gave the financial institutions a commanding presence in the corporate sector. As the financial institutions were under the control of the government, theoretically the government controlled a large part of India's private corporate sector.

Thanks, however, to a close nexus that developed between the political system and the family groups, both new and old, the commanding presence of the financial institutions was used more to the advantage of the family groups, rather than to their detriment. Some malpractices in corporate governance were either condoned or connived at. It was common practice for the groups to obscure corporate accounts or divert funds for making political contributions to the detriment of the small investors. There was hardly any transparency. It was common for family members to start independent trading companies which would act as agents for procurement of raw materials or sales of the finished product and divert funds through an unfair transfer-price mechanism. Promotion to senior management positions was not based on merit but closeness to the family. Family disputes leading to separation invariably resulted in a division of the company, much to the detriment of individual shareholders. Manipulation of prices in the stock market was not unusual and the small investors enjoyed little protection. Financial institutions not only turned a blind eye to such practices, but a cardinal principle of their policy was to support the family group's management of the companies.

There were of course several notable exceptions to this otherwise widespread phenomenon. There were industrial groups which functioned on professional lines with much greater transparency and ethical standards, but they were few. More importantly, there were not many large public corporations with a complete separation between ownership and management.

The third phase in the development of the Indian corporate sector began in 1991 with the liberalisation and the globalisation of the Indian economy. With competition replacing the old protected environment, the corporate scene in India is undergoing a sea change. Indian corporations are seriously engaged in re-evaluating their strategy. Under the former regimented system, diversification of the industrial base was dependent on the availability of industrial licenses. When that system withered, the corporations began applying their minds seriously to the concept of core competence. Businesses are being divested, new businesses acquired and efforts being made to scale up operations to international size. This process also raises important issues of corporate governance, including a much greater degree of professionalism of the management. Nonetheless, there are no immediate signs of a division taking place between the ownership and the management.

In recent times however, a new factor has emerged which is triggering off a crisis in corporate governance. Thanks to liberalisation, the Indian economy is today moving at a much faster pace than at any time in the past. In particular, the Indian corporate sector is experiencing a growth rate of more than 12 per cent, and several segments of the industry are registering growth rates of well over 30 per cent. The economic reform has unleashed a very strong demand for quality products and Indian industry is responding to this challenge with a great deal of enthusiasm. Even though the degree of inefficiency still leaves Indian industry internationally uncompetitive, international competition has not yet become significant notwithstanding the opening of the Indian economy. Indian industry has been taking advantage of the time lag to increase productive efficiency and achieve international competitiveness. There is a mood of optimism in the air.

However, this accelerated growth has led to a major problem for the corporate sector. In the past, most expansion plans were financed comfortably by the financial institutions and banks on terms which could be considered quite liberal. Access to the capital markets was also fairly easy as the financial institutions controlled much of the capital market's activities. As the industrial groups continued to enjoy a cozy relationship with the financial system, funding of expansion hardly presented any difficulty.

With the acceleration of the process of development, however, a severe liquidity squeeze has gripped the economy and it has become imperative for the corporations to seek more and more cross-border funding. Several leading corporations are now entering the international capital market for debt as well as equity. Thus foreign investment institutions now hold a significant proportion of the equity in Indian corporations. As the Indian corporations are gradually globalising their funding, a transformation is taking place in corporate governance because of the requirements of the international capital market. Certain immediate changes are visible, such as greater transparency in accounts, appointment of professional managers, greater sensitivity to shareholders' interests and a closer attention to profits. There is still no evidence, however, to suggest that the family ownership is giving way to broader public ownership and more professional top management.

There is evidence to suggest that the close relationship between financial institutions and the Indian corporate sector is undergoing a change. Public financial institutions are now going to the capital market to meet their capital needs and in the process they are acquiring a large body of vigilant individual shareholders. Foreign institutional investors are also acquiring a significant stake in the Indian financial system. The financial sector is now realising the need for much greater accountability to its own shareholders and this, more than anything else, is bringing a change in the attitude of the financial institutions towards recalcitrant borrowers.

One of the significant features of the economic reform is the change that is taking place in the government-corporate relationship. The government has so far played the role of manager in the corporate sector. While in the East Asian models this role has become transformed into that of a "coach", for a variety of reasons, this is unlikely to occur in India. On the other hand, there is greater likelihood of India's moving towards the Anglo-American model, with the government emerging as a "referee". In large measure, this would be close to the pattern of the political and bureaucratic system that emerged during the last four decades. To what extent this will inhibit India from emulating the East Asian pattern of growth remains to be seen.

The Nature of the MAI

William Witherell

A year ago the OECD Ministers launched negotiations among our Member countries on a Multilateral Agreement on Investment (MAI). At their May 1996 meeting this year the Ministers received a progress report on these negotiations. This report indicated that: "Overall the negotiations are on course. Most substantive issues have been examined and a framework for the MAI is evolving." The Ministers committed their governments to "reach an agreement by the Ministerial meeting in 1997, with high standards of investment liberalisation and protection and effective dispute settlement procedures, and to aim at achieving a higher standard of liberalisation". They also committed themselves to "engage in an intensified dialogue with non-OECD countries, in particular those most interested in acceding to the MAI."

The objectives of the MAI negotiations are clear:

— To provide a broad multilateral framework for international investment with high standards for the liberalisation of investment regimes and investment protection, and containing effective dispute settlement procedures;

— Creating a free-standing treaty open to all OECD Members and the European Communities, and to accession by non-OECD Member countries which will be consulted as the negotiations progress.

The OECD governments set these objectives after determining that the time is ripe for developing multilateral rules of the game for international investment. Companies making cross-border investments are confronted with a vast array of different legal frameworks as they consider where to invest. Although investment regimes have become much more open and welcoming in the recent past, there is no assurance that they will remain so in the years to come. Foreign investors still encounter investment barriers, discriminatory treatment and legal and regulatory uncertainties. These remaining restrictions are a potential source of international friction, not the least because they are barriers to market access. The MAI initiative aims at providing a strong and comprehensive framework for foreign direct investment activities, widening the scope of existing liberalisation and providing legal security for international investors. It will seek to "level the playing field" and ease market access, essentially by embodying the principle of national treatment in a multilateral and most-favoured-nation context. To give it teeth, the MAI will be legally binding and contain effective dispute settlement provisions.

The Uruguay Round negotiations, of course, addressed some investment issues in the agreements on Trade-Related Investment Measures (TRIMS), Trade-Related Intellectual Property Measures (TRIPS) and the General Agreement on Trade and Services (GATS). These agreements are important steps in the development of international disciplines, but they only address the investment concerns we have mentioned to a rather limited extent.

Within the OECD, our governments have co-operated for many years on investment matters on the basis of a framework of OECD investment instruments. These are the Declaration and Decisions on International Investment and Multinational Enterprises, and the Codes of Liberalisation of Capital Movements and of Current Invisible Transactions. The principal motivation behind the MAI negotiations was to consolidate and strengthen these disciplines among the OECD countries. Several years of preparatory work had been accomplished by the OECD's investment committees. Another consideration behind the choice of the OECD as the forum for the negotiations was the good prospect of reaching agreement relatively rapidly among our Members on a comprehensive agreement containing the strongest features of existing agreements — a truly "state-of-the-art agreement".

An agreement is expected by May 1997. The alternative suggested by some of directly moving to pursue such negotiations in the WTO would clearly have been a much more prolonged process. Although many countries around the world have unilaterally adopted more liberal policies on investment, a number are not yet at all convinced of the desirability of having binding international disciplines covering investment.

Also, it should be recognised that the OECD countries account for some 85 per cent of all international investment outflows and 65 per cent of all inflows. The MAI, therefore, while not including all countries in the world, will cover a significant share of the world's international investment.

These factors underlie the choice made last year of the OECD as the forum, but it is important to understand that the MAI is not intended to be an OECD instrument per se. The negotiating mandate makes it clear that the MAI is to be a "free-standing international treaty" and, as such, it will be open to accession by interested non-OECD countries. This is a major innovation for, with a few exceptions, the usual practice in the past has been for participation in OECD agreements to be limited to the OECD Member countries. In the case of the MAI, a number of non-OECD countries are being consulted as negotiations proceed. If non-Member countries interested in the possibility of future accession to the MAI have views on the developing agreement, the OECD wants to hear them and the negotiators will try to take them into account. There is no intention of presenting a *fait accompli* to such countries.

The independent status of the MAI also means that its implementation will not be an OECD responsibility but, rather, the joint and equal responsibility of all the eventual Parties to it, working through a "Parties Group".

Why might some non-OECD countries want to accede to the MAI, once it has been developed, and commit themselves to the international disciplines that it will contain? Our mandate is to develop an agreement that represents high standards in every respect. It will be a "quality agreement", a fact that is likely to deter some countries, but which should be attractive to countries already committed to high standards of treatment for foreign investors. Signing up to the MAI will mean saying loud and clear to investors and to the investment community that the country concerned subscribes to the highest standards in offering legal protection, market access and equitable treatment. For countries that are also a source of outward investment — and that includes a number of countries in the Asian region — the MAI will offer the additional attraction of assuring market access and legal protection for all forms of their investment into other MAI countries.

As we have seen, the negotiations are taking place among the 27 OECD Member countries. Our Ministers decided not to invite other countries to take part in the negotiations, as such, mainly because experience shows that the larger the number of countries involved, the slower the pace of work. This does not mean that the MAI is being offered on a "take it or leave it" basis. First, we are politically committed to consult closely with interested non-Member countries during the course of the negotiations. Moreover, if any country should seriously wish to adhere to the MAI, we would have to negotiate the conditions upon which that country could become a party. This does not mean re-opening negotiations on the text of the MAI itself, but rather identifying the reservations, if any, that the country would have to lodge to the various MAI provisions. There are likely to be core conditions that all parties must meet; for example, the investment protection and dispute settlement provisions and a commitment to the basic underlying principles. There could be transition periods for some other provisions by mutual agreement. In the case of a country that would like to accede to the agreement but which needed technical assistance to develop its investment regime, a programme for providing such advice could be developed, perhaps along the lines that the OECD already is following with respect to some of the economies in transition to market economies. It is important to note here that the WTO Secretariat has been invited to participate as an observer in the MAI negotiations to assist us in avoiding conflicts with the WTO instruments. For similar reasons, observers from the IMF and the World Bank are also assisting in the negotiations.

All this being said, it is likely that the eventual participation in the MAI will fall considerably short of the full membership of the WTO. To use a Geneva term, it will be a "plurilateral" agreement. At their recent meeting our Ministers affirmed their interest to "begin an examination of trade and investment in the WTO and work toward a consensus which might include the possibility of negotiations". There is particular emphasis on the term "consensus" in that commitment. The question of whether or not the WTO will eventually seek to develop its own disciplines in the investment area is obviously a matter for the WTO membership as a whole to decide. Should such negotiations be undertaken at some future date, it is likely that the MAI would serve as a reference, as would other agreements such as NAFTA, the Energy Charter, bilateral agreements and regional agreements among developing countries. Any WTO agreement would, naturally, have to be designed for the full WTO membership and in the framework of WTO disciplines and institutional arrangements.

The MAI negotiations, the work on investment in other international organisations and in regional groupings such as APEC, NAFTA and Mercosur should be viewed as complementary processes. Over time, they will contribute to a broad consensus on an international framework for investment in parallel and integrated with the one we now have for trade. We fully expect the MAI will prove to be an important step in that process, and for any country wishing to participate, the door will be open.

PART TWO

DYNAMICS AND OPPORTUNITIES

Part Two

Dynamics And Operations

Introduction and Overview

Charles P. Oman

The Attraction of Asia

The Asian developing countries — including China, India and Pakistan, the four newly industrialising economies of East Asia (NIEs) and the seven members of the Association of Southeast Asian Nations (ASEAN) — constitute, by far, the world's most populous, and economically its most dynamic, region. Moreover, all signs point to that economic dynamism — growth over the last decade averaged about 8 per cent annually in the region as a whole — as likely to continue for some time to come. Strong economic performance, rapidly growing markets and profitable investment opportunities, even more than a strong yen driving Japanese firms to invest abroad, have in turn made Asia the largest recipient of foreign direct investment among developing countries since the mid-1980s, when it overtook Latin America. The stock of FDI in developing Asia has more than doubled since 1988, and annual FDI inflows have grown from about $30 billion in 1992 to some $60 billion in 1994 and close to $100 billion in 1995. Equally important, the region's demand for FDI is likely to increase enormously as it seeks in the coming years to overcome major infrastructure bottlenecks (see Brooks and Leuterio in this volume), to upgrade technology and strengthen competitiveness in many industries, and to create new production capabilities, especially in capital goods and modern services.

Europe's Investment in Asia

Together, the countries of the European Union are the largest suppliers of FDI in the world. Since 1990 they have accounted for over half of global FDI outflows, as compared to the US share of 20 per cent and Japan's share of about 12 per cent. Nevertheless, a significant share of EU countries' foreign direct investment goes to other EU countries — intra-EU FDI amounts to 18 per cent of global FDI — and only 2 per cent of EU FDI goes to Asia, as compared to 12 per cent of Japanese and 11 per cent of US FDI. The EU countries' combined share of developing Asia's total FDI inflows since 1990 is thus only 10 per cent, as compared to 16 per cent from Japan and 11 per cent from the United States[1].

More worrisome, perhaps, is the fact that the EU countries' share of FDI flows going to China and the ASEAN countries, which together host over 80 per cent of recorded FDI flows into all Asian countries (see Estanislao in this volume), has actually declined in recent years. Part of the reason for this decline is the rapid growth of FDI in China and the ASEAN countries by the NIEs, whose overseas investment accounts for slightly over half of all FDI in Asia since 1990. But EU FDI in China and the ASEAN countries has also failed to keep pace with the flows coming from Japan and the United States.

EU-based firms' relatively poor investment performance in the world's most populous and economically most dynamic region appears to have several causes[2]. One has undoubtedly been European perceptions of business needs and opportunities closer to home. Particularly important have been the European Community's Single Market process ("EC 1992") launched in 1985; successive enlargements of the European Community and Union; and the far-reaching changes, still underway, in Central and Eastern Europe. All these transformations may have diverted European managers' attention to some extent from developing Asia.

A second cause, more worrisome, is that many European executives appear to have underestimated the growth potential of the dynamic Asian developing and newly industrialising economies, especially in the early stages of that dynamism.

A third cause, also troublesome, relates to the apparent failure of many Europeans today fully to appreciate the recent speed and importance of the opening-up of developing Asia, and of the loosening of traditionally more closed business practices there (see both Estanislao, and Chakwin and Hamid in this volume). That opening-up is creating a "window of opportunity" for non-Asian as well as for Asian investors (see also Lehmann in this volume) to contribute to, and profit from, developing Asia's dynamism.

A further cause might be a phenomenon whose political significance grew considerably when Europe's economic growth slowed in the early 1990s, though its influence on European firms' investment decisions is difficult to judge: widespread popular perceptions that "globalisation", the relocation of production destined for European consumers to low-wage production sites in developing countries, and the competitive dynamism of Asia are causing high unemployment and constitute a threat to living standards in Europe. Those perceptions — essentially mistaken[3] — must be dealt with constructively by European business leaders, as well as (and especially) by European politicians and policy makers.

Strengthening Euro-Asian Business Ties

The time is thus ripe for Europe and Asia to make more determined efforts to strengthen business and investment relations between their two regions. For both European and Asian firms, prospects to continue increasing exports to one another's regions — and for European firms, the ability to profit from Asia's dynamism — will depend largely on willingness to invest. Globalisation is increasing, not reducing, the importance of proximity between firms and their customers.

Strengthening business ties between the two regions is above all the responsibility of corporate executives in the two regions. Policy makers and governments nevertheless have a key role to play. Not least important is drawing attention to the need for more determined efforts to strengthen business and investment relations between Europe and Asia, for the benefit of both regions.

The five chapters that follow, briefly summarised in the remainder of this chapter, seek to inform those efforts. They focus on the changing institutional environment for investment in China and the ASEAN countries; the economic environment in Asia; Asian infrastructure and natural resources; systems of corporate governance in Europe and Asia; and Euro-Asian corporate alliances.

The Institutional Environment for Investment in China and the ASEAN Countries

Starting from the observation that the lion's share of the rapid growth of FDI in Asia since the mid-1980s has gone to China and the ASEAN countries, the chapter by Estanislao clarifies both the extent to which those countries have liberalised their investment regimes as they have shifted from import substitution to export promotion strategies, and the current limits to that liberalisation. Particularly valuable is the country-by-country breakdown of information on specific policy reforms presented in the extensive tables, which allow for cross-country comparisons as well.

For each of the seven countries covered, the tables offer an assessment of policies towards FDI, and of many policies and factors that condition the investment climate. The former include FDI policy provisions, government priorities and the general direction of FDI policy orientation; also included are restrictions and regulations on foreign equity participation, conditions for 100 per cent foreign ownership, negative lists that preclude or restrict FDI in certain activities, and policies with regard to special zones or special sectors for FDI. The tables also look at tariff and non-tariff barriers to trade, trade-related investment measures, policies on privatisation, subsidies and public procurement, and provisions for dispute settlement. They assess the extent of public-sector involvement in the economy, the location of power and the influence of special-interest groups, bribery and corruption, and attitudes and practices toward foreigners. They also examine labour-market regulations, government-labour relations, and their influence on government-business relations.

The picture that emerges is one of significant unilateral trade and investment liberalisation, with the trend likely to continue as competition intensifies to attract FDI. Significant exceptions persist, however, especially in the form of non-tariff trade barriers and policies that favour nationals over foreigners in the realm of investment[4].

The Economic Environment in Asia

The chapter by Chakwin and Hamid begins with a discussion of globalisation and of what investors look for in a host country. Noting important similarities among the fast growing economies of Asia, including relative price stability and high domestic saving and investment rates, the authors stress that the region is composed of countries with important differences in culture and history as well as in economic policies and performance. They focus their analysis on Indonesia, Malaysia and Thailand, on China, and on India.

Particularly interesting is the authors' discussion of likely future trends. Starting from the arguable assumptions that globalisation will sustain the growth of FDI flows to developing countries and that "protectionism in developing countries will become a thing of the past" — the issue being the *pace* of liberalisation — the authors highlight a widespread fear in the region: China, with its huge potential market, strong growth, insatiable demand for investment funds and immense potential supply of both low-wage and educated labour, may crowd out FDI from other countries; it may also overwhelm labour-intensive exports of other Asian countries that are just starting on a process of export-led growth. The authors explain why they do not share this fear.

With the exception of Indonesia, whose restrictive, anti-competitive and high-cost environment for FDI to serve the domestic market may persist, the chapter presents a very positive picture of likely FDI trends in virtually all countries in the region. Discussion of their paper, on the other hand, raised important questions not only about the authors' view of globalisation but, crucially, about their assumption of continued high growth in the region which ignores any "downside risks", including those that stem from the vulnerability of some countries in the region to balance-of-payments or political shocks (Thailand, for example, might be vulnerable to the former).

Discussion also focused on the considerable significance for foreign investors of the trend in several countries towards a decentralisation of power, from central to state or provincial governments, which creates new obstacles or complications as well as new opportunities. The issue of local business practices (see also Lehmann in this volume) and corruption, which some foreign investors see as a big problem in a few countries, and the question of how much regional integration through AFTA, APEC, etc. will attract FDI, were also discussed.

Natural Resources, Economic Structure and Infrastructure in Asia

The chapter by Brooks and Leuterio highlights well the critical role of infrastructure in raising the productivity of natural resources, labour and capital, and in improving the quality of life, sometimes dramatically, in countries at all levels of development. As the authors note, "infrastructure converts constraints to opportunities", and the cost of inadequate infrastructure can be enormous. The environmental repercussions of infrastructure can also be significant, as shown by Asian Development Bank estimates of between $13 billion and $70 billion per year as the cost of investment required in the coming few years to improve the state of the environment in Asian developing countries. At the same time, technological change is significantly reducing the number of natural monopolies in the provision of infrastructure services — e.g. in power generation, communications and the operation of roads — thus increasing the scope for competition to improve efficiency in the provision of infrastructure services.

The ADB estimates that between 1994 and 2000 total demand for investment in infrastructure in Asia, excluding Japan and the NIEs, will be about $1 trillion, or about 7 per cent of the region's gross national product. This figure includes $300-$350 billion in the power sector, a similar amount in transport, $150 billion in telecommunications and $80-$100 billion in water supply and sanitation. The high rate of domestic saving in developing Asia allows a high rate of domestic investment, and the public sector is likely to remain responsible for a large share of investment in water development, rural roads and mass transit. But the opportunities for private investment in power, telecommunications, environmental services and the maintenance of existing infrastructure, for example, both directly and through private-public and foreign-domestic partnerships, such as build-operate-transfer (BOT) arrangements, are significant and growing rapidly.

Underdeveloped financial markets constitute a serious constraint to infrastructure development in Asia. Part of the solution, for some types of infrastructure, may be to charge users fees which, among other advantages, generate revenue to help cover investment and maintenance costs or finance new investments. Multilateral finance organisations can help to develop local capital and financial markets, notably bond markets that help transform high saving into long-term investment, as well as through direct financing, loan guarantees and helping to mobilise co-financing. Large foreign investors, in addition to the technological know-how they can contribute, may have a comparative advantage in pooling risk across countries, and in access to export credits and to non-recourse loans in OECD financial markets.

Corporate Governance Systems

European worries about the ability of non-Asian firms to contribute to, and profit from, Asia's economic dynamism tend to stem less from perceptions of any formal *de jure* barriers to trade or investment in Asia, than from feelings that *de facto* business practices in Asia can make it difficult for "western" firms to succeed as investors in Asia. What some see as significant "cultural" differences are seen by others as differences in systems of corporate governance — different "capitalisms" — in the two regions. As the rich and informative chapter by Lehmann points out, corporate governance issues have moved to the centre of attention of business leaders and officials responsible for international policy negotiations. As globalisation advances and FDI grows in importance, relative to trade, interest in corporate governance systems will grow.

Lehmann's argument, however, is that it is wrong to believe that corporate governance in the "West" differs fundamentally from that in the "East". The situation is more complex, and the notion of a fundamental cultural contrast must be dispelled. Diversity among systems of corporate governance within each region is greater than any inter-regional differences. Many similarities exist between business practices found in the two regions, depending on what role governments play. The dividing line, in other words, is not between Europe and Asia, but between countries in which government adopts a more or less "hands-on" approach to business affairs, and those in which it adopts a more or less "hands-off" approach.

This chapter also addresses the question of convergence: as globalisation proceeds will there be international convergence towards a single system of corporate governance? Moreover, as is often assumed today, will such a convergence be towards the Anglo-American system? After looking in some detail at the world's three dominant approaches to corporate governance — the German, the Japanese and the Anglo-American — as well as at the Korean *chaebol* and the Chinese "bamboo network", the author concludes that all are under considerable pressure to change, but the answer to the later question, at least, is no: there is no convincing reason to believe that globalisation is synonymous with Americanisation. Nor, he argues in response to the first question, is there any clearly emerging "global order" of corporate governance, but "a somewhat chaotic transition to uncharted international business territory". The policy objective, he concludes, should not be to achieve homogenisation, but transparency. Also, European executives need to make the effort to understand Asian enterprises, while Asian executives need to make the learning easier by becoming more transparent.

Euro-Asian Corporate Alliances

The chapter by Sigurdson starts from the observation that in the current context of globalisation, inter-firm alliances have become increasingly important as even the largest and most powerful companies, in Europe and other OECD countries, are driven by the speed of technological change and the pressures of competition to share investment risks and costs, reduce time in research and product development, and gain access to rapidly changing markets. Particularly important are *strategic* alliances, defined as such because they directly impinge on partners' long-term competitiveness in global markets. The benefits to partners of sharing costs and reciprocal access to markets are important motivations, though the single most important is access to knowledge, especially technology.

Until recently, few Asian companies outside those of Japan, Korea and Chinese Taipei participated in strategic alliances. That picture is changing due to developing Asia's rapidly expanding economies and growing availability of such critical assets as skilled engineers and research personnel. A strong motivation among developing-Asian firms is to acquire technology and/or market expertise.

Most strategic alliances in Asia have been with US firms or, inter-regionally, with Japanese firms. European firms have been less active through alliances in Asia. One reason, according to the author, is that EU R&D policy has tended to support EU regional corporate "champions" in key sectors, such as electronics, where EU governments' policies to support national champions have been less than fully successful. That policy, he argues, reflects a poor understanding of the implications of technological and industrial globalisation today. Support for national champions in the 1960s focused on trying to close the technology gap with the United States, and shifted in the late 1970s and early 1980s to try to meet the Japanese challenge, notably in electronics, with limited success. European national and EU regional policies must change from a parochial to a global perspective, in which Asian firms must play an increasingly important role as partners, as well as competitors.

Notes

1. These data refer to the period 1990 through 1994. The EU countries' share of global FDI stock, as source countries, was over 45 per cent (about 25 per cent excluding intra-EU FDI) as of end-1994, as compared to 26 per cent for the United States and 12 per cent for Japan (figures reported in European Commission and UNCTAD, *Investing in Asia's Dynamism: European Union Direct Investment in Asia*, Interim Report, March 1996).

2. See also European Commission and UNCTAD, *ibid.*

3. See R. Lawrence, *Single World, Divided Nations? International Trade and OECD Labor Markets*, OECD Development Centre and Brookings Institution, forthcoming. See also, C. Oman, *The Policy Challenges of Globalisation and Regionalisation*, Policy Brief No. 11, OECD Development Centre, Paris, 1996.

4. It is in some ASEAN countries, in particular, that one therefore finds strong reservations about OECD negotiations toward a Multilateral Agreement on Investment, to be completed in 1997, which will be open, on a negotiated, case-by-case, basis, to non-OECD countries.

Corporate Governance in East Asia and Western Europe: Competition, Confrontation and Co-operation

Jean-Pierre Lehmann

Corporate Governance: Who Cares?

Globalisation is having a dramatic impact on the landscape of international business. As the 21st century approaches, companies will be divided between those that participate in global business and those that do not. Those that do not will be the losers; and even those that do will continually have to struggle to survive and compete very hard in order to flourish. Inefficient domestic firms will no longer be able to bask in the protection of governments, less because of regional trends and the WTO, than because of the global industrial and technological developments.

The recent great increase in foreign direct investment provides a good illustration of how the landscape of international business has been changing. This greater volume of FDI helps explain why corporate governance has become a more important international issue. While multilateral or bilateral trade negotiations have traditionally focused on resolving or reducing frictions "at the borders", attention now is shifting towards what is happening "within borders". International debate and negotiations focus on how corporations manage their affairs and how they relate to partners and competitors, relationships conditioned by national systems of corporate governance.

A good early example is the Structural Impediments Initiative (the so-called SII negotiations) launched in the late 1980s by the US government in a context of escalating US-Japanese "trade frictions". Washington argued that the *keiretsu* system gives Japanese firms an unfair advantage, and that it should be dismantled. Tokyo countered that the American corporate problem was its short-termism (excessive attention to short-term profits) which, in turn, reflects the undue influence of external actors, namely shareholders, as opposed to the system in Japan where employees come first.

Experience shows that debate over the pros and cons of different systems of corporate governance can intensify frictions between countries, but it can also provide companies from different cultures with a means to learn from each other. One of the reasons why some leading US companies have significantly improved their performance in the auto, electronics and office equipment sectors, for example, has been their ability to learn from the Japanese.

Companies must adapt as the world economy changes, especially as it globalises. The external environment is the major factor. Companies now recognise the need for transformation in industrialised and industrialising countries. The Korean *chaebol* are under pressure to change their system of corporate governance from having owner-managers to the employment of professional managers. In Italy, the scions of the leading families who are assuming positions of corporate power openly admit that change and internationalisation are imperatives[1].

Corporate governance, therefore, is currently one of the main issues facing those who deal with the international political economy, with relations between states and between regions, and in the field of international business studies.

The Bangkok Summit of 1-2 March 1996 of European and East Asian heads of government has provided a new impetus to the relationship of their two regions after many years of neglect. As Europe and East Asia seek a closer relationship, it is vital for it to be open and dynamic: Europe "and" as opposed to "versus" East Asia. Corporate governance must be addressed for the reasons already noted and because of a tendency to use pseudo-anthropological distinctions between European and East Asian business cultures.

This chapter seeks to demystify some of the false assumptions frequently encountered with respect to corporate governance in Europe and East Asia. It also aims to provoke discussion, not pretending to be the final word on the subject. To that end, both the external contexts and the internal dynamics of corporations in both continents are assessed. In the following section, we begin by looking at the international business environment. In a second section, we try to find the truth behind the myths of corporate governance in East Asia. In particular, we emphasize the diversity of corporate governance in the region, as opposed to an often assumed unity or homogeneity. Diversity is also a feature of European businesses, as we underscore in a third section. In spite of the unification of the European market, companies tend to retain their national identity. "European companies" per se do not yet exist, and mergers have been difficult, as systems of corporate governance remain distinct.

With that background, in a fourth section we discuss similarities and differences in the world's three dominant forms of corporate governance: the German, Japanese and so-called Anglo-American models. It is stressed that while the differences between the three may be highlighted when placed under a "microscope", in the broader context of the international economy their similarities distinguish them from the rest of the world.

Extending the analytical horizon in a fifth section to include a larger number of economies and corporate systems in both East Asia and Europe, we turn to a critical factor, namely the role of the state. Here we argue that three types of government-industry relationships can be identified, all three of which can be found both in East Asia and Europe. The dividing line is not between Europe and East Asia, but between economies in which governments take a hands-on or a hands-off approach to business affairs. There are many similarities in business practices in European and East Asian environments, depending on the role governments play.

As East Asian corporations are the "new neighbours" in the global economy, a sixth section looks in some detail at the three main actors in that region: the Japanese *keiretsu*, the Korean *chaebol*, and the Chinese "bamboo networks". They differ considerably from each other and all three are under considerable pressure to change. The deep recession in which Japan has been mired since the beginning of this decade is seen, *inter alia*, as a crisis of corporate governance. The appointment of a Scot (Henry Wallace) by the American majority owner (Ford Motor Company) of a Japanese company (Mazda) is likely to remain an exception for the foreseeable future. Nevertheless, it is emblematic of the crisis in the Japanese corporate world and of the imperative need for some adjustment. In Korean and Chinese businesses, the generational change from founder-owner to heir and the aspirations of the companies to be global are having a very strong impact.

A leitmotif of the chapter is the question of convergence. As the globalisation of the world economy occurs, will there be a globalisation (that is, harmonization) of corporate governance? In particular, will there be a globalisation of corporate governance in favour of the Anglo-American model, as is generally assumed? In the conclusion, we state that the answer to the second question is, in our view, an emphatic no. There is no reason *a priori* to believe that globalisation is synonymous with Americanisation. This is the case for many reasons, including the fact that while cultures are dynamic and subject to change, cultural change nevertheless tends to occur relatively slowly. What is certain, however, is that change is occurring both in Europe and in East Asia. No new "global order" of corporate governance is clearly emerging at present, but there is a somewhat chaotic transition to uncharted territory in international business. For that reason, among others, corporate governance will be a dominant theme in the economic affairs of men and women in East Asia and Europe in the years and decades ahead.

East Asia and the International Business Environment

Much current discussion about international business and the global economy is based on an assumption that there are fundamental differences between "Western" and "Eastern" approaches to corporate governance and economic management. These dissimilarities are said to "explain" differences in economic and business performance between the West and Asia and/or are portrayed as causes of an inevitable conflict.

Samuel Huntington wrote about geopolitical trends towards an ultimate "clash of civilizations"[2], and increasingly it is alleged that Western and Asian capitalism will clash[3]. Even when not portrayed so apocalyptically, it often considered that the West and Asia are separated by a "Bamboo Wall" which, in turn, is often held responsible for the "misunderstandings" that occur with greater frequency as the centre of global economic activity continues to shift from the Atlantic to the Pacific.

The main message of this chapter is that reality is a bit more complex for various reasons of which two are:

1.   There is considerable diversity in corporate governance both in East Asia and in Western Europe. To be sure, certain characteristics such as cultural, economic or development factors may define one region or the other. However, parallels can be found between approaches and systems in some East Asian forms of corporate governance and some of their Western counterparts. The prevalence of small and medium-sized enterprises in Italy and in the Chinese business sphere[4], for example, reflects a comparable structure and culture of corporate governance. Similarly, bank-industry relationships in Germany are very different from those in Japan, but Germany and Japan have more in common on that score than Germany and the United Kingdom. It is therefore a serious error to say there is unity or homogeneity in either East Asian or Western European forms of corporate governance which *a fortiori* implies a clash between the two.

2.   For various reasons, the probability of continued occasional confrontation between Western Europe and East Asia remains high. The protectionist tendencies of some Western European countries lead to attempts to set up barriers based on "moral" principles and/or perceived fundamental structural disparities. Some people allege that because corporate systems in East Asia rest on very different legal and moral foundations, labour standards are different and inferior to those in the West: child labour, prison labour, exploitative wage rates, suppression of unions, etc. are widespread and confer an "unfair advantage" on East Asian enterprises. Alternatively, the predatory exporting prowess of East Asian enterprises is held up as a *raison d'être* for protectionism.

However, not only will there be conflict *between* regions, but it will also occur within regions. Conflict has become somewhat attenuated in the European Union (EU) where there are recognised means of redress and arbitration, but nevertheless differences, occasionally acute[5], will persist[6]. In East Asia, as the economies of the region become increasingly interdependent, competitive and mature, more scope for conflict will emerge, and moreover, without the benefit of an independent regional forum for arbitration, redress or appeal.

As long as the international economy remains geared towards more open trade and the momentum following the completion of the Uruguay Round is sustained, enterprises in Europe, North America, East Asia and elsewhere will intensify their globalisation strategies. Global markets give rise to competition and cross-border alliances between multinational corporations on a global scale. Competition, confrontation and co-operation therefore will co-exist.

Certain recent events, developments and trends in the international environment will have considerable influence on the behaviour and direction of enterprises:

— The East Asian region has been the fastest growing part of the world economy for the last three decades and will remain so for the foreseeable future. Its economic and business fundamentals are very healthy. Although the region's geopolitical vulnerability and fragility could jeopardise prosperity, East Asia's economic prospects are good in a "no hot-war scenario";

— For that reason, East Asia has become and will increasingly be *the* business battlefield par excellence. Western European businesses will have to focus on North America and East Asia[7] because the EU's own markets remain somewhat anaemic, the promise of an Eastern European economic dawn remains unfulfilled, Latin America is a very mixed patchwork of only a few bright spots (e.g. Chile) with economic turbulence elsewhere, and the Middle East and Africa are plagued by socio-political turmoil. Expansion of European activity in North America, a territory that is quite familiar, is normally carried out by merger and/or acquisition and European enterprises rarely establish greenfield sites or enterprises. On the other hand, East Asia is much less charted territory and European corporate expansion there often takes the form of greenfield sites with East Asian partners, rather than more traditional Western mergers and/or acquisitions;

— A growing number of European captains of industry believe that East Asia is "where the big battle is"[8]. European firms will face their biggest challenges in East Asia, especially in the areas of management and human resources, hence their strategic thinking will be increasingly oriented towards the region[9];

— The East Asian battlefield will be crowded by all the familiar players from Western Europe, North America and Japan, and also by increasingly assertive non-Japanese East Asian corporate players. Therefore, corporate governance patterns and practices in East Asia are not simply theoretical or academic issues. The business world is becoming more and more "Asianised", if only because a great deal more of the "action" will depend on Asia. East Asian corporations are among the most aggressive foreign direct investors, not only in their own region, but increasingly also in North and South America, and Europe. A 1995 headline was a sign of the times: "Taiwan Group to Build $368 million Plant in Scotland: Investment Seeks to Compete with Koreans"[10].

A major theme of this chapter is that differences between East Asian approaches to business are as important as the similarities, and, as often as not, there are closer parallels between East Asian and Western European forms of corporate governance than between different forms in East Asia. Nonetheless, certain characteristics and/or attitudes currently define the East Asian region. They are:

— "Success" is a characteristic of the region, but high economic growth in most though not all countries and territories of the region is based on differing social, political, economic, business and other factors. The driving force of technology in Japan, Korea and Chinese Taipei, and to some extent in China, has been largely absent elsewhere, notably in the Southeast Asian countries. Northeast Asian countries have developed their own enterprises, but Southeast Asia depends to a much greater extent on direct investment from foreign multinationals. In a word, East Asia's high growth has varying patterns;

— East Asia's success has generated its own momentum. The area bristles with activity, rapid development and new construction. Kuala Lumpur has the tallest building in the world, Shanghai is getting a new, contemporary airport, etc. The momentum in turn generates self-confidence and increasing interaction between the countries of the region;

— There is some argument in academic and policy-making circles in the West over whether East Asia truly constitutes an economic "region" with respect to cohesiveness and homogeneity, as opposed to a region in a purely geographic sense. East Asians themselves increasingly perceive or portray East Asia as a region, as a geographic space with a degree of economic, political, cultural and social integration. This perception of East Asia is quite widespread;

— Regional success, cohesion and greater integration have perhaps inevitably led to references to common Asian values. Asian leaders and some of their Western admirers speak of "Asian approaches", the "Asian way" and "Asian values". Concretely, they are generally referring to things like close family ties, high levels of education, a strong work ethic, respect for elders and hierarchy, discipline, frugality, harmony, consensus, emphasis on personal rather than contractual relationships and social obligations. In fact, there are significant differences in Asia. For example, whereas family ties have traditionally been strong in Chinese society, in Japan they are weak. Although high levels of education tend to characterise Northeast Asian societies, this is far less the case in Southeast Asia. The existence or prevalence of Asian values is a myth. However, myths can be influential;

— Corporate networks are a characteristic of East Asia. There are significant and striking differences between the three primary networks, the Japanese *keiretsu*, the Korean *chaebol*, and the Chinese "bamboo networks". However, they are all quite closed. An outsider can do business with or form an alliance, e.g. a joint-venture, with a corporate member of an East Asian network, but cannot join one. This applies as much to outsiders from within the region as from the rest of the world. For example, core members of a Japanese *keiretsu* remain core members, but peripheral members to a much greater extent come and go. However, both core and peripheral members are *exclusively* Japanese.

What applies to membership in the corporate networks also applies to management. Leading Japanese corporations tend to recruit management from a very small number of academic institutions, where admission is primarily meritocratic[11], while promotion within the firm is generally reserved to university graduates who are lifetime career employees. Among leading Korean firms, recruitment and promotion is reserved for meritocratic university graduates from a limited number of prestigious institutions, and also for members of the *chaebol* owner families. Chinese corporations have been somewhat more flexible in occasionally bringing in outsiders, including non-Chinese. However, such cases are temporary. Recruitment and especially promotion are primarily family affairs. Often the offspring of leading first-generation Chinese capitalists are sent to be trained in elite business schools in the United States.

A key characteristic of the business environment is the emphasis given to relationships. As one observer wrote: "business in North America is based on law, in Europe on logic, and in Asia on relationships"[12]. Considerable business is conducted by Japanese in expensive hostess bars over whisky, by Chinese in restaurants over cognac and dinner, while in Korea's highly "macho" society, whisky, cognac and other things are all mixed at one sitting. Close relationships, sustained and lubricated by frequent informal meetings, pervade the business world.

There undoubtedly has been a much greater degree of intraregional business penetration in East Asia during the past decade than before. There has been a greater flow of investments, trade, technology transfer and tourism within the region. Until the mid-1980s, the economies of East Asia were primarily directed towards the United States. The American market represented 50 per cent of exports for Chinese Taipei, over 40 per cent for Korea and some 35 per cent for Japan. Though Western markets remain important, the 1990s has witnessed a boom in intra-Asian trade.

A final feature of East Asia that might be noted here is that the region has shifted from being a passive to an active player in the international economic arena. Although APEC was conceived by Australians and then launched to a higher plane by the Americans at the Seattle summit (1993), since then Asian governments have been an equally powerful driving force. The Asia-Europe Summit Meeting (ASEM), held in Bangkok on 1 and 2 March 1996, was also an East Asian initiative. East Asian activity has not been limited to regional forums. Although East Asian governments tended to be passive in the GATT and during the Uruguay Round, they have become far more forceful in the WTO, whose first ministerial conference will be held in Singapore in December 1996. Also, the economic muscle of East Asian enterprises arises from increasingly higher value added and technological sophistication. While Japanese high-tech firms such as NEC, Fujitsu and Kyocera have been on the scene for some time and are well known, more recent, less well known, forceful entrants into high technology include companies with diverse national origins such as Mitac (Chinese Taipei), Samsung Electronics (Korea) and Alphatech (Thailand).

To what extent then is the region's greater commercial drive, technological dynamism and economic integration caused by and/or reflected in regional patterns of corporate governance?

Mythology of Homogeneous East Asian Corporate Governance

Political and academic circles have tended to see a single East Asian form of corporate governance, whereas in fact diversity is predominant. Among the reasons for the erroneous views (in no particular order of priority) are:

— Although there has been much greater East Asian intraregional economic integration since 1985, intellectual integration and cross-fertilization remain limited.

— There is simple ignorance which is related to two complementary factors. One, to the extent that East Asian economic integration exists, it is hardly more than a decade old[13], which implies that there has been limited time for research, study and reflection. Moreover, because most of the economies of the region have very high growth rates, it has seemed reasonable to assume that they also had similar socio-economic structures and cultures.

— The Japanese dimension has loomed large. Japan's economic success since the late Edo era (1860s) has been due in considerable measure to its assiduous study of and selective borrowing from the West. Shortly after the Meiji Restoration (1868), Japan effectively joined the Western camp, as advocated by one of its most influential intellectual leaders, Yukichi Fukuzawa, namely *Datsu-A*, the "shedding of (or exit from) Asia". From that time, Japan became a "Western" power, learning from and closely allied to three successive Western partners: Britain, Germany and, since the end of World War II, the United States.

— The development of greater East Asian integration in the second half of the 1980s occurred simultaneously with growing economic friction between Japan and the United States. As a reaction against the hitherto dominant American influence, some Japanese having influence on public opinion began to "rediscover" the country's Asian roots and "re-Asianisation" became the slogan.

Furthermore, in the period roughly from the mid/late 1970s to the mid/late 1980s when "Japanese management" became a subject of interest, leading Japanese thinkers tended to draw primarily socio-cultural distinctions between "Japanese" and "Western" management. Two important elements of this phenomenon were: (a) the "West" tended to be lumped together and generally held to be synonymous with America; (b) Japanese culture, on the other hand, was perceived as being unique. More recently there has been a tendency in Japan to see alleged Japanese business traits on a greater East Asian canvas[14]: the "East Asian model" is often presented as a Japanese model writ large.

With the end of the cold war, economic frictions between the United States and East Asian countries, Japan and China in particular, have become more acute. When the Clinton administration came to power, there was a view in influential intellectual circles that the age of geopolitics was being replaced by "geo-economics". During the cold war rivalry between two military superpowers, the battle had been between capitalism and communism. However, the demise of the Soviet Union in itself proved the growing irrelevance of the conventional means of power. To rephrase Mao Zedong, power no longer emerges from the barrel of a gun, but from financial and technological resources. The battle is no longer between capitalism and communism, for capitalism has prevailed, even in supposedly communist countries, e.g. China and Vietnam. The 21st century battlefield, according to this school of thought, is one that will pit different types of capitalism against each other[15]. Although Japan has been the *bête noire* of the "geo-economists", some of these writers have also tended to see Japanese corporate governance characteristics in a broader East Asian arena.

European presence and influence in East Asia in recent decades has been comparatively weak. The major encounter between "East" and "West" since the mid-1950s has been almost overwhelmingly with the United States. European awareness of the vital economic importance of East Asia has increased significantly in the last five years or so. The European business presence in East Asia, though still small compared to that of the United States, is also increasing, even though European influence may remain marginal at present[16]. Nevertheless, with greater European activity in East Asia, and vice versa, with the enhanced reciprocal interest generated by ASEM and other initiatives, the more complex patterns of corporate governance that exist may also come to be recognised.

Limitations of European Integration

East Asians are relatively unacquainted with each other. In the modern epoch, with the exception of Japan, they did not trade, invest or do much business among themselves until recently. For more or less two centuries, individual East Asian economies were dominated by and directed towards their colonial masters, e.g. Indonesia towards the Netherlands, the countries of Indochina towards France, Malaysia towards Britain, or, as in the case of China, were exploited by various Western imperialist powers and Japan. The main economic partner became the United States after the demise of European colonial domination and imperialism.

In contrast, the European nations have been engaged in economic exchanges with each other for centuries, and besides making war among themselves, a portion of their populations have migrated to other European countries and intermarried, and knowledge has easily spread from one country to another. Furthermore, while East Asian discussions about regional co-operation are of recent vintage, the construction of a European common space has been in the making for a half century. The inauguration of a single European market in 1993 has not yet created a single European business community. The distinctive approach of individual European nations to business, and the persistence of national barriers, has prevented a large-scale fusion of European businesses.

For example, the great shakeout in the European automotive industry that has been heralded for well over a decade has yet to materialise. BMW acquired the Rover Group and Volkswagen acquired Seat, but both were minor players. The much trumpeted merger between Renault and Volvo ultimately failed. The collapse of the merger was in part held to be the incompatibility between two very different forms of corporate governance, namely the fact that Renault was state owned — even though the French government had promised to privatise it in part — while Volvo was a public company[17].

Cross-border European mergers, acquisitions or alliances tend to fall into one of several distinct categories:

— Extremely large projects, whose existence depends on extensive cross-border co-operation, which are deemed to be of strategic significance and where the role of governments looms large. Thus Europe would not have a sizeable civil aircraft industry, let alone be able to compete with Boeing, without a four-nation Airbus consortium;

— High-tech areas, also deemed of strategic significance, where the size of the project may not be so great, but resources in R&D need to be pooled, e.g. the Franco-Italian joint venture between SGS and Thomson in the semiconductor industry;

— Acquisitions by dominant European players of much smaller companies tend to occur in relatively low-tech industries such as the acquisitions of Rover by BMW and of Seat by Volkswagen, though this kind of activity has been perhaps the most prominent in white goods and consumer electronics;

— Cross-border companies that predate and therefore have little, if any, connection to current European integration, e.g. Royal Dutch Shell and Unilever.

There are exceptions to these rules, though, apart from ABB, the merger of the Swedish Asea and the Swiss Brown Boveri, none are of major proportions.

What is striking about the European business community is how "national" companies have remained[18]. Thus, in spite of its acquisition of Rover, BMW remains a very German company, as is the case with Volkswagen in spite of Seat. Mercedes remains very German, just as Renault and Peugeot remain very French, Saab — even though half-owned by GM — and Volvo remain Swedish, and Fiat remains quintessentially Italian. It could be said that the most "European" car companies are Ford and GM[19].

The observation about Ford and GM underscores a predominant pattern of American presence in the European market and European corporate strategies vis-à-vis the United States. For a long time IBM was one of the biggest European employers. Although IBM's fortunes have waned recently, it was the only company in Europe to have value-added activities in all European Community countries. It succeeded rather brilliantly in both creating a broad and universal IBM "church", while at the same time integrating in local communities. IBM Deutschland is both IBM and German. No European company has come anywhere close to achieving that kind of synergy between pan-Europeanism and local integration.

While American companies remain dominant players in Europe, they are also key partners, or "targets", in European corporate strategies. In the pharmaceutical industry, for example, major European companies in one country have acquired minor companies in another country. However, cross-border mega-mergers and/or acquisitions have been primarily between European and American companies such as between the Swedish Pharmacia and Upjohn, or between the French Rhône-Poulenc and Rorer. The other recent mega-merger in pharmaceuticals was between two companies from the same country, Ciba Geigy and Sandoz of Switzerland. Relationships between European and American companies generally appear to be easier to manage than between European companies from different countries.

Why should relationships with Americans be easier? For one thing, Americans tend to have a far more flexible attitude towards corporate ownership. Companies are aggregates of economic assets which exist to be bought or sold, and it generally does not matter whether the buyer is American or foreign[20]. In contrast to prickly, often nationalistic Europeans, Americans are much more easy-going. Furthermore, in Europe, even in cases of publicly traded companies, governments are far more likely to become involved not only in the details of the merger or acquisition, but also in subsequent management activities. For reasons related to corporate governance, management practice and the broader political environment, in the business world Europeans find it easier to deal with Americans than with other Europeans.

Americans have been key and often prominent —sometimes dominant— players for some decades in the European market, while more recent arrivals have come primarily from East Asia. It would have been very interesting if the possible acquisition of Fokker from Daimler Benz by Samsung had proceeded a bit further[21], as it would have created something of a precedent. Although Japanese, Korean and Chinese companies have made acquisitions in Europe, they have been largely in areas such as real estate, including hotels, vineyards and distilleries, retailing, fashion and luxury goods.

The only prominent case of an East Asian acquisition of a European high-tech manufacturing company was that of the Japanese Fujitsu acquiring the UK information technology company ICL. The UK attitude towards buying and selling companies, especially as fostered by former Prime Minister Margaret Thatcher, is much closer to an American than to a Continental European pattern. In automobiles and electronics, the sectors where Japanese, and more recently Korean companies, have tended to be most prominent in Europe, investments have been primarily in greenfield sites and in some cases joint ventures, e.g. in automobiles between Mitsubishi Motors and Volvo in the Netherlands.

Have the Japanese, and other East Asians, been restrained from making acquisitions in Europe because of possible European resistance — whether active or passive — or has it been because of the incompatibilities in corporate governance and the fears of management problems that would subsequently arise? The answer would seem to be a combination of the two.

Corporate Governance in the Japanese, German and Anglo-American Models

Comparing corporate governance in different cultures can be done from a number of different perspectives. Comparisons can overlap with contrasts. The framework here reviews the characteristics of Japanese, German, and the Anglo-American "models". Models are based on reality and perception but portray "ideal-types". Inevitably there are variations and distortions. In assessing these three models, corresponding to four countries, the following points should be kept in mind:

— The United States, Japan, Germany and the United Kingdom are four of the world's largest economies. Together they account for the bulk of the world's foreign direct investment. The other members of the G-7, France, Italy and Canada, have much less overseas investment, while Asian foreign investment, apart from Japan's, is a recent phenomenon and is still relatively limited. American, Japanese, German and British firms are the most numerous and prominent global players;

— The four countries also have the world's most influential and best-known economies and business systems. The United States, Japan and Germany rank first, second and third respectively in GNP[22], and although the United Kingdom is comparatively weaker, it remains influential for a number of reasons, such as the role of the city of London in international finance. They are the best known economies in the sense that the most has been written about corporate governance of these four countries in scholarly journals and the business press;

— State control of industry is minimal in these four countries, unlike in France and Italy. Most of their large companies belong to the private sector;

— Again unlike in France and Italy, most large American, Japanese, German and British companies are no longer owned or dominated by individual families, although there may still be some instances of family shares in the large companies, e.g. the Siemens family in Siemens corporation, the Kobayashi family in Fuji Photo Film, the Ford family in Ford Motor Corporation, the Sainsbury family in Sainsbury's, etc;

— The United States, Japan and Germany all tend to be active players across a very broad spectrum of sectors and technologies. Their relative strengths, e.g. the United States in aerospace, Germany in chemicals and Japan in consumer electronics and components are derived more from historical experience than from differing forms of corporate governance;

— Two general differences stand out in particular. The first is that friendly or hostile take-overs are a part of everyday industrial life in the United States and the United Kingdom, whereas they are rare in Germany and Japan. Second, whereas the United States and, to a more limited extent, the United Kingdom generate many start-up companies and have a strong and active venture capital market, in Germany and Japan start-ups are rare and the venture capital market is weak.

With the exception of this last point, it should be emphasized that there are many similarities in the industrial fabric of these four countries. What is striking is how much the United States, the United Kingdom, Japan and Germany have in common in contrast with 90 per cent, or more, of the rest of the world's economies, including those of industrialised countries such as Italy, France, Spain and Korea. One further feature they share, which is perhaps obvious but bears recalling, is that all four countries' business systems have been successful, and on balance remain so.

A comparison of the three "models" reveals what can be called a permutation of priorities towards the "three Ps", people, products and profits. The differing priorities will be outlined below. Later, we will consider whether these models are changing and whether they converging.

Japan	Germany	US/UK
People	Products	Profits
Products	People	Products
Profits	Profits	People

Large Japanese companies have so-called lifetime employment. The fact that there may be many exceptions to this rule — e.g. women, temporary workers, foreigners — is irrelevant from the viewpoint of corporate governance. It is definitely part of the discourse of Japanese capitalism that people in companies come first, that they are community-oriented enterprises and that senior management has a social responsibility[23]. In Japanese the word for corporation, *kaisha*, and the word for society, *shakai*, are composed from the same two characters (*kanji*), albeit in reverse order. Some Japanese are fond of saying that in Japan there are lots of *kaisha* (corporations), but no *shakai* (society). Among the many implications of this state of affairs, most of which will be disregarded here for our purposes, one needs to be noted. This lack of *shakai* is manifested, among other ways, by the absence of a welfare state. On the other hand, employees in large corporations expect the companies to provide the welfare. One of the many reasons why there are very few start-ups in Japan, is that life is so much more comfortable in established large companies. Security, social prestige, better pay and excellent fringe benefits, including good marriage prospects[24], are among the advantages to be gained. Traditionally, lay-offs in Japanese companies are rare, certainly the last resort. In exchange, the employee is supposed to provide loyalty to the company.

German corporations do not have quite the same fixation with employees as the Japanese. The union structure is also different. In Japan unions tend to be vertical corporate unions as opposed to horizontal trade unions, which are the prevalent form in Germany. Japanese companies do not have legal requirements for union representation on the board as in Germany, nor is it the custom. Since most Japanese company unions are de *facto*, if not *de jure,* closed shops, at one time or another all employees, including senior managers, will be union members.

Traditionally German companies' reputations and claims to excellence lie in their technology, specifically the engineering quality of their products. Consequently products take precedence over other considerations. German automotive companies, for example, have been reluctant to adopt either American or Japanese (lean production) manufacturing techniques because they might jeopardise the quasi-craftsmanlike nature of their vehicles. Therefore, German cars cost a great deal more to produce than do Japanese cars, or, for that matter, American cars.

People have a lower priority in German companies than in Japanese companies, but rank well ahead of traditional Anglo-American corporate concerns. Considerable investment in Germany goes into training workers, for example, through an intensive and extended apprenticeship system. Job-hopping between major German companies is rare. Although lifetime employment does not exist as in Japan, layoffs are rare compared to the United States and United Kingdom, and employees tend to remain with their companies throughout their careers. Both in German and Japanese companies promotion is primarily internal.

Unlike in the United States and United Kingdom, in Germany and Japan take-overs are very rare and hostile take-overs virtually non-existent. It is generally stressed that a key reason for this contrast lies in the very close bank-industry relationships in Germany and Japan[25]. However, there are also important cultural reasons. In particular, because of the high priority given to people in Japan, and their relatively high priority in Germany, take-overs are socially and ethically frowned upon as akin to buying and selling people.

Until recently, IBM could have been described as a German/Japanese-style company, just as some other American and British companies (e.g. Boeing and British Petroleum) might also correspond to the community-centred type of enterprise. As a general pattern, however, in American corporate life, people are the last of the three priorities. Lay-offs are frequent and reflect the business cycle, people being hired when times are good, fired when times are bad; appointments to senior positions will more often than not result from external horizontal moves, rather than internal promotions; American and British companies spend a far lower proportion of their resources than their German or Japanese counterparts on training; job-hopping is virtually the way of American professional life and take-overs are endemic.

The implications of these differences in priorities are quite profound and can be depicted in tabular form as follows:

Japan →	People have priority →	Emphasis on market share →	CEO is a "generalist"
Germany →	Products have priority →	Emphasis on technology & engineering →	CEO is an engineer
US/UK →	Profits have priority →	Emphasis on share-holder value →	CEO is an MBA or an accountant

Some clarification is necessary to understand what it means to describe a Japanese CEO as a "generalist". The members of Japan's managerial elite tend to be graduates of law, engineering or economics faculties. However, graduates of law faculties of prestigious Japanese universities, the so-called former "imperial universities", e.g. Tokyo, Kyoto and Osaka, are very rarely lawyers. For reasons not discussed here, a Japanese university law faculty may be more accurately described as a general social science faculty, combining law, political science, economics, modern history, etc. More important, however, is one of Japan's paradoxes. While the population has a reputation for working hard, Japanese university students in most social science, engineering, humanities and science faculties generally do not study very hard. Getting into a good Japanese university is very tough and possible only through highly competitive entrance examinations, while graduating is practically a formality. In contrast, primary and especially secondary school pupils study extremely hard.

At the university Japanese students are expected to "network". Ability to develop relationships and assume leadership positions in extra-curricular activities are the most important criteria Japanese companies look for in new recruits. Since lifetime employment in large companies is virtually guaranteed, which means in the company as such, *not* in a particular job or skill[26]. Rotation in the company is also a characteristic of Japanese corporate culture. For promotions, corporations put a high value on qualities such as those required to foster team spirit, create consensus, motivate, etc. Therefore, a Japanese CEO and his senior colleagues will typically be generalists, namely people who have worked in many different departments and have acquired a good bird's eye-view of the company.

In comparing priorities with respect to the three P's in the three models, what was said about *kaisha* (corporation) versus *shakai* (society) should be kept in mind and it should not be concluded that people count for more in Japan than in American and UK societies. In fact, community spirit in the United States and United Kingdom is quite strong outside the corporation, as reflected in churches, non-governmental organisations, school groups, guilds, etc. which tend to be absent in Japan. Furthermore, in the Anglo-American model an individual's worth will normally be based on his or her specific skill. In the Japanese model, an individual's worth will more normally be based on loyalty to and longevity in his[27] company. The value of a good Intel or GEC engineer is that he/she is a good engineer. The value of a good Toshiba man is that he is a good Toshiba man.

From this standpoint, the frequency of lay-offs in the United States/United Kingdom as opposed to their absence in Japan, can be seen in perspective. For example, an Intel or GEC engineer has his/her skill to sell in an open labour market. If he/she is made redundant, transferring the skill to another company is relatively straightforward. If a Toshiba employee is made redundant, the fact that he knows a lot about Toshiba is not much use, except of course if he knows so much that he can help the competition, in which case he is unlikely to be made redundant. For that reason when large Japanese companies do layoff or prematurely retire their employees, they normally place them among the company's suppliers, where they will still provide an advantage to the parent company.

Another point regarding the different corporate governance cultures of the three models is made by Ronald Dore[28]. He has contrasted the Japanese community-oriented enterprise with the British market-oriented enterprise, by noting, among other things, how language and patterns of behaviour differ. In regard to remuneration, for example, in British companies directors get fees, managers get salaries, workers get wages. Furthermore, traditional British companies would generally have separate eating facilities — directors' dining rooms, managers' restaurants, workers' canteens — separate car-parks, separate toilets, different unions, not to mention different accents, after-hour social activities, consumption patterns, newspapers, etc. In Japanese companies, emphasis is put on vertical integration, hence the same canteens and other common facilities for all employees, and in many companies, wearing the corporate uniform.

A ramification of these different attitudes is that workers in the Anglo-American model are not expected to feel loyalty towards the corporation, specifically to their bosses, nor do directors feel loyalty to the company. This absence of loyalty no doubt explains the exorbitant fees, bonuses, stock-options, and other forms of remuneration which British and American bosses pay themselves. Corporate life is transient, *carpe diem*. The income spread in Japanese companies is much narrower than in the United States and the United Kingdom, and consequently Japanese executives are paid far less[29], while in Germany the situation tends to be somewhere in the middle.

A good deal of comment, often negative, has been made about the fact that Japanese corporate boards, and, to a somewhat lesser but nevertheless comparable extent, German boards, are rather ingrown, with great power concentrated in the hands of the CEO. Although the legal form of German and Japanese boards differ, especially in that the former have a two-tier system of separate supervisory and management boards, in fact this will more often be cosmetic than effective in terms of the balance of power[30]. The main disadvantage of the German/Japanese models with their priorities on people and products, as opposed to maximising shareholder value, and their more limited role for shareholders, is the relative absence of efficient monitoring of top management. The *folies de grandeur* which gripped Japanese and German companies in the 1980s, culminating in huge losses due to reckless diversifications, and the scandals that beset Japanese companies in particular[31], would not have occurred with more careful, closer and more objective monitoring. A remedy that is often proposed[32] is the appointment of outside directors.

Internal dynamics of the corporate governance systems in the Japanese, German and Anglo-American models have been emphasized in this analysis. Passing reference was made to the crucial difference in the nature of bank-industry relationships in Japan and Germany on the one hand, and in the United States and the United Kingdom on the other. As this is a more widely known feature of the corporate governance systems of the different models, it requires less attention here.

Although profits have lower priority in the Japanese and German models than they will typically have in the United States or United Kingdom, that does not mean that profits do not count or shareholders do not matter. Since German and Japanese institutional/network shareholders have a much higher profile, the emphasis will tend to be on *stable* returns. A priority on profits/shareholder value clearly has important implications. Dividends in the United Kingdom typically will be nearly twice as high as German dividends and three times as high as Japanese. Moreover, as V. Handy (1993) observed: "During the ten years 1972-82 one-third of the 730 biggest quoted companies in Britain changed ownership, with all the complications and expense and distractions which such change involves. The comparable figure for Japan was 8 per cent. In Germany, of the 450 companies quoted on the stock exchange, only 30 or so are actively traded. In contrast, there are 2 400 companies listed on the London Stock Exchange, almost all of them candidates for the auction ring at any time."[33]

Despite the differences between these three major models of corporate governance, it should be noted that there is a consensus that convergence will occur and that German, Japanese and similar systems will emulate or follow the American model. This trend is considered to be an inevitable consequence of globalisation, whether it is seen as a good thing, as by the *Economist* [34], or viewed with regret and resignation, as in the case of M. Albert[35].

As Aron Viner has remarked: "Japanese boards, not unlike those in Germany, have despotically maintained their own priorities. The interests of employees, customers, politicians, and established corporate and banking relationships have traditionally come before those of institutional investors and individual shareholders. Today in Germany there is a growing recognition that management must be committed to maximising the long-term value of the company's shares for the shareholders"[36]. Yoshimori notes that "Japan and Germany are edging towards the Anglo-American model for increased openness and transparency, emphasis on shareholder interest and short-termism. . . . Increased reliance on the New York capital markets and the future location of the EU's central bank in Frankfurt will certainly accelerate the Anglo-Americanisation process. Disclosure by Daimler Benz of its hidden assets to conform to the SEC regulations for listing on the New York Stock Exchange is symbolic"[37].

Certainly there is a crisis in Japan. The economy has been in the doldrums for half a decade, unprecedented in Japanese post-war history and pretty lacklustre compared even to the generally more sluggish European economies. One can agree with the statement made by Robert Monks that Japan's economic crisis is, to some extent, a corporate governance crisis[38]. There are both internal and external pressures for change, some of which were incorporated in amendments made to the Japanese Commercial Codes in 1994, e.g. in requiring the establishment of at least one outside auditor[39].

Three points conclude this section.

First, one must be careful to distinguish between lessons and hasty conclusions. In the 1980s it was fashionable to argue that American companies needed to learn from their Japanese and German counterparts, and that the latter societies enjoyed a higher and more effective form of capitalism[40]. Though a number of American companies did absorb some lessons from Japan, especially in production technology and human resource management, the culture and structure of American corporate governance did not undergo fundamental change. Today many American companies are doing very well, and in many instances better than their Japanese and German competitors. However, it is too early to say whether this derives from a systemic superiority. The relative German and Japanese disadvantages may be temporary.

Second, efforts to change deep-rooted cultures are difficult and can have all sorts of serious consequences. If Japanese companies were to heed the advice that they should abandon the lifetime employment system in order to focus on boosting profits and thus maximise shareholder value, the economic and social consequences would be very different from those that occur with lay-offs in the United States and the United Kingdom. The skills and even the identities of employees of large Japanese firms are closely linked to their companies. Japanese companies can of course change and begin emphasizing the development of individual skills rather than the fostering of a collective spirit. The Japanese system of corporate governance before World War II was quite different from what it is now. Priority was not given to people in the past, and the working class had to rely on their individual skills. Hence, what is considered Japanese corporate culture is mainly a feature of the post-war era, as opposed to something traditionally embedded in Japanese society. Corporate culture has changed before and it can change again. However, a transition to the kind of change that is being talked about, namely ending lifetime employment and leaving employees to deal with an open labour market, will require at least one generation.

Third, although the world is changing, Japanese, German and American companies, and to some extent the British as well, will continue to dominate global markets and their models will remain the most prominent for the foreseeable future. However, different patterns of economic management and corporate governance are emerging. The world economy is becoming more multipolar, but there is no objective evidence that globalisation will inevitably take the form of Americanisation.

Corporate Governance and Models of Government-Industry Relations

In the book *Capitalism versus Capitalism*, Michel Albert discusses the main differences between the Anglo-American model and the "Rheinal" model. The latter includes: Germany, Austria, Switzerland, the Netherlands and the Scandinavian countries[41]. He considers Japan as basically an Asian extension, or variation, of the Rheinal form of capitalism[42]. In this analysis, we add a Mediterranean form in Europe, while a distinction is made between the Japanese *keiretsu*, the Korean *chaebol* and the Chinese bamboo networks in Asia. Corporate governance is thus divided into six systems:

—   The Anglo-American.

—   The Rheinal.

—   The Mediterranean.

—   The Japanese *keiretsu*.

—   The Korean *chaebol*.

—   The Chinese bamboo network.

There is some overlap between the different systems. Furthermore, greater similarities can be identified among the advanced industrialised countries which are dominated by large, private-sector companies (the United States, Japan, Germany and the United Kingdom) than between the others. From the perspective of economic dominance by large private-sector companies, Switzerland and the Netherlands are the closest to the German "model" among Albert's Rheinal countries. Large Austrian enterprises are dominated by the state, while in Denmark there are very few large corporations and indeed comparatively little industry outside agriculture. Sweden is *sui generis* in that it includes a considerable number of large private-sector companies across a broad spectrum of industrial activities, but there is a heavy concentration of family ownership and control, in particular by the Wallenberg family. In the other three models, the Mediterranean, the Korean and the Chinese, only the Korean has large private corporations, although here too family ownership and control loom large.

The core of a good deal of the argument in Francis Fukuyama's book, *Trust*, is that in societies where there is limited trust outside the family, large corporations are unlikely to emerge, let alone flourish. In France, Italy and in the countries or territories where Chinese enterprises operate, trust, especially in public institutions, like courts, government agencies, etc., tends to be conspicuous by its absence[43]. Therefore, in the Mediterranean and Chinese models the predominant pattern is that of small and medium-sized, family-owned and generally family-managed enterprises. Indeed in the Mediterranean countries, well-known companies such as Benetton and Fiat of Italy, and Rémy Cointreau and Peugeot of France, among others, tend to be family fiefs, in which professional managers may be retained in much the same way as feudal lords employed mercenaries. To compensate for the absence of large corporations, the state has intervened and created them. In France, Italy, Spain, Chinese Taipei and some of the economies of Southeast Asia, large enterprises have usually been owned and managed by the state.

Four models cover the impact of government-industry relationships on corporate governance[44]:

— The government as referee.

— The government as manager.

— The government as coach.

— The government as crony.

It should again be indicated that these models are "ideals", which correspond to prevailing doctrine or principles, but not necessarily to reality in all respects. There are also exceptions in certain sectors. The government-industry models broadly correspond to the corporate governance models.

In the first model of the government as referee, as implied, the government is expected to remain totally impartial with respect to the market, standing on the sidelines and only intruding if or when abuses need to be prevented (e.g. monopolies or cartels) or perpetrators of illegal acts (e.g. insider trading) have to be punished. The government's role in this model is to be as unobtrusive as possible, to promote fairness, grant recognition and respect to the market, and thus minimise regulations. As the government must exercise its role of vigilant referee, this system also places stress on transparency and visible observance of the law. Auditors and lawyers have an important role to play. Corruption tends to be low.

Ideally, this is supposed to be system that prevails in the United States and also the United Kingdom, especially since the Thatcher "revolution". It is also the system that has existed for the last half century or so in Hong Kong. Furthermore, while some countries have undergone "conversions" from one system to another, they have generally tended to be gradual and have mainly involved moving from the second (manager) to the third (coach). Australia provides a rare case of a relatively radical conversion to the first model from a hybrid of models two and three, which occurred under the Hawke and Keating Labour governments.

In summary, the model of the government as referee can be summarised as shown in the following table

Government as referee	United States United Kingdom Hong Kong Australia New Zealand	Sidelines Impartiality Prevention and punishment of abuses Emphasis on fairness and unregulated market forces Open transparent, accountable forms of corporate governance

In the second model of the government as manager, the government's role is at the other extreme. Not only does the government neither recognise nor respect the market, it does not trust it. Although in democratic societies, the application of the models may vary depending on parties in power (e.g. in the United States the Republicans tend to be less intrusive than the Democrats), the models by and large apply irrespective of the party in power. In France, which is the epitome of the government as manager in Europe, there is continuity whether the right or left is in power. The socialists nationalise and the right privatises, but certain Gallic attitudes remain ingrained. This point can be illustrated by former Prime Minister Edouard Balladur's reference to the "jungle" of the market while he was a presidential candidate in 1995.

The ideology of the government-as-manager is known in France as *dirigisme*. In this model, the government knows best. The government is intrusive, regulations are numerous and often labyrinthine, trade policies incline towards protectionism and corruption tends to be rampant. Although the government-as-manager model normally includes a significant proportion of state-owned and state-controlled industry, especially in so-called strategic sectors, the main point about the government as manager is that it is quite intrusive even when industries are not owned by the state. French economic life is suffocated with regulations, the bureaucracy is powerful, lots and lots of paper is required for everything and anything. Another major *raison d'être* of the government as manager is to promote national industrial champions.

In France there has traditionally been an absence of professional managers in senior management positions. The French elite comes from the *grandes écoles*, institutions of tertiary education, for which entry is by a competitive exam. They differ from and are far "above" the ordinary universities. The elite of the elite are graduates of the École Nationale d'Administration (ENA). *Enarques*, as graduates of the ENA are known, will typically spend their careers alternating between bureaucracy and business as they climb (usually quite quickly) the rungs of these parallel ladders.

In the government-as-manager model, corporate governance is opaque, secretive and, consequently, closed. In summary, the government as manager model can be presented as follows:

Government as manager	France, Italy, Spain China and Viet Nam Singapore Indonesia, Malaysia Thailand Korea (ca 1962-90) Chinese Taipei (ca 1949-86)	Economic nationalism and protectionism Government intervention and control Promotion of national corporate champions Corporate governance is opaque, secretive and closed, with little public accountability

The distinction between government as manager and government as coach will be discussed further below. However, two things should be noted here: first, most hybrids involve these two systems, especially in East Asia; second, complementary to the first, most of the changes in East Asia have also involved these two models. Korea, for example, was quite clearly a case of the government as manager, although in recent years it has moved in the direction of the government as coach. This would apply to other East Asian countries, and thus they will feature under both models, with the differences either determined by stage of development or other circumstances. For example, the Malaysian and Indonesian governments tend to play the role of coach with respect to Chinese enterprises, but have a much more hands-on role with respect to management of *bumiputra* enterprises in the case of Malaysia and *pribumi* enterprises in Indonesia.

There are variations in all the models. Italy is closer to a government as manager than any other model. The government's role in the Italian variant of this model is much less pronounced than in the French for various reasons, of which an important one of course is the fact that Italy often does not have a government. Spain does not have national champions to promote. On the other hand, neither the Suarez nor the Gonzalez governments succeeded in breaking totally with the Francoist state-corporatist and protectionist legacies. Also, just as there are efficient and inefficient managers in business, the same applies to governments. The French government has been reasonably successful. Without large private corporations, especially high tech, it is difficult to imagine how France could have developed a successful nuclear power industry without the government. The Italian government has been less effective, though the Italian economy, especially the myriad small family enterprises, has been quite successful in spite of the Italian government. On the other hand, Singapore has one of the developed capitalist world's most intrusive governments, and yet it has been remarkably successful.

Korea and Chinese Taipei, as noted, have made the break from government as manager to government as coach. This is partly the result of their successful policies in previous decades, as well as the result of economic growth, increasing industrial complexity and the greater independence and the corporate sector's aspirations to power[45]. It is also no doubt a consequence of democratisation in both societies.

Indonesia, Malaysia and Thailand manifest both models, i.e. manager and coach. Although all three countries have been successful economically compared to most countries of the Third World, none of the three can match the success of Korea or Chinese Taipei. Indonesia, Malaysia and Thailand are developing countries and are likely to remain developing countries for the foreseeable future, rather than joining the ranks of the NIEs (newly industrialising economies). There are a number of reasons for this state of affairs[46], one of which is that none of the three countries' governments has had the management capability of Korea, Chinese Taipei or Singapore.

The economic reforms launched in China and in Vietnam — and possibly ultimately in Laos and Myanmar — are aimed at giving industry more leeway and thus coming closer to the coach model. As things currently stand, however, governments in both countries remain quite intrusive. The trend at this stage is no more than that, a trend, and it could still be reversed. Thus China and Vietnam for the time being remain in the second model.

This chapter will not attempt to cover the recently emancipated economies of Central and Eastern Europe or the former Soviet Union. There are those who have urged these countries to leap from communism (which might be described as the government-as-dictator model) to the government-as-referee model, while others have favoured a more gradualist Chinese type of approach. However, events are too recent and the situation too volatile to draw any firm conclusions.

There are variations of the government-as-coach model, as in the others. A coach can actively shout from the sidelines, or he/she can be detached. In Europe, the Rheinal-capitalist countries will tend to conform to the government-as-coach model. Among other things, this is a natural outcome of the welfare state and the social contract that characterise these economies. Furthermore, while all of the Rheinal countries have had both centre-right and socialist governments, none of the latter sought extensive nationalisation of industry like President François Mitterrand's socialist government in France. In the Rheinal countries, Socialists are content to remain coaches, rather than aspiring to become managers.

Although the Socialists have been in power in Sweden for most of the last seven decades, and a number of the policies that they implemented were quite extreme — e.g. in incomes policy — they never attempted to dismantle the Wallenberg industrial empire. Although the Rheinal countries tend to be far less protectionist than the Mediterranean countries, there may be significant protectionism in certain sectors, especially in agriculture, and like telecommunications, sausages and beer in Germany. Many forms of direct and indirect subsidies for industries are more characteristic of the government-as-coach Rheinal countries. On the whole, however, the Rheinal coach tends to be rather laid-back and detached.

There has been a growing body of literature and a quite intense debate among Western scholars and others as to whether the Japanese government has or has not been prominent and/or effective in the country's economic development. Members of the school which portrays the Japanese government as having been weak and/or ineffective[47], among other things, point out that Japanese business has tended to be strong precisely in those sectors (e.g. cars) where there has been least government interference and the most successful companies such as Sony and Honda have had the most distant relationship with government. While all this is to some extent true[48], the consensus among social scientists specialising in Japan is that the Japanese government's role has been very important[49], but perhaps also quite subtle.

The Japanese have been refining and developing[50] the government-as-coach model since the mid-Meiji era (1880s-1890s). As far as coaches go, the Japanese can be said to have been among the best. However, when Japanese officials intruded beyond the limits of coaching, they tended to fail. In contrast with the coaching provided to the electronics, office equipment, machine tool, factory automation, telecommunications equipment and specialty chemicals sectors, the Japanese government engaged in outright managerial interference in financial services, aerospace, pharmaceuticals, petroleum refining and agriculture and these five sectors are among Japan's weakest[51].

France and Japan have similar systems of essentially meritocratic elites. Parallels can be drawn between France's *grandes écoles* and the half dozen or so prestigious Japanese universities[52] from which the *crème de la crème* of Japanese managers and bureaucrats tend to be recruited. While the graduates of Japan's elite universities, as in France, form a sort of nomenklatura, there is a critical difference. In France, with its government as manager, graduates of the *grandes écoles* move between government and industry throughout their careers. In Japan, elite university graduates run the government and corporations but do not move between the two. However, they know each other well, drink together, play golf together and plot together. Much of their contact is informal.

In Japan there is no movement at all from corporation to government. Those bureaucrats who do leave government in early or mid-career will normally go into politics, in some cases into universities, and in a few cases they may join foreign companies. Government bureaucrats do not, except in cases of temporary assignment due to special circumstances, work in private corporations during their careers. At the end of their careers as bureaucrats, there is a practice known as *amakudari* (descent from heaven), whereby bureaucrats are recruited by private companies as executives for the board or as "senior advisers".

These two different approaches to government and corporate careers in France and Japan reflect the differences between the government as manager and government as coach.

Other East Asian societies, including China, are seeking to emulate the Japanese model of government as coach. Chinese Taipei and Korea have been the most successful. The fact that both were colonies of Japan and that close, even if occasionally hostile, links have been maintained is surely not irrelevant. Indonesia, Thailand and Malaysia are also striving to follow the Japanese model.

The fashion in the mid-1990s is to argue that all economies should go the American way. However, it was widely asserted in the United States in the 1980s that only by adopting an industrial policy could America hope to compete against Japan. However, there is some uncertainty whether the role of coach assumed by Japan actually constitutes an industrial policy. Its approach has been also been described as a system of "administrative guidance"[53]. However that may be, it would have been rather difficult to "Japanise" the United States, partly because the culture of the bureaucracy has been very different since time of American independence. For analogous historical reasons, it will be difficult for the Japanese and others to "Americanise".

MBAs tend to be conspicuous by their absence in both the coach and manager models, in contrast with the referee model, but this is changing. For example, in the Chinese bamboo networks more second generation managers are getting MBA training in American business schools. In France of the *grandes écoles* and in Japan of the elite universities, however, there is not much room for an outsider. Both the French and the Japanese meritocratic/education systems are nationalistic. This in part explains why neither Japanese nor French enterprises have been particularly successful in the management of their foreign operations. French and Japanese graduates of elite institutions do not readily accommodate to corporate governance of other cultures.

Like a referee, a coach stands on the sidelines. However, unlike the referee, a coach is not impartial. He wants his team to win. As Richard Whitely notes about East Asia, "support and connections are often a crucial aspect of business activities in these societies and form a key component of their dominant business systems. This support does not, though, usually extend to the granting of monopoly powers or toleration of sustained inefficiency. Rather it tends to reward success and punish failure and so 'accelerate market forces'"[54].

Unlike a manager, a coach does try to promote national champions. The coach recognises that competition is good, especially on the home turf. The more competition faced, the better one becomes. To avoid wasting energy and resources, however, it is best to ensure that competition is orderly. In contrast with France which tried to promote one key computer maker (Bull), Japan has four major computer makers (Fujitsu, NEC, Toshiba and Hitachi) which actively compete against each other, all the better to compete against IBM. The same principle applies to many sectors of Japanese industry. One of the reasons why the aerospace industry in Japan has been somewhat of a failure so far is that although there are also four major players (Mitsubishi Heavy Industry, Kawasaki Heavy Industry, Fuji Heavy Industry, and Ishikawajima-Harima), they do not compete against each other. The Japanese government decides which company will do what, get which project, receive which technology, etc.

The coach model is close to the manager model as it naturally implies cosy relationships between government and industry. Consequently, there is considerable scope for corruption, although this appears to be more widespread in the East Asian cases of the model than in the European. Indeed, the Rheinal societies are among the world's least corrupt, though this may have more to do with religion (the "Protestant ethic") than with forms of government-industry relationships or corporate governance.

The coach model can be summarised as shown in the following table:

Government as coach	The Rheinal economies, Japan, Korea and Chinese Taipei (Thailand, Malaysia & Indonesia)	Sidelines partiality Administrative guidance Support systems, subsidies, etc. Organised competition Semi-transparent/semi-opaque corporate governance with limited public accountability

There is no need to consider the fourth model. Unlike the others, which have their strengths and their weaknesses, "crony capitalism" is an entirely negative model. The term was coined to refer to the Philippines at the time of the Marcos regime. Although there have been some attempts at reform, and the economy is doing better under the presidency of Fidel Ramos, it is nevertheless still difficult to categorise the Philippines in any of the other models. There is a bit of management, a bit of coaching, but cronyism remains — even though the cronies may not be the same cronies. There is an element of crony capitalism in many economies. The scandals that have been rocking France in recent years, reveal the extent to which favouritism prevails in that country and, consequently, a lot of insider information circulates. Crony capitalism in various forms permeates most Southern European and East Asian societies.

Corporate Governance in East Asia: Trends and Implications

The Japanese Keiretsu

Not all Japanese companies are necessarily members of a *keiretsu*. However, most, are closely or loosely associated with one, or, in many cases, several *keiretsu*. *Keiretsu* is a rather loose term which can mean several things.

Companies joined together in a horizontal group, e.g. the Mitsui or Dai-Ichi Kangyo groups, represent one form of *keiretsu* (also known as *kigyo shudan*). These horizontal *keiretsu* are all associated with a major bank[55], they include companies from most, or certainly many, industries in the primary, secondary and tertiary sectors, from mining to insurance, they have significant cross share-holdings[56] and the presidents of the core *keiretsu* companies meet on a regular basis in the association of presidents (*shacho-kai*). *Keiretsu* companies normally have privileged mutual trading relationships. Among the six major horizontal *keiretsu*, Mitsui, Mitsubishi, Sumitomo, Dai-Ichi Kangyo, Sanwa and Fuji, only Mitsubishi uses its name extensively among the companies of its network: e.g. Mitsubishi Motors, Mitsubishi Heavy Industries, Mitsubishi Kasei, etc. The Mitsubishi group also owns a great deal of the real estate in the business district of Tokyo, Marunouchi, between the Tokyo railroad station and the Imperial Palace, and thus the area is commonly referred to by city residents as "*Mitsubishi mura*" (Mitsubishi village)[57].

Even companies which are theoretically not members of a *keiretsu* will nevertheless be part of a "main bank" system. The main bank has the most exposure to the company (i.e. debt) and/or is the bank with the largest share in its equity. Main banks are normally the principal city banks, i.e. those that are at the core of the six groups mentioned above, or long-term credit banks, or some of the provincial banks, e.g. the Tokai bank in Nagoya.

A second form of *keiretsu* links the chain between suppliers and manufacturers. These are vertical groups. In the horizontal groups, in principle, equality reigns between the companies, though a handful will normally be more equal than the others, but among the vertical companies there is a clear and strict hierarchical order. Large manufacturers, e.g. Nissan, Kobe Steel and Matsushita, have first, second, third or higher tier suppliers, organised in pyramidal fashion. Virtually all small and medium-sized manufacturing companies in Japan belong in one form or another to a vertical *keiretsu*, although some of the vertical *keiretsu* companies can be huge. Nippon Denso which is part of the Toyota *keiretsu* has a turnover of some $14 billion.

The nature of the vertical relationship can take various forms. In terms of equity, it can range from total ownership to none. The relationship is more historical, industrial, commercial and possibly social, than contractual. In the late 1980s, when the American corporate raider T. Boone Pickens made a hostile takeover bid for Koito, an automotive lighting manufacturer, he sought representation on Koito's board. After much publicity and rancour, Pickens ultimately had to give up as he was thwarted by Toyota. Although Pickens had a greater proportion of the shares of Koito than Toyota, "everyone" (in Japan) knew that Koito "belonged" to Toyota.

A third form of *keiretsu*, also vertical, is in the distribution chain. Manufacturers have their distribution chain, which normally involves distributors selling their products exclusively. For example, Shiseido, which introduced the vertical distribution system in 1924, has some 45 000 retail outlets in Japan which exclusively sell Shiseido products. Market share is, not surprisingly, often in direct proportion to the number of retail outlets in the distribution *keiretsu*. Thus, Shiseido's major domestic competitor, Kanebo, has roughly half the number of outlets as does Shiseido and about half Shiseido's market share in Japan.

As large Japanese companies have internationalised through direct foreign investments, they have tended to take their *keiretsu*, especially of the first and second variety, with them. For example, Mitsubishi Shoji (the general trading company) has invested together with Mitsubishi Motors in the joint venture they have in the Malaysian national car project (Proton Saga), partly because Mitsubishi Shoji, like the other major trading companies (*sogo shosha*) has vast international experience and quite a few networks in Malaysia. Similarly, the arrival of Japanese automobile manufacturing companies in the United States brought in its wake hundreds of Japanese parts and component makers who, as the suppliers in the individual companies' *keiretsu* chain, were instructed to establish operations in America.

The origins of Japan's *keiretsu* are complex and will be discussed only briefly here. The story begins with Japan's industrial revolution in the late nineteenth century, which was primarily led from above, that is by the government which quickly recognised that it could not run industry profitably. In the late 1880s most government-owned assets were sold to the private sector. However, they were not sold on an open-market, highest-bid basis. They were sold on preferential terms to certain leading family groups (the *zaibatsu*). An overriding concern of the officials of the modernising government was their commitment to the principle and practice of *order*. They also wished to ensure that private sector corporate interests and national interests (as determined by the government) should converge. Thus, while private entrepreneurs might be entrusted to "manage", the government remained the "guide" (or "coach"). The sale of national assets to the *zaibatsu*, of which the four leading ones at the time were Mitsui, Mitsubishi, Yasuda and Sumitomo, was carried out in orderly fashion[58]. In essence, therefore, the Meiji era (1868-1912) economic edifice became a government-guided oligopolistic industrial system.

The American occupation authorities (1945-1952) tried to break things up. In the immediate post-war period, however, the Japanese had very little, or no, capital, markets, products and natural resources. Japan had lost the war, but the siege mentality was retained in economic affairs and, especially with respect to economic security. When under siege, co-operation provides an advantage and the Japanese chose to co-operate. Many of the business networks of the prewar era were revived. When the *défi américain*[59] began reaching Japanese shores in the late 1950s and early 1960s, the prewar *zaibatsu* were reconstituted in a modified form and new groups were created around major banks. A collective defence mechanism to prevent Japanese industry from being taken over by American capital led to the emergence of the horizontal *keiretsu*. These *keiretsu* companies together owned majority shares in each other's firms, which would prevent the Americans from buying majority, or even significant proportions of the shares of Japanese companies.

The *keiretsu* also correspond to something which is far more profound and extensive in Japanese capitalism: they represent the structural embodiment of the principles of *interdependence*. This points to the most striking difference between the Japanese and Anglo-American models of capitalism. In the Anglo-American model, economic entities operate independently in an environment with free-for-all market forces. In contrast, the one word that best epitomises the culture and structure of every aspect of Japanese economic life is interdependence. In the United States and United Kingdom, banks are independent from industry, but in Japan they are closely associated. In the United States and United Kingdom, manufacturers select suppliers on the basis of costs and through short-term contracts. Both remain independent unless they are taken over. In Japan, interdependence is fostered by long-established and constantly "massaged" relationships.

The extent of Japan's interdependence and the corresponding form of governance have come under some severe criticism outside of Japan, in the United States in particular. Americans long-believed that Japanese government policies were preventing American companies from getting into the Japanese market, but then they began to think that perhaps the structure of industry, and the *keiretsu* system in particular, was more to blame[60]. *Keiretsu* featured prominently among the subjects the Americans wished to have discussed, with a view to their being dismantled, in the Structural Impediments Initiative (SII) talks during the Reagan and Bush administrations. Among the American grievances against Japan is the fact that whereas Japanese companies can acquire American companies, foreign companies cannot acquire Japanese companies, not because of law, but because of the nature of the system of corporate governance[61].

Given Japan's interdependent, possibly nationalistic industrial structure and culture, corporate governance is intrinsically different from what it is in the United States, whatever the law books may say. As Ulrike Schaede has written: "The Japanese system of corporate governance builds on mechanisms that are not commonly recognised in the West. . . . It is true that Japan is undergoing rapid change, and the role of the government may change accordingly. However, it is likely that the Japanese system of corporate governance will remain distinctive from that in the US, even if shareholders in Japan do obtain more rights and proceed to assert them"[62].

The Japanese government, in principle, is committed to deregulation. Progress is slow, possibly because the Japanese bureaucrats' predilection for order remains steadfast. While there can be no doubt that the Japanese system of interdependence has been outstandingly successful in the era of building national economies, it is difficult to envisage how the structure and culture of interdependence will evolve as Japanese companies globalise.

Korean Chaebol

Korea is the world's newest industrial country and, no doubt largely for that reason it is the least studied. One of the world's poorest countries as recently as the early 1960s, when the GNP was lower than in countries such as Ghana or Togo, Korea now has a *per capita* income greater than $10 000 and has applied for membership in the OECD. Conventional wisdom about Korea's astonishingly rapid economic development portray the government, especially the military dictatorship of General Park Chung-hee, as the *deus ex machina*. There can be no doubt that the role of the government was crucial and that the Park Chung-hee regime successfully applied a number of "Japanese lessons".

As pointed out by Jung Ku-Hyun, "although economic literature pays a great deal of attention to the government role in economic development in Korea, one should not underestimate the role of entrepreneurs in the process. For example, we cannot imagine the Hyundai group or Samsung group without such entrepreneurs as Chung Ju Yung or Lee Byung Chul"[63].

Korea was one of the last Asian countries to be "opened" to foreign relations and trade. It was long part of the Chinese empire, though from the 1870s it was primarily Japan that began encroaching upon it. Unlike the reformers in Japan of the Meiji period, the Korean court and aristocracy (*yangban*) remained resolutely conservative. However, the Japanese invaded Korea and in 1910 made it a colony, which it remained until Japan's defeat in 1945.

With liberation and the cold war, Korea was divided into two, the Democratic People's Republic of Korea in the North and the Republic of Korea in the South, whose territories corresponded to the Soviet and US zones for supervising the surrender of Japanese troops. The country was left devastated by the Korean War from mid-1950 to mid-1953, in which the US forces participated in support of South Korea and Chinese troops supported North Korea. From liberation in 1945 until 1962 the South Korean government was headed by Syngman Rhee. He was overthrown in a coup d'état by General Park Chung-hee in 1962. In that year Korean GNP per capita was $80 and over 80 per cent of the working population was engaged in agriculture.

Many Koreans have studied in US universities and American influence is strong in Korean tertiary educational institutions. (The prestigious Yonsei University was founded by an American Christian missionary.) There is now a sizeable Korean-American community in the United States. Largely as a result of American missionary activity in Korea, it is one of the few Asian countries that has a relatively large number of Christians, the others being the Philippines and Viet Nam, A generally friendly disposition towards the United States and hostility towards Japan, has not prevented the Korean economy and business environment from looking more like Japan's than America's.

Although the predominant form of large Korean enterprises, the *chaebol*, are frequently compared to the Japanese *keiretsu* — the same Chinese characters are used to express *chaebol* and *zaibatsu* — there are some important differences between the Japanese and Korean enterprise systems and environment.

First, although Korea's symbiotic relationship between government and industry is shifting from "manager" to "coach", as late as the early 1990s state-owned enterprises still accounted for 10 per cent of GNP. Korea Electric, Korea Telecommunications, Pohang Steel Co (Posco) are in the top ten business groups if they are compared with private firms in terms of sales[64]. Thus the government's role in the economy is greater than Japan's.

Like in Japan, close relationships between the government and oligopolistic companies resulted from state support, especially in the form of low-interest loans and other types of subsidy[65]. Korean enterprises were "invited" by the government to enter certain sectors after the 1960s, much as Japan did in the pre-World War II era.

Second, although *chaebol* and *zaibatsu* both literally mean financial clique, the *chaebol* do not include banks. Korea's financial sector is still dominated by the state.

Third, the Korean *chaebol* do not include the vertical supplier and/or distribution chains that exist in Japan.

A fourth difference, is that while the *keiretsu* (and before them the *zaibatsu*) include companies in many different sectors, individual companies tend to be highly specialised. Even today Japanese manufacturers typically make 90 per cent of their profits from their core business. In the Korean *chaebol*, by contrast, individual companies are highly diversified. The *chaebol* have been compared to department stores: first floor, heavy engineering and shipbuilding; second floor, construction; third floor, footwear; fourth floor, textiles; fifth floor, chemicals; sixth floor, electronic components; seventh floor, consumer electronics; eighth floor, cars; ninth floor, hotels, etc. The government has tried to get the *chaebol* to specialise from the mid/late 1980s, but with hardly any success. For example, the government tried to prevent Samsung from entering the car business, but gave up in 1993.

Fifth, the Korean *chaebol* are predominantly owned and controlled by entrepreneurs and their families and/or descendants: domination by the founder and his family is one of the most striking distinguishing features of the Korean *chaebol*. As Whitley comments:

> "Despite state pressure to sell shares on the stock exchange and dilute family ownership, only 20-30 per cent of *chaebol* firms were listed in 1986. Nearly all the unlisted firms are owned and controlled by the founding family, who often used the group holding company or trading company to control all the firms in the *chaebol*. This pattern of family ownership, despite high growth rates and large size, has been maintained by widespread reliance on debt financing, with debt/equity ratios of 3.6 for the top ten *chaebol* in manufacturing in 1983 and 6.8 in construction. In contrast to Japanese firms, even with the prewar family-owned *zaibatsu*, family ownership in Korea means strong family control. Nearly all the top management posts in the *chaebol* are held by close relatives of the founders, and it is a common saying in Korea that founders create subsidiaries for each member of the family to manage"[66].

A sixth difference between the Japanese and Korean business environments is that lifetime employment is not customary in Korea, perhaps because of the dominant role of the family. Although the *chaebol* claim to be paternalistic and develop close ties of loyalty with the core labour force, this assertion would seem to be mainly cosmetic. There is mobility between large firms and job-hopping exists. Labour unions in some instances have been extremely militant. However, this may be due to recent political change, democratisation, and to the fact that hitherto unions — apart from government unions — were banned in Korea and labour conditions were quite difficult.

Jung[67] argues that with democratisation the balance of power between government and the *chaebol* has tilted in the direction of the latter: "the top five business groups have become so powerful that their influence reaches not only to the marketplace but also such diverse areas as culture, welfare and the political arena". In the heady new atmosphere of democracy in Korea, there is heavy public criticism of the excessive concentration of economic power in the hands of a few *chaebol*. This concentration is aggravated by the lack of separation between ownership and management in the Korean *chaebol*.

The founder families often control the entire business with less than 10 per cent of the total outstanding capital. This is made possible by the presence of cross-shareholdings. As Jung stresses, there is an anomaly, namely that private family power is concentrated in enterprises that are nevertheless public, in the sense that over 50 per cent of the shares are owned by private investors, including small shareholders and institutional investors. In addition, the large companies are heavily dependent on borrowing from public financial institutions. For these reasons, among others, it is quite alarming that virtually no monitoring is provided for under Korea's family form of corporate governance.

It follows from what has been said that the composition of the board of Korean companies is entirely at the discretion of the chairman. In Japan it is also the CEO who appoints the members of the board, though in Korea the chairman is both owner and CEO. As Jung says, "it is apparent that the board does not function as a decision making body but as a meeting where the chairman directs and gives orders to its members".

Jung argues that things will change. Korean *chaebol*, he says, are going through a transitional period.

Large companies are currently about 40 years old and thus there is a transition towards the second generation of the founding families. Inheritance taxes will also contribute to the dilution of capital. The Korean government, now being democratic, is more accountable to the public and can engage in less favouritism. Laws have been introduced with a view to making financial transactions more transparent. However, one of the main reasons why families will have to rely more on professional management is that the companies have become much bigger and the technologies have become far more complex.

Take the example of Samsung. As described in a 1995 article in the *Economist*: "It is leading a Sino-Korean venture into aerospace, building new semiconductor plants, even eyeing up Hollywood. The group's planned investments this year alone come to a staggering 7.8 trillion won ($10.2 billion), about a fifth more than is planned by the 17 firms that make up the core of Japan's Mitsubishi empire. All this investment is aimed at quadrupling Samsung's sales by 2001. That means over $200 billion worth of goods, more than the entire output of a country the size of Sweden"[68].

The Korean economy is doing well, growing at 7 per cent in 1996. It is not facing a crisis or recession as in Japan. Nevertheless, much in Korea is changing and the country is facing simultaneous discontinuities: domestic political change, international geopolitical change, technological change and social change. There are many challenges ahead. As Jung observes, "how to develop a Korean-style governance system commensurate with the current and future ownership structure is the major challenge that Korean business groups are faced with in the next decade".

"Globalisation" has been the slogan and alleged goal of the current Korean administration under the President Kim Young-sam. From the ruins of war to a global power is a big leap. Also, the rate of Korea's economic change has been dramatic. Most Koreans were peasants until recently. Although it is counted among the "NIEs" (or "Asian tigers"), it is much bigger than Hong Kong and Singapore, and has more than twice the population of Chinese Taipei. Unlike the Chinese entrepreneurs of the other three NIEs, there is not a global diaspora that Koreans can depend on. There is also the very thorny question regarding the North. South Korea seems to be in a no-win situation: the financial burden of North Korea's possible collapse are so great that it has become a taboo subject in the south.

Korea has one more unenviable trait in common with Japan: most foreign businessmen believe the Korean market is closed, that it is an extremely difficult environment in which to operate, that Koreans believe the ends justify the means, and hence, among other things, intellectual property rights are regularly violated. For these reasons, although Korea had been a leading star in the World Economic Forum's *World Competitiveness Report* for years, in the 1995 edition it was "demoted" to rank 16. The stated reason for the demotion was Korea's excessive economic nationalism and its hostile environment for foreign direct investment.

Changes are bound to occur. The tremendous national solidarity which characterised the first decades of Korea's industrial revolution will have to give way to greater internationalism and more international management skills.

Chinese Bamboo Networks[69]

The most obvious difference between the Japanese and Korean enterprises on the one hand and the Chinese on the other, is that the former operate from secure, often captive, certainly highly protective, domestic bases, while Chinese enterprises are operating in insecure environments. Not only does this include the Southeast Asian countries, but also the Chinese outposts, Chinese Taipei and Hong Kong, where there is a great deal of uncertainty. Trust among the Chinese is a scarce commodity beyond the confines of family and clan. For this reason, among others, the approach to corporate governance by Chinese enterprises does not include any basic commitment to social responsibility, public accountability or to good corporate citizenship. Political circumstances may occasionally dictate lip service to social responsibility. In Southeast Asia, governments claim to be becoming concerned about the apparent growing gaps between rich and poor. A large proportion of the rich in Southeast Asia, especially the super rich, are Chinese[70].

In the summer of 1995 the Indonesian government summoned about 100 (primarily Chinese) businessmen to a conference in Bali aimed at fostering greater adherence to the state ideology *Pancasila*. In particular, they were urged to devise measures of contributing to alleviating problems of poverty and thereby to exercise a higher level of social responsibility. At the end of the conference the businessmen issued the "Bali Declaration", which, among other things, pledges to narrow the gap between rich and poor by fostering the growth of small businesses. However, the businessmen also took a swipe at the government by calling for more transparency in government policy and in the bureaucracy[71].

The first point to stress is that while it has been said that all of the major East Asian systems of corporate governance are secretive, generally quite opaque, this clearly applies to the Chinese enterprises. They use "innovative" accounting systems and normally keep several distinct account books. The extent of family ownership and control in Chinese companies, as Whitley writes, is such that "enterprises are often viewed as part of the family property rather than as separate administrative entities"[72]. The *Economist* points out that although some Chinese firms "display all the trappings of a modern corporation, such as professional managers, stock market listings, or even a public relations department . . . the choicest assets are frequently ferreted away in a maze of private companies and trusts"[73].

Chinese enterprises are also relatively small (although there are some exceptions), thus forming another contrast with Japan and Korea. While the Korean economy is dominated by large enterprises and the small and medium-size sector is weak, conversely the Chinese Taipei economy is dominated by small and medium-sized enterprises and the sector of large enterprises is weak. The Korean government is seeking to restrain the large companies and encourage the small and medium-sized companies, while the Chinese-Taipei government wants to encourage the creation of large enterprises and, by projects like the Hsinchu science park, it wants to get small enterprises to co-operate in R&D[74]. The small size of Chinese companies is a handicap for meeting the new challenges of moving into technology-intensive sectors.

The bamboo network is also far more informal than the Korean or Japanese forms. In the Chinese scheme of things, firms are connected to a large number of other firms through a "complex web of deals, obligations, personal ties and joint activities"[75]. Trust is crucial, but relations are far more fluid than in the Japanese *keiretsu*, and, unlike them, the Chinese networks may also change. Relationships are between individuals, not between firms. The general *informality* which pervades

Chinese enterprises is also reflected in financing: preference is given to informal sources, including family members, friends, credit associations, or unregulated "curb" markets, rather than formal institutions such as banks.

In the internal functioning of the firm, personal autocratic leadership is complemented by a preference for recruitment and promotion of kin for top and key positions. The centralised decision-making does contribute to two of the Chinese firms' strengths, namely their high degree of production flexibility and strategic adaptability. Garments today, semiconductors tomorrow, no problem. Owner-entrepreneurs are also obviously far more sensitive to matters of costs and financing than outside managers. On the other hand, businesses are generally small scale, with low capital intensity, limited product diversification, and concentration on a few markets[76].

Until about 1985, Chinese enterprises tended to be players in their local environments. Since 1985, not only have Chinese enterprises become regional players, but in China and in most Southeast Asian markets, they are the most active foreign players. Companies from Chinese Taipei and Hong Kong needed to go abroad because their currencies (especially in Chinese Taipei) appreciated, labour and land became more expensive and scarce, and new opportunities beckoned. The trade regimes of the other countries in the region also improved significantly. Chinese companies in the ASEAN countries have engaged in considerable cross-border investments.

The regionalisation of Chinese companies has been one of the most significant recent business developments. The push abroad has been mostly spurred by changes in external conditions, rather than internal corporate strategies. However, the foreign operations of the Chinese companies are greatly facilitated by a number of key non-market forces, in particular ethnic resources and networks, kinship and personal links. These links include those fostered among Chinese studying in American universities. From their community networks, Chinese businessmen can obtain information, business partners, distribution channels, etc. Although organisational structures and control systems of overseas Chinese enterprises tend to change with the degree of internationalisation, these changes are more apparent than fundamental.

Chinese companies could be described as hyperactive small entities. Thus although their networks have achieved phenomenal success in stimulating the growth of the Chinese and Southeast Asian economies, the fact that the individual companies are small compels them to remain at a fairly low technological level, for they cannot afford large R&D costs, and they are also unlikely to become major global foreign investors. The Chinese bamboo network extends to the United States, but not to Europe.

Although the Chinese and Southeast Asian economies are booming and are expected to continue to be the fastest growing economies for the foreseeable future, and Chinese business enterprises are the driving force of the region's economies, serious challenges of transition also lie ahead.

Control of the companies is now passing from the elderly founders to new generations. In some cases, the new generation consists of bright, American-educated, professionally inclined executives. There are also some incompetents who obtained their position purely through nepotism. Presumably the sheep will be separated from the goats.

International activities will require greater organisational skills and also greater transparency. As Asian governments liberalise trade and deregulate their domestic economies, the key asset of the Chinese, their *guanxi* (connections) may become less important.

If Chinese companies wish to remain competitive with their Western and Japanese counterparts, they will require greater separation of ownership and management to recruit well qualified and highly motivated staff. If promotions are made on a nepotistic basis, clearly non-family members will prefer to look for better career prospects elsewhere.

One of the key challenges is being large enough to afford expensive R&D. There are some large and even very large Chinese firms, but they are mainly engaged in real estate or in commercial operations. There are also some in the high tech industrial sectors, such as Acer and Mitac in Chinese Taipei, and Alphatech in Thailand, but they are few and far between.

One of the most successful Chinese enterprises is the Thailand-based Charoen Pokphand (CP) Group. The company appears to be extremely ably run by two brothers, Sumet and Dhanin, grandsons of the founder. In their case, the often quoted Chinese proverb that in the third generation everything tends to go to pot, would not seem to apply. CP is active throughout East Asia, including in China where it has made large investments which are providing good returns. The "Chinese-style" approach which, according to Sumet, accounts for their success, can be illustrated from comments he recently made in an interview. CP's performance in China is guided by "flexibility", in contrast to the "inflexibility" of non-Asian companies: "American and European companies have adapted themselves to a very sophisticated legal-based society. In China there is no law. There is no system. It is a government by individuals, by people"[77]. While CP is clearly attuned to the Chinese way of doing things, it also understands the ways of international businesses, and its partners include the American Nynex (in telecoms), the Japanese Honda (in motorbikes) and the European Makro (in retailing). From having been primarily an agribusiness company, a sector in which it remains extremely strong, CP has moved into aquaculture, real estate, transport equipment and telecommunications. Although CP has listings on a number of stock exchanges, including New York's, as a company it is characterised by rather opaque corporate governance. The Jiaravanon family still reigns and rules.

The bamboo network has emerged as a highly dynamic force in the Asia Pacific Regional environment. As the *Economist* noted, it inspires "both fascination and fear" in the West[78]. However, it remains to be seen how the bamboo network will accommodate to globalisation and conversely, the global economy to it.

Conclusion: Corporate Governance in Europe and Asia

The subject of corporate governance in Europe and East Asia constitutes a very rich field for research. There is a great deal of work to be done. This is all the more true for some of the societies in East Asia like Korea where the subject is very new.

One important conclusion of this discussion is that it is incorrect that corporate governance in the West and East differ fundamentally. The situation is more complex than that. In some respects, the stage of development obviously has an influence. The business environment in China today is perhaps not dissimilar from what it was in North America a century ago. Some convergence tends to occur as economies mature.

However, it is wrong to assume that convergence will invariably lead to globalisation of the Anglo-American model. The fact that the economies of the Anglo-American model at present may be doing better than the Rheinal and Japanese keiretsu models does not necessarily prove anything. What is happening in America and Britain today does not provide the basis for long-term global projections.

As the world becomes politically "multipolar", a similar trend will be follow in business affairs. The objective of the World Trade Organisation is transparency, not homogenisation.

As the global industrial centre of gravity continues to shift from the Atlantic to the Pacific, businesses will increasingly face challenges and opportunities and even perceive threats. In this chapter we primarily focused on Europeans looking at Asia. As East Asian companies globalise they will have to look more closely at Europe.

As investments become a greater driving force in the world economy, increasingly companies will be meeting and competing in more and more markets. The scope for co-operation will be enhanced, but so will potential for more frictions. Greater understanding of each other's economic and political systems and forms of corporate governance will increase the scope for co-operation and decrease confrontations.

ASEM has been a substantial step in the right direction. Some of the activities planned following the summit, especially university exchanges, linkages between think tanks and business forums should be encouraged. There is a need to create more European-East Asian networks of influential public figures and policy makers, including businessmen, government officials, academics and journalists.

Europeans need to make the effort to understand East Asian enterprises and the latter should be encouraged to make learning easier by becoming more transparent.

Notes

1. For example, see Ruth Sullivan, "Inheritors of Italy's Industrial Legacy", *The European*, 9-15 May 1996.

2. Samuel P. Huntington (1993), "The Clash of Civilizations?", in *Foreign Affairs*, Summer.

3. For example, see James Fallows (1994), *Looking at the Sun: The Rise of the New East Asian Economic and Political System*, Pantheon Books, New York; and the works of Chalmers Johnson, including, *Japan: Who Governs? The Rise of the Developmental State*, Norton, New York and London, 1995; *MITI and the Japanese Miracle: the Growth of Industrial Policy*, Stanford University Press, Stanford, 1982; "Capitalism: East Asian Style", The 1992 Panglaykim Memorial Lecture, Jakarta, 15 December 1992.

4. The Chinese business sphere (CBS) encompasses the People's Republic of China (PRC), Chinese Taipei, Hong Kong, and those parts of Southeast Asia heavily dominated by Chinese business culture.

5. The "cow war" between the UK and its European "partners" has produced a level of bad feelings comparable to the "car wars" between the United States and Japan.

6. The UK is often depicted as the outlier because of its refusal to accede to the EU's social charter and because of its more "open" approach to foreign direct investment from outside the EU, notably from East Asia. Conflict exists and will persist between other European countries as well: the single market has not eradicated the tendency to create individual national champions, while battles over air transport, telecommunications, government procurement, defence, agricultural products, etc. within the EU are likely to continue.

7. The position of India has been somewhat marginal in international business discussions. Quite apart from the sheer size of its population, India has Asia's second largest middle class after Japan. The Indian government's economic policies have become more oriented towards liberalisation and its current strategy seeks to emulate its East Asian neighbours. Certainly there is a great deal more foreign interest in India, including from both West and Asia, e.g. the recent entry of Korean car manufacturers. In certain respects corporate governance in India should be more familiar and transparent to the West than that of East Asian societies. Nevertheless, India has been and remains a comparative outsider in international economic and business affairs and consequently has featured less in the strategic horizons of Western and East Asian corporations, though this will probably change.

8. The quoted comment was by Percy Barnevik, chairman of the giant Swiss-Swedish conglomerate, Asea Brown Boveri (ABB). Cf. the *Financial Times*, 29 February 1996.

9. See the speech given by Sir Michael Perry, chairman of Unilever, to the Royal Institute of International Affairs (Chatham House), reprinted in *World Today*, August-September 1994.

10. *Financial Times*, 14 November 1995.

11.	There are approximately 500 institutions of tertiary education in Japan. Major blue-chip Japanese companies recruit managers and engineers from about 20, at most, of these institutions, which are the same ones that supply recruits for the elite of the higher civil service.

12.	Cited from Charles Voi, in "Asia-Pacific Telecommunications", *Financial Times*, 9 April 1996.

13.	In 1984 Deng Xiaoping's economic reforms, which had been initiated in the countryside, were instituted in the PRC's urban and industrial areas, thereby bringing the Chinese economy into the world and regional business environments. In 1985 the Plaza Accord resulted in the first massive phase of yen appreciation, thereby precipitating the outflow of productive Japanese investment into Asian countries. The appreciation of the Korean Won and the New Chinese-Taipei Dollar had similar effects on their offshore manufacturing investments. Thus 1984-85 marks the genesis of East Asian regional economic integration and a quantum change in its business environment.

14.	The Japanese tend to oscillate between presenting their business culture as unique and emphasizing its universality, or at least universality with respect to Asia. Concerning the difficulty that the Japanese have making up their minds whether to be unique or universal, Francis Fukuyama (1995) observes in *Trust: The Social Virtues and the Creation of Prosperity,* Free Press, London: "With the rise of Japan as an economic superpower, there has been talk among certain Japanese of a 'Japanese model' that should be followed by other nations of Asia, if not by other parts of the world more generally. . . . In terms of industrial structure, however, there is a wide gap between Japan and other East Asian cultures, and some reason for thinking that it will be very difficult for Sinitic societies to adopt Japanese practices" (p. 347).

15.	See Lester Thurrow (1992), *Head to Head*, William Morrow, New York; Chalmers Johnson (1995), *Japan: Who Governs?*, Norton; Edward Luttwak (1993), *The Endangered American Dream*, Simon and Schuster, New York; Laura d'Andrea Tyson (1992), *Who's Bashing Whom? Trade Conflicts in High Technology Industries*, Institute for International Economics, Washington; Clyde V. Prestowitz, Jr.(1988), *Trading Places: How We Allowed Japan to Take the Lead*, Basic Books, New York; James Fallows (1994), *Looking at the Sun.*

16.	US influence in East Asia derives from the fact that not only is it a major economic power in the region, but it is also the guarantor of East Asian security, as well as having an enormous amount of "soft power", especially through its university networks and kith and kin relations across the Pacific. Europe does not and will not have that kind of presence in East Asia in the foreseeable future.

17.	See, Jean-Pierre Lehmann, "Volvos franska Šktenskap passar inte in I globalt nŠtverk", *Svenska Dagbladet*, 13 November 1993.

18.	By companies remaining "national" is meant that major shareholders and senior management tend to be primarily, sometimes exclusively, citizens of the company's home nation, their R&D tends to be in or near home, they dominate their domestic markets, e.g. Fiat in Italy, and generally convey a distinct national image, e.g. the German engineering image of Mercedes Benz, the solid Swedish safety image of Volvo, etc.

19. By "most European" we mean something that is recognised and consumed by the greatest number of Europeans across national and language borders. By such criteria the "most European" newspaper is the International Herald Tribune, the "most European" television news station is CNN, the "most European" restaurant is McDonald's, etc.

20. There are exceptions. When the "American" IC manufacturer Fairchild was to be sold by the French company Schlumberger to the Japanese company Fujitsu, there was a cacophonous nationalistic uproar about key high-tech American strategic assets falling into "foreign" hands, with the result that Fujitsu had to back down. Similarly, when Sony bought Columbia Studios there was a great outbreak of emotional chauvinistic sentiment — epitomised by a Newsweek article that complained about how Sony had acquired a "piece of the American soul". Generally, however, when acquirers have been Europeans, Australians or Canadians, there have been no outbursts and no opposition. This would give some credence to Japanese complaints of American racism. On the other hand, Japanese tend to prevent any form of foreign acquisitions in Japan.

21. "Fokker Studying New Plane with Asians", *International Herald Tribune*, 8 May 1995.

22. China's GNP may be catching up and, according to come calculations, has already surpassed Germany's and Japan's. However, in the terms being discussed here, China's business system is not influential.

23. See Ronald P. Dore (1987), *Taking Japan Seriously: A Confucian Perspective on Leading Economic Issues*, Athlone Press, London, and Mark Fruin (1992), *The Japanese Enterprise System*, Clarendon Press, Oxford.

24. About 60 per cent of marriages among employees of large corporations are so-called *"shanai-kekkon"*, i.e. intra-firm marriages. Women (known in Japan as OIs, office ladies) are hired in considerable numbers by large Japanese corporations, even if their tasks are minimal and often unnecessary, e.g. serving tea, to provide a suitable marriage pool for male employees. If male employees choose a partner from within the company, this has the benefit for the corporation that they will be happy to work late hours in the company rather than running around looking for women, at least that is the theory.

25. See Masahiko Aoki and Hugh Patrick (1994), eds., *The Japanese Main Bank System: Its Relevance for Developing and Transforming Economies*, Oxford University Press, Oxford, including the chapter by Theodor Baums, "The German Banking System and Its Impact on Corporate Finance and Governance".

26. Richard Whitley (1992) in *Business Systems in East Asia: Firms, Markets and Societies*, Sage, London, notes that "high levels of mutual dependence between large employers, their 'core' workers and suppliers/customers in Japan is unlikely to generate effective business systems if they are combined with highly specialised tasks and formalised control systems"(p. 23).

27. The feminine pronoun would be somewhat inappropriate here as women are still not really part of the corporate system in Japan.

28. Ronald P. Dore (1973), *British Factory - Japanese Factory*, Allen and Unwin, London.

29. On the other hand, it is true that fringe benefits for Japanese senior management make a considerable difference. Chauffeur-driven company cars are much more common in Japan than in the United States or Europe, while Japanese corporate entertainment expenses are gargantuan, as are the membership fees for golf clubs, etc.

30. Elmar Gerum, "Aufsichtsratstypen-Ein Beitrag zur Theorie der Organisation der Unternehmensführung", *Die Betriebswirtschaft*, 6, 1991, quoted in Masaru Yoshimori, "Whose Company Is It? The Concept of the Corporation in Japan and in the West", LENS: The LENS Academic Page, http://www.lens-inc.com/academic.html.

31. Japanese companies have close links with organised crime and in that respect greatly differ from American and German firms. In this domain Japanese corporate governance (or lack of governance) comes much closer to the Italian model.

32. See, for example, Robert A.G. Monks, speech given before the Japan Investor Relation Association, Tokyo, Japan, 2 November 1994, LENS: The LENS Academic Page, http://www.lens-inc.com/academic.html.

33. Victor Handy, "What is a Company For?", *Corporate Governance: An International Review*, Vol.1, No. 1, January 1993, p. 15.

34. See, for example, the article on "Stakeholder Capitalism" in the *Economist*, 10-16 February 1996.

35. Michel Albert (1991), *Capitalisme contre Capitalisme*, Seuil, Paris.

36. Aron Viner, "The Coming Revolution in Japan's Board Rooms", in *Corporate Governance: An International Review*, Vol. 1, No. 3, July 1993, p. 118.

37. Masaru Yoshimori, *op cit.*

38. See Robert A. G. Monks, speech given before Japan Investor Relation Association, Tokyo, 2 November 1994, LENS: The LENS Academic Page, http://www.lens-inc.com/academic.html. Watanabe and Yamamoto, "Corporate Governance in Japan: Ways to Improve Low Profitability", *Corporate Governance: An International Review*, Vol. 1, No. 4, October 1993, also point out that "... the current economic recession can be called a 'governance recession'", p. 208.

39. See Aron Viner, *op cit.*

40. See, for example, Lester Thurow (1992), *Head to Head*, William Morrow, New York, and Jeffrey E. Garten: *A Cold Peace: America, Japan, Germany and the Struggle for Supremacy*, Time Books, New York, 1992.

41. Michel Albert. *op cit.*

42. Japanese industrial society and law in the pre-World War II era owed quite a lot to German influence. The Japanese constitution of 1889 was inspired by a Bismarckian model, a German professor of jurisprudence, Hermann Roesler, drafted Japan's commercial code, and the emphasis in Japanese tertiary education on engineering rather than science was also "copied" from Germany.

43. This point is also extensively developed in Richard Whitley, *op. cit.* For example, "the lack of strong institutional trust mechanisms in Hong Kong and Taiwan inhibits the development of impersonal authority and trust relations within firms and limits the size

of Chinese family businesses as well as leading to extensive reliance of personal networks between enterprises" (p.23). Fukuyama makes virtually the same point about Italy, cf. *op. cit*, Chapter 10, "Italian Confucianism".

44. Consideration here is being given only to capitalist models, thus communist models are excluded. However, China and Vietnam are included even though they retain a Leninist form of government with the Party in command, for the reforms undertaken in both countries serve to enhance the role of market forces.

45. These transitions are not necessarily smooth. In Korea, there has been a considerable degree of confrontation between some of the *chaebol* and the government.

46. See, for example, James Clad (1989), *Beyond the Myth: Business, Money and Power in Southeast Asia*, Unwin, New York, and on Indonesia, Adam Schwarz (1994), *A Nation in Waiting: Indonesia in the 1990s*, St Leonards, Sydney.

47. One of the strongest "anti-government" cases can be found in Karl Zinsmeister, "MITI Mouse: Japan's Industrial Policy Doesn't Work, *Policy Review*, No. 64, Spring 1993, pp. 28-35. I am grateful to Patricia Nelson for drawing this article to my attention.

48. The government's role in the development of the Japanese automobile industry, however, should not be too lightly dismissed. For one thing, for several decades the government imposed outright protectionism, following which non-tariff barriers were erected to keep out foreign competition.

49. A recent excellent study on this subject is David Williams (1994), *Japan: Beyond the End of History*, Routledge, London, and see also the remarkable book of Shigeto Tsuru (1993), *Japan's Capitalism: Creative Defeat and Beyond*, Cambridge University Press, Cambridge.

50. This is a subject treated at some length, in Jean-Pierre Lehmann (1982), *The Roots of Modern Japan*, St Martin's Press, London and New York.

51. Different ministries have jurisdiction over different sectors. The record of the Ministry of International Trade and Industry (MITI) is on balance quite good, although it would have to assume responsibility for the failures in the Japanese aerospace industry. The Ministry of Health and Welfare, on the other hand, has stifled the industries it supervises, which partly explains the hitherto weak performance of the Japanese pharmaceutical industry and its fragmentation. There are some 2 200 pharmaceutical companies in Japan and the market share of the largest, Takeda, is less than 6 per cent. The Ministry of Finance's influence has greatly handicapped Japan's financial services industry. The Ministry of Agriculture in Japan resembles its counterparts in other industrialised economies.

52. The *necs plus ultras* are in fact five: the University of Tokyo (*Todai*), the University of Kyoto (*Kyodai*), Keio, Waseda and Hitotsubashi.

53. The government could intervene directly in a number of ways to guide industry during the 1950s and 1960s, e.g. through exchange controls, preferential interest rates, etc. For the most part in recent decades, government activity largely consists of providing information and infrastructure to industry.

54. Richard Whitley, *op cit*, p. 22.

55. In the prewar era this kind of group was referred to as *zaibatsu*, which literally means "financial clique". A number of features distinguish the prewar *zaibatsu* from the postwar *keiretsu*: e.g. in the *zaibatsu* the founding families retained significant ownership and control, including through holding companies, whereas the families were divested of their ownership by the postwar occupation forces and holding companies have been forbidden by law. There is some pressure especially from the Keidanren (the federation of large companies) to revise the code so that holding companies may be legal.

56. See, Paul Sheard, "Interlocking Shareholdings and Corporate Governance", in Masahiko Aoki and Ronald Dore (1994), eds., *The Japanese Firm: Sources of Competitive Strength*, Oxford University Press, Oxford.

57. In contrast, the main electric and electronic company in the Mitsui group is Toshiba, while the Sumitomo group's is NEC, and their respective automotive companies are Toyota and Mazda. Lavish use of the Mitsubishi name has advantages in terms of name recognition and corporate clout but it can also have disadvantages. For example, when the Mitsubishi Trading Corporation (Mitsubishi Shoji) was accused of ecological devastation through massive deforestation of tropical forests in Southeast Asia, environmentalists called for a boycott of all Mitsubishi products. In the sexual harassment case now facing Mitsubishi Motors of America, other Mitsubishi company presidents have expressed concern that they too might suffer consequences from the company's bad reputation in America.

58. Leading Japanese government officials and zaibatsu families further cemented their relationships by marrying their children to one another.

59. *Défi américain* literally means "American challenge". It was the title of a highly popular book, published in 1967, translated into numerous languages, written by the French author Jean-Jacques Servan-Schreiber. In it, he forecast, among other things, that superior American capital, management and technology would overtake European business.

60. See Dennis Encarnation (1992), *Rivals Beyond Trade: America versus Japan in Global Competition*, Cornell University Press, Ithaca, and Mark Mason (1992) *American Multinationals and Japan: the Political Economy of Japanese Capital Controls, 1899-1980*, Council on East Asian Studies, Harvard University Press, Cambridge, Mass.

61. Strictly speaking it is not impossible for foreign companies to acquire Japanese companies. It is however extremely rare. There are only two cases of first stock-exchange listed Japanese companies acquired by foreigners. One was the acquisition of Banyu by Merck, Sharp and Dome, the other was the acquisition of Osaka Gas by British Oxygen Corporation (BOC).

62. See Ulrike Schaede, "Understanding Corporate Governance in Japan: Do Classical Concepts Apply?", *Industrial and Corporate Change*, Vol. 3, No. 2, 1994, p. 321.

63. Jung Ku-Hyun (1995), "Ownership and Governance Structure of Korean Business Groups", unpublished. I am very grateful to the author for having given me his paper.

64. Jung, p. 3.

65. Also, there is a great deal of corruption. In Korea, however, politicians, including former presidents (as in the current cases of Chun Doo-hwan and Roh Tae-woo) are prosecuted and imprisoned, whereas in Japan they go scot-free, with rare exceptions.

66. Whitley, *op cit*, p. 44-45.

67. This and a several paragraphs immediately following are borrow quite extensively from Jung's paper cited above.

68. "South Korea Survey", *Economist*, 3 June 1995, p. 15.

69. My use of the term "bamboo network" was borrowed from articles have occasionally appeared in the *Economist*. While writing this chapter, I had neither read nor seen the recent book, Murray Weidenbaum and Samuel Hughes (1996), *The Bamboo Network: How Expatriate Chinese Entrepreneurs are Creating a New Economic Superpower in Asia*, Martin Kessler Books, New York.

70. According to the *Economist*, "The Overseas Chinese - Inheriting the Bamboo Network", 23 December 1995 - 5 January 1996, nine out of every ten East Asian billionaires is Chinese. Gordon Redding (1990) in *The Spirit of Chinese Capitalism*, Walter de Gruyter, New York, claims that overseas Chinese are brought up to value three things: work, family and money, and to understand the connection between the three.

71. Manuela Saragosa, "Leaders of Indonesia's big business return fire: Bureaucracy and a lack of transparency irk the mostly ethnic Chinese tycoons", *Financial Times*, 1 September 1995 and "Time to loosen the ties that bind", *Financial Times*, 17 October 1995.

72. Richard Whitley, *op cit*, p. 54.

73. "The Overseas Chinese - Inheriting the Bamboo Network", the *Economist*, 23 December 1995 to 5 January 1996.

74. "The Hsinchu companies, which employ 42,000 people, spend around 5.5 per cent of their turnover on research and development (against a national average of 1 per cent)". "A Survey of Business in Asia", the *Economist*, 9 March 1996.

75. Whitley, *op cit*, p. 56.

76. See Rajeswary Ampalavanar Brown (1995), ed., *Chinese Business Enterprise in Asia*, Routledge, New York, and Gordon Redding *op cit*.

77. "When Family Empires Shape Asian Expansion", *International Herald Tribune*, 16 November 1995.

78. "A survey of Business in Asia", *Economist*, 9 March 1996.

Globalisation and Corporate Strategic Alliances: A European Perspective

Jon Sigurdson[1]

Strategic alliances have come to the forefront since the early 1980s as a major factor in understanding the changing character of the firm. The number of strategic alliances formed by large global companies and smaller companies also affects our understanding of the global economy.

Alliances include almost any type of organisation that involves co-operation of one or more firms with customers and suppliers, with universities and national research institutes, or with other companies and competitors. There is a vast array of co-operative industrial arrangements, but only those that directly affect partners' competitiveness in a global context should be classified as strategic alliances.

In the past, co-operative ties between companies have been strategic in a broad sense, whereas alliances formed in recent years are often strategic in a narrower sense. The types of strategic alliances include technical relationships (often licensing), R&D collaboration, production contracts (including OEM agreements and co-production), marketing agreements, the formation of joint ventures at all levels (from product development through production and marketing), as well as minority equity investments in other companies. While licensing agreements may be seen by the licensor as spot transactions, rather than as "strategic", the licensee often has a strong interest in the relationship, which may develop into a comprehensive strategic alliance.

The strategic elements of alliances have increasingly become more prominent and more focused in three ways. First, the establishment of new alliances increasingly involves core skills and processes of the companies involved. This reflects a new understanding of the company as a network of core skills and processes which form the basis of its competitiveness at a time when it is no longer sufficient or possible for all activities to be under a single company. Thus alliances have become essential for enhancing a company's competitive strength. Second, capital has been replaced by information and knowledge as the most important element in corporate partnerships and information and knowledge have become essential elements of strategic alliances. While such relationships are more loosely controlled than those based on capital, and are potentially unstable, they generally give a company a great deal of flexibility as it can withdraw from the relationship on short notice and with little immediate loss of resources. Third, alliances have been focusing more on the long term, guiding economic parameters towards long periods of investment rather obtaining immediate returns.

Already in the 1950s there was a proliferation of partnerships between Western industrial firms and local firms in the Asia-Pacific region. Those partnerships were mainly in the form of licensing agreements or equity joint ventures, as firms in Asia which lacked technology joined up with large Western companies which had strong technological bases. Why did these partnerships come into existence, and what effects did they have on reshaping the traditional firm? In understanding the changes that have occurred since then, it is useful to identify the major driving forces at the time.

The early partnerships were mainly for one or two reasons: *(i)* to capture possibilities in a special market, *(ii)* to exploit local resources such as labour or raw materials. Regarding today's global partnerships, Lasserre and Schütte observe: "Global partnerships are co-operative ventures in which partners combine their resources, assets, and competencies to improve their overall competition in major global and regional markets. . . . Partnerships come in various legal forms. They can consist of long-term supply or management contracts, and cover licensing and franchising operations. In general, agreements can regulate joint research and marketing activities and set up consortia"[2].

They note that foreign investors are driven by three major factors in choosing to enter into a joint venture rather than a wholly owned venture. One is the political imperative which follows from the will of local governments to impose restrictions or offer incentives. A second is the competitive imperative which results from a firm's need for local resources, assets and competences in order to compete more effectively. A third is the risk-sharing imperative which challenges the firm to come to terms with high risks involved in developing or marketing new products, a situation that arises when an investment is very costly, say for high technology projects, or when the return on investment is unusually uncertain.

The economic benefits of sharing costs and access to markets are becoming important factors, although access to knowledge probably remains the most important. In the past most companies would have preferred embedded knowledge as it is easier to protect, on the assumption that the transfer of knowledge could be controlled. However, a globalising company requires that an increasing share of the knowledge under its control be codified in order to be transferred easily and used in different parts of a global network.

The globalisation of knowledge is an important development that helps explain the changing shape of the modern firm, and suggests the following four propositions. First, the global system has a vast pool of potentially marketable knowledge that requires new approaches to be exploited successfully. Second, a growing number of actors are adding to this pool of knowledge, including universities, independent research organisations, niche companies, large companies, and many others. Successful exploitation of emerging knowledge requires new linkages, knowledge links, many of which are likely to be organised in the form of strategic alliances.

Third, certain parts of the knowledge pool are easily transferable. This is true for almost any codified knowledge that exists in manuals or books, in pieces of machinery, and in formulas and specific designs. By obtaining them an individual or organisation with suitable capabilities will also be able to master such codified knowledge. Fourth, much of the knowledge existing or being created in the global knowledge pool is non-codified, or is embedded, and can only be transferred slowly because such knowledge resides in complex relationships that are usually social in nature.

Forms of alliances

It may be useful to recall some of the traditional reasons why a firm enters into an alliance[3]. First, the companies that form an alliance want to reduce the costs of research, marketing and distribution, production, etc. Second, firms want to reduce technological risk, financial risks etc., and by joining together they are able to take on projects that are considered too large or too precarious for a single company. Third, companies want to get access to complementary resources, whether in research, production or marketing. Fourth, companies often collaborate in order to gain access to markets where they are weak or absent. Finally, a group of companies want to reduce the competition within an industry in order to "cartelise" the sector to increase profits.

The competitiveness of large global companies is mainly based on four factors:

1. Long-term perspective and the existence of global opportunities.

2. Acquisition of competitive advantages on an international scale.

3. Creation of strategic capacity that enables a company to act on a global scale in key sectors.

4. Sufficient profitability to cover the costs of globalisation, as well as the risks associated with such a strategy.

A new, emerging relationship is developing between the state and global companies. The most crucial decisions, which relate to the allocation of technological and economic resources, are mainly made by large global companies. Single decisions by ABB, Siemens or IBM often concern several countries and regions of the world. States superficially appear to be playing an increasingly less important role, as they seem to react to rather than anticipate major changes in global markets. However, the state is increasingly active in technological and economic spheres of the world economy, though it does not act as a leader.

The reasons for this major change in the relationship between the state and global companies are threefold. First, the growing integration arising from information and telecommunication technologies compels companies to participate in all sectors and markets that are likely to affect their future development. Second, the rapidly rising costs of R&D compels companies to makes alliances which reduce costs as well as technological and financial risks. Third, a relative scarcity of engineering and R&D personnel forces companies to go after human resources wherever they can be found, and prompts the state to invest in R&D programmes and universities to provide students with highly advanced training that meets the companies' needs.

Globalising companies expect the state to support them in various ways, of which the following are the most important:

1. Cover the costs of basic infrastructure, which includes basic and high-risk research and funding for universities and vocational training systems.

2. Provide tax incentives needed for investment in industrial R&D and innovations and support for regional investments.

3. Guarantee that companies have a sufficiently stable industrial base with privileged access to the domestic market via public procurement contracts.

However, there can be no doubt that the emerging characteristics of a global economy have changed and reduced the role of the state, while greatly enhancing the importance of co-operative relations between companies. These relationships exist across the spectrum of company activities. See Figure 1 for details.

The figure shows that alliances exist in R&D, in manufacturing, marketing and distribution. The reason for entering a R&D alliance arises from a desire to share risks and costs or to gain access to technology. Manufacturing alliances are mainly aiming at cost reduction and include joint ventures for manufacturing and various licensing and patent agreements. Access to markets is the main justification for alliances which aim at joint marketing, territorial allocation or trademark licensing. A strategic alliance may involve only one element or all elements mentioned above.

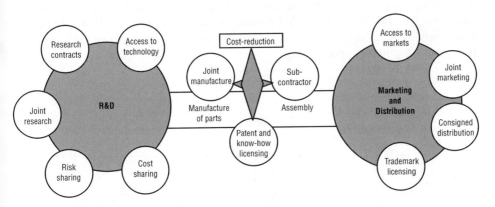

Figure 1. **Forms of Alliances**

Technological Clusters

It is useful to look at some illustrations of international partnerships that are increasingly eroding the role of an industrial group, or an industrial conglomerate. For example, Hitachi Ltd., in one of its major areas, semiconductor development, has entered into a far-reaching, long-term agreement with Texas Instruments. This agreement has been supplemented with partnerships for microprocessors, one with Hewlett Packard and another with Sun Microsystems. Another important semiconductor partnership is with Mitsubishi Electric for flash memory. Furthermore, Hitachi has an extensive partnership with General Electric in nuclear power plants and in gas turbine technology. Rockwell International provides partnerships in process control equipment and in factory automation systems while TRW is an equally important partner in space technology that is jointly developed with Nissan Motor.

Canon Inc. has also entered into a wide array of partnerships. These include joint ventures for semiconductor devices with both Texas Instruments and Hewlett Packard and a three-party joint venture for the manufacture of semiconductor memories in Singapore. These partnerships include various distribution agreements. Canon is Hewlett Packard's major supplier of laser printers, in which Canon maintains a leading position in the world. A similar agreement links Canon with Apple. Canon also maintains important partnerships with Motorola, Eastman Kodak and IBM.

Fujitsu is one of the most internationalised companies in Japan. It has a controlling interest in Advantest, the leading company in the world for advanced testing equipment used in the semiconductor industry. Fujitsu also has a controlling interest in Amdahl, in the United States and has a majority of the equity of ICL in the United Kingdom. Furthermore it has a number of important partners in Japan and overseas, and has recently given special attention to software alliances. Figure 2 provides details of some of the most important partnerships. Most of Fujitsu's partnerships are with US companies. The relationship with ICL began with a partnership in the early 1980s. Full control, achieved in the early 1990s, led to the expulsion of ICL from several R&D programmes which were organised under European Community sponsorship.

Figure 2.

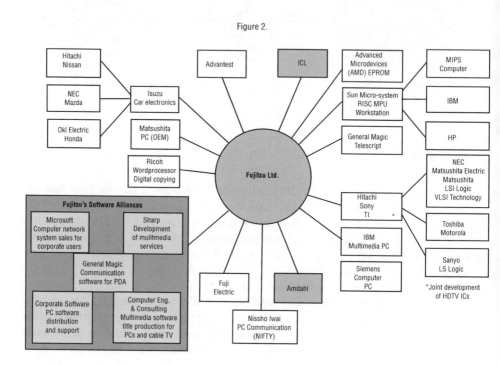

Marketing Clusters

The examples cited above indicate that there is a growing role for alliances for developing or sharing technology. However, many of these alliances include agreements to share or develop markets jointly. In other agreements the marketing aspect dominates, as will be illustrated for Mitsubishi Heavy Industries (MHI). MHI has a number of collaborative arrangements with major companies in the United

States and Europe, which include joint ventures with Caterpillar and Dresser Rand, and with International Aero Engine. MHI is also sharing technology and engaged in business co-operation with Corning Glass. See Figure 3 for details.

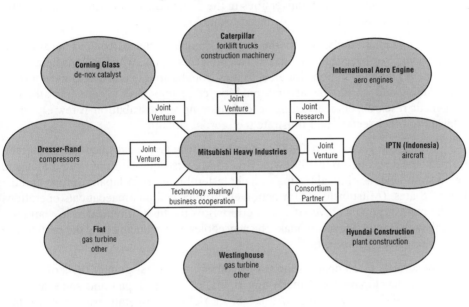

Figure 3. **MHI Major International Partners**

Source: Adapted from data provided by Mitsubishi Heavy Industries

MHI, which manufactures high-capacity gas turbines, has agreements in power plant technology with both Fiat and Westinghouse, though the relationship with Fiat is rather weak. The company has benefited from the collaboration with Westinghouse Electric Corp. which has provided gas turbine technology for many years. In 1986 the two companies entered into an agreement under which MHI would supply gas turbines on an original equipment manufacturing (OEM) basis to the US company, which had terminated its own production in this area.

In 1991 MHI signed an agreement to promote new technical and business co-operation with Westinghouse Electric covering gas turbine and co-generation know-how. Until then, Mitsubishi had been paying technology fees to Westinghouse. However, under the new agreement both companies will co-operate on an equal basis in technology and management to compete with General Electric Co. of the United States on the world market.

After marketing turbines supplied by MHI on an OEM basis, Westinghouse has been producing gas turbines developed by the Japanese company since 1993. As a result, General Electric, a leading producer of stationary gas turbines, is facing strong competition from a consortium of MHI, Westinghouse and Fiat in Italy.

MHI is also engaged in the development and manufacture of products that are based on "strategic alliances". This includes the design of aircraft together with Boeing, which provides an important element of risk-sharing for both companies. MHI has a number of relationships with universities in the United States and Europe whose aim is obtaining access to the most advanced technologies.

Only a small number of pharmaceutical companies have acquired the status of "megaplayer", or have the potential of reaching this status, which means being able to maintain global operations for all activities from basic research and clinical testing to marketing and worldwide distribution. Most companies have to enter into alliances for genetic research, clinical testing or for marketing and distribution. A few examples relevant to other sectors will illustrate the present situation.

Mitsubishi Kasei Corp. (MKC), now Mitsubishi Chemical since a 1994 merger, formed a business tie-up in 1990 with Bristol-Meyers-Squibb of the United States to begin simultaneous clinical testing of a cholesterol reducer in Japan, Europe and the United States. (Mitsubishi's information/electronics and pharmaceuticals operations are the mainstays of its diversification efforts.) At the time, it indicated it would use the link with Bristol-Meyers to make the new cholesterol-reducing drug the centrepiece of its pharmaceutical efforts.

According to company sources, Mitsubishi Chemical granted Bristol-Meyers worldwide development and marketing rights, excluding Japan and some areas of Southeast Asia. The two firms will establish a close co-operative relationship that will include exchanging clinical test data and will proceed with clinical tests in their own countries. The tie up was formed after Bristol-Meyers, which produces a similar cholesterol reducer, found the MKC drug more effective than its own product, which had annual sales in the United States alone of 60 000 million yen but was losing ground to a Merck drug. The tie up will allow Mitsubishi to reach a global market, and in 1990 the company announced a programme to triple its current pharmaceuticals sales to 100 000 million yen by the year 2000.

Mitsubishi Chemical and Marion Merrell Dow of the United States, both grappling with the soaring cost of drug development, formed a strategic alliance in 1993 to develop and market pharmaceuticals each company would have first option for a set period of time to license promising drugs developed by the other. In addition, Mitsubishi, which was already Japan's largest diversified chemical firm, and Marion Merrell, which ranks in the world's top 20 pharmaceutical makers, would exchange research information and continue talks on possible joint-research projects. The link would also extend to marketing, giving Mitsubishi access to the US marketing network of Marion Merrell.

The agreement was the first strategic link between chemical concerns from the United States and Japan in pharmaceuticals. Among other benefits, the licensing options should lighten the burden of new drug development, which can require an investment of $100-$200 million and can take 10 to 15 years. On the marketing side, Mitsubishi gained a key foothold in the United States. Eventually, the present Mitsubishi Chemical aims to develop independent sales bases in the United States with the assistance of Marion Merrell. In the meantime, the US firm gains access to Mitsubishi's strengths, including work on drugs related to the central nervous system and the circulatory system.

The evolution of strategic alliances

Strategic alliances have evolved through several stages since the late 1950s. Initially most alliances were in food processing, mining and mechanical and electrical engineering, and were based on a desire to access local resources and local markets. Many alliances were FDI or turnkey projects where technology transfer played an important role. The focus shifted to consumer goods, electronics, chemicals and packaged brands in a second stage, and equity investment and various types of joint ventures became more prevalent. Licensing became important in moves to pass national barriers in order to gain access to markets and local production facilities.

Local production became more prominent in a third stage which saw a new focus on microelectronics, pharmaceuticals and civilian aircraft, with alliances based on a desire to gain access to human resources. Subcontracting, licensing and marketing became more prominent as technologies for information processing and communication made it possible to achieve a division of labour between affiliates and the principal producer.

In the present stage strategic alliances are increasingly motivated by a desire to gain access to engineering and R&D resources. Advanced product and process innovation for global and regional markets is carried out within a network of alliances. Technology co-operation has come to the forefront, which requires changes in intellectual property regimes and changes in various other regulatory mechanisms.

The four stages are briefly outlined in Table 1. The flood of alliances started among the early industrialisers in Asia, i.e. Japan, Korea and Taiwan, but the development has now spread throughout the region. Countries are at different stages of economic development and have different forms of corporate governance, both of which greatly affect the possibilities for making alliances. However, the larger countries in Asia are hosts to alliances which cover all industrial categories included in Table 1.

Table 1. **The Evolution of Strategic Alliances - An Elementary Taxonomy with a Focus on Technology**

	Category of industry	Major driving forces	Type of activity	Type of alliance	Facilitating factors	Attribute	Examples
Stage 1 (1960s)	food processing, mining, mechanical & electrical engineering	access to local resources, and local markets	basic production capabilities, adaptation, reverse engineering, assembly	FDI & turnkey projects, subcontracting, and OEM	closeness to local resources and markets, closeness to production resources	Technology transfer to subsidiaries	US-Japan alliances
Stage 2 (1970s)	consumer goods, electronics, packaged brands, chemicals	shares in local markets, crossing national barriers	product development for local market, local upgrading for quality and speed, also innovations in production	equity investment and JVs in core business, licensing, and subcontracting	large and protected markets, closeness to customers and production facilities	Technology growth in acquired or greenfield investments	... Taiwan-US, and Korea-US alliances
Stage 3 (1980s) Maturity	microelectronics, pharmaceuticals, civilian aircraft	access to markets and human resources	full production skills, process innovation, product design capability (for global markets)	equity investment and JVs in core business, subcontracting, licensing, marketing	enabling information and communication technologies, division of labour between affiliates and principal producer	Maturing technology in JVs and in own R&D facilities, inter-firm co-operation	... ... MNCs in expanding Asian markets
Stage 4 (1990s) Take-off	microelectronics, pharmaceuticals, civilian aircraft	access to markets and human resources access to engineering and R&D resources	competitive R&D capability, R&D linked to market needs, advanced product & process innovation for global and regional markets	FDI & JVs, JVs with MNCs in domestic markets, technology co-operation, marketing	divisibility of core and non-core activities, changes in intellectual properties, deregulation	Learning advanced technology in JVs and in own R&D facilities, inter-firm co-operation, local manufacture and design	... ... chemical, telecom, and aircraft alliances in all major Asian markets

Sources: Reddy, P. (1996), *Emerging Patterns of Globalization of Corporate R&D and Implications for Innovation Capability in Developing Host Countries: The Case of India.* (Ph.D. Dissertation); and Hobday, M. (1994), *Export-led Technology Development in the Four Dragons: the Case of Electronics.*

Technology Sharing Versus Market Access

It is of interest to look into the assessment of certain specific technologies by the research community in Japan, technologies that are also at the centre of international strategic alliances. Every five years Japan makes a forecast to identify how quickly certain technologies might be achieved and to identify the constraints on their realisation. Information technology and electronics are naturally areas that will require new devices with greater capacity. These include very large memories, logic devices with higher speeds and so on. Two areas have been singled out for special attention, the technology for manufacturing gigabit chips and the technology for using such chips. Today chips in common use have a capacity of 4 or 16 megabits, only one-250th, or one-60th of a gigabit chip.

The latest technology forecast in Japan predicts that the chips and the enabling technologies will be developed by about 2003 and 2002 respectively. Both technologies are considered highly important by those who participated in the study, most of whom were working in the R&D departments in Japanese companies. Very few of those questioned considered that international joint development was necessary. A majority also believed that Japan was leading in both areas. Only 4 per cent believed that Japan was less advanced than other countries.

In spite of this assessment of Japanese leadership, major research consortia are being formed to develop these two technologies. These alliances are of a global character extending beyond the national borders of Japan. This is partly explained by the constraints on realisation. The study reports that technical constraints on realisation are very high, followed by cost and funding considerations, while all other constraints were almost negligible. Table 2 provides further details.

The new situation can also be illustrated by the international alliances appearing in the semiconductor field. The struggle among companies to become or remain technological leaders requires very large investment in research and development. Declining profit levels are forcing companies to look for international partners in financing very costly development projects, as illustrated by the alliance formed by Toshiba, IBM and Siemens to develop the technology for manufacturing future generation semiconductors (256 megabit DRAM). In the summer of 1992 the three companies announced that they "will co-operate in the development of a 256-million-bit dynamic random access memory (DRAM) chip. This sophisticated submicron technology will be a basis for production of future generations of highly dense chips[4]."

Table 2. **Forecasting Technological Advances and Constraints for IC Development**

		Use of 10nm line patterns for gigabit chips	Practical use of gigabit chips
Year of realisation		2003	2002
Degree of importance (%)		90	90
Necessity of international joint development (%)		13	6
Comparison of current R&D level between Japan and other countries (%)	• Japan is more advanced	57	75
	• Equivalent	30	12
	• Japan is less advanced	4	4
Constraints on realisation (%)	• Technical	88	84
	• Institutional	1	1
	• Cultural	0	2
	• Cost	41	57
	• Funding	25	25
	• Human resources	7	2
	• R&D system	6	5

Sources: *Future Technology in Japan, The Fifth Technology Forecast Survey*, National Institute of Science and Technology Policy/Science and Technology Agency (Japan) and the Institute for Future Technology, Tokyo 1993 (originally published by the Institute for Future Technology under the title "2020 nen no Kagagijitsu").

The Economics of Forming an Alliance

A major reason for this tripartite alliance is the considerable savings that the participating companies are making. Toshiba estimates that it can reduce the development costs by approximately 60 per cent, costs that may be in the region of US$200 million[5] or more. The reduction in development costs by entering into an alliance is illustrated in Figure 4.

The figure indicates that a major cost saving will be achieved by joining up with the first partner, and the additional saving is still substantial when accepting a third partner, after which the savings are less. We can expect that major companies in Japan, and elsewhere, will be striving to become attractive partners for such alliances. Companies involved in such globalisation will partially loose their national allegiance.

However, it still must be explained why Japanese companies are choosing foreign partners if their scientists and engineers believe that they are actually at the technological frontier. We have to look for other reasons than purely cost and technological considerations that have prompted companies like Toshiba, Hitachi and NEC to enter into international collaboration for 256 megabit DRAM, a pattern that is more than likely to be continued for the succeeding generations of chip technology. The companies apparently find partners in order to reduce costs and have chosen partners outside their home country in order ease trade frictions and get improved access to markets. Naturally this reduces Japan's ability to promote national champions, and, it also reduces the ability of the European Union to use transnational research consortia as a platform for improving EU company performance.

Figure 4. **Economics of Forming an Alliance**

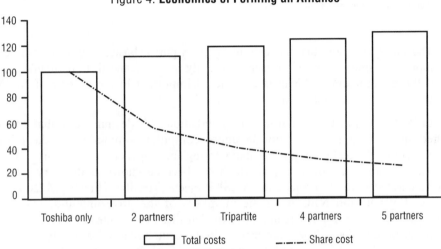

In an attempt to handle the perceived technology gap vis-à-vis the United States in the 1960s, a number of European governments directly or indirectly supported companies, usually referred to as "national champions". They were expected to enter the top league and compete successfully in the international arena. This was most notable in mainframe computers and related equipment, where IBM was perceived to be the enemy. Supporting champions shifted to a European level when Japanese electronics companies threatened their European counterparts in the late 1970s and early 1980s. An ambition to support "European champions" can still be discerned in the EU Framework Programme for R&D and in the Eureka Programme. The latter, which is strongly influenced by European firms, is expected to engage in R&D that is close to the market, although receiving substantial national subsidies.

In areas in which Japan is more advanced, the forecasted realisation time is relatively short and there is little need for international joint development, according to those surveyed, whereas the cost factor is seen as a major constraint. In areas where other countries are more advanced than Japan, on the other hand, the forecasted realisation time is longer and it is seen as desirable to engage in international joint development. See Table 3.

Table 3. **Views On Constraints and the Need for International Collaboration for Future Technologies**

Topics in which Japan is:	Realisation time	Main constraint on realisation	Need for international joint development
more advanced	Relatively early	Costs	Low
less advanced	Relatively late	Funding	High

Source: Future Technology in Japan, p. 12.

The study concludes that "Japan must actively pursue basic, long-term or large-scale topics in which other countries are presently more advanced. In particular, the role of the government in Japan is considered important in the aspects of R&D investment and international joint development."

In 1975 the Ministry of Industry and International Trade announced that it had reached an agreement with major Japanese computer companies for the joint development of the technology for manufacturing future-generation memory chips. That was the beginning of a project which has become known as the Very Large Scale Integrated Circuits Project, the VLSI Project. Toshiba, Hitachi, Mitsubishi Electric, Fujitsu, and NEC were the members of the government-sponsored partnership. However, it has become obvious that these companies today no longer rely on Japanese partners. Their partners are in the United States, Europe and Korea, primarily in the United States, with Korean companies playing the second fiddle. See Figure 5 for an overview of the major partnerships.

Making an Alliance Work

Strategic alliances may be considered important to reduce costs, but also to ease trade frictions and become a global actor. Toshiba has stated: "Partnerships are effective tools for speeding the technological development process, reducing costs, increasing business opportunities and sharing the risks involved. Toshiba firmly believes in the value of pooling resources with other companies in order to complement our strengths and to maximise future benefits for both partners, as well as to address customers' needs in a comprehensive manner. Alliances at Toshiba take two forms: those with other electronic companies, and those with companies in other industries[6]". Major joint programmes of the first type include work on large-scale liquid crystal displays with IBM Japan in the joint partnership Display Technology Inc. and the 256 megabit DRAM project with IBM and Siemens, for which the cost-reduction considerations were already discussed.

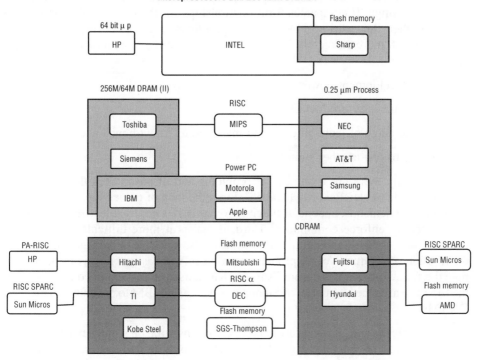

Figure 5. **Partnerships for developing Semiconductors, Microprocessors and 256 Mbit DRAM**

Toshiba's annual report gave two other examples of tie ups with companies in other industries. One is an agreement with Time Warner Inc. and the other is a lithium ion battery venture with Asahi Chemical Industry. Toshiba expects strategic alliances of both types to be increasingly central to the company's success during the remainder of the 1990s and beyond.

Toshiba is in no way unique. Hitachi also says that, as a way of reducing the burden of escalating development costs, the company is expanding its joint development partnerships. For example, an agreement was signed with Texas Instruments relating to the joint development of a 256-megabit DRAM, while an arrangement with General Electric Company covering the joint development of gas-turbine technology was strengthened.

Let us briefly look into the justification of these agreements, taking as a starting point the companies' need to deploy world-class resources in order to compete effectively on a global scale. One possibility, at least in theory, is to buy other

143

companies to get access to markets or technologies. However, only certain companies are available and affordable, and not necessarily the best ones. Another option, as illustrated above, is to form strategic alliances and build multinational networks. Mikio Ohtsuki of Fujitsu stresses that the main objective of strategic alliances is collaborative creativity, stating: "If companies form relationships for the purpose of collaborative creativity, then they will be able to solve problems, make discoveries, and create products much more efficiently." According to Ohtsuki the most important synergies are:

1. joint development power;

2. complementary product lines;

3. the exchange of technological and managerial "know-how;" and

4. access to one another's markets[7].

Naturally there are a number of problems and disadvantages that have to be solved, or at least satisfactorily handled[8]. First, the lack of ownership creates crucial co-ordination demands. Second, following from this, it is impossible to dictate strategy or unilaterally enforce compliance. Third, it makes it more difficult to establish a common set of values and culture. Fourth, it is also difficult to manage an equitable distribution of returns. Not all problems can be solved easily, but it is of interest to note the following comment from Tsuyoshi Kawanishi of Toshiba in connection with the tripartite alliance composed of Siemens, Toshiba and IBM to develop 256 megabit DRAMs:

> "Americans and Germans are very assertive, insisting on what they believe
> to be best, so you need a good conductor to orchestrate the alliance unit.
> Being modest and patient, we have found ourselves ideal coordinators [9]"

From the beginning, the joint research facility in the United States, where some 200 researchers and engineers from the three companies have been assembled, has been directed by a manager from Toshiba, supported by deputy directors from Siemens and IBM.

However, it is important to have a vision of one's industry and how networks are likely to evolve. Only then is it possible to find which capabilities will improve a competitive position, to be able to select and join the right alliances, and to use the networks to advantage. Ohtsuki sees the future of collaboration in the following way:

> "I think that companies that survive in the future are those which
> understand the need for collaborative creativity, those which make their
> strategic alliances work, and those which are able to efficiently focus their
> management resources on their core technologies[10]."

Thus, it is essential for a company to build up its own technological strength in order to be able to choose and select according to its aims. Yasuo Kato, executive vice president of NEC, stresses the importance of the following factors:

1. Each alliance partner should have a core competence in an area that can be exchanged, and must be willing to contribute to the alliance;

2. The partners should reciprocate benefits as much as possible;

3. The alliance should produce synergy, a multiplier effect;

4. Mutually weak points are reinforced;

5. The relationship is based on mutual trust rather than legal contractual terms alone; and

6. Alliance partners must be patient, especially when faced with difficulties and differences[11].

Efficient advanced R&D and protecting one's own turf are important for being able to enter meaningful strategic alliances. The control of intellectual property rights, in particular patents, has become more important to most industrial companies today for a number of reasons. First, a strong patent position is basic in order to ward off claims from competing companies. Second, patents are of primary importance in providing a basis for access to technology from competitor companies and to establish alliances with other companies. Third, patents are of great importance for establishing a strong foothold in emerging new technologies. The technological basis for standards is often rooted in patent rights. Finally, the width and depth of a company's patent portfolio is more often than not a good indicator of the company's technological strength, not only in its research laboratories but also in the market place.

Patent practices and management today are undergoing important changes following from major transformations which, in brief, have two key characteristics. First, the globalisation of the world economy has created close links between the major markets in which globalising companies are the main actors. Second, innovations are becoming increasingly important for most sectors, and for almost all large corporations in the industrialised countries.

The efforts to develop a new type of video disk in recent years provides an illustration of the close linkages between patent positions and the de facto standardisation of major electronics products, and the emergence of a multimedia industrial sector. In addition, the speed of technological change in the domain of information technologies clearly indicates that standards are no longer established by international bodies, assisted by a number of formal committees, that gradually reach a consensus. Instead, IT standards are increasingly established by ad hoc corporate groups which organise informal technology panels that work closely with the companies' R&D departments.

In September 1995 the leading companies in consumer electronics announced that they had agreed on a common format for the new generation of digital video disk systems. A compromise was reached when a group of companies led by Toshiba agreed to a proposal from the opposing group led by Sony and Philips Electronics that they would adopt an amended version of the disk system developed by the Super-

Density (SD) Alliance led by Toshiba. The compromise averted a conflict like the technology battle of the 1980s when a Matsushita group with its VHS video system eventually defeated Sony's Betamax system. The greater storage capacity of the SD-system proposed by Toshiba gave an initial advantage which was further strengthened when Matsushita Electrical Industrial Co. decided to work with the Toshiba group after previously having almost opted for the Sony group.

In accepting the compromise, Sony agreed to make considerable changes in its proposal, although at the same time the Toshiba group recognised the need to adopt Sony's signal format, based on existing CD technology, which is preferred by the computer companies because of its higher data reliability. This is important for Sony and Philips as they will be able collect large royalties from their strong patents for CD technology. However, Toshiba and other companies in its group have been able to amass a large number of patents for the SD disk technology and will also be able to benefit from patent royalties.

Countries in Asia differ greatly in population and level of development. This is also true in Europe, although the ranges are considerably narrower. Thus in the past, Asian companies from Japan, Korea and Chinese Taipei have been dominant in forming strategic alliances, mainly with partners in the United States. This situation is now changing dramatically due to the economic boom in Asia, expanding markets and the availability of critical inputs such as skilled engineers and researchers.

From the changes mentioned in this chapter it is possible to draw several conclusions. First, the advanced industrialised countries in Europe and North America are less and less a base for the development and manufacture of products for export and market exploitation/penetration. Second, small advanced countries are even less a basis for product development, which is increasingly dominated by market considerations. Third, strategic alliances are becoming increasingly important in the development of many technology sectors where very high costs and increasing risk force companies into forming alliances.

Available evidence indicates that not even the largest Western multinational companies can market their products equally well in all parts of the global economy. Nor is its possible for them to support leading-edge research and development activities in all areas that are essential for their products or systems. Furthermore, many find it difficult to remain sufficiently competitive in all parts of the added-value chain. Thus strategic alliances offer the option of concentrating on core competencies and accessing the remaining inputs from partners. However, the main interest of Asian partners, aside from those in Japan, Korea and Chinese Taipei, is usually a desire to acquire technologies and/or market expertise.

There can be no doubt that a strong patent portfolio is a key asset for many companies when successfully negotiating an alliance. A strong patent position also offers possibilities for earning substantial license revenues to offset high R&D costs, or to offer substantial deliveries as an original equipment manufacturer (OEM). Both alliances and OEM products enhance the possibility for establishing what may be referred to as "technology families" that create a group of companies with common interests for the promotion of certain technologies, a de facto standardisation. A similar form of protection for technology standardisation is found in the new alliances between the makers of electronic hardware in Japan and the producers of entertainment software in the United States. The underlying changes indicate that many companies have been transformed from manufacturing to knowledge-creating firms, which may offer greater possibilities for forming strategic alliances.

Many economists have already understood that the size and behaviour of multinational companies have radically undermined conventional approaches to industrial theory and policy. The significance of what is often referred to as meso-economics is that it not only represents a new power structure of multinational companies but also has an indirect impact on both micro- and macroeconomic variables and thereby undermines the function of many traditional economic policies. The total value of production by multinational companies already exceeded the total value of world trade by the late 1970s. National borders are being eroded by the internationalisation of both business and technology, a development reinforced by supranational research programmes in Europe.

It is to expected that the globalisation of R&D facilities will continue rapidly for three reasons. First, the ongoing process of mergers and acquisitions naturally leads to more and more R&D facilities being controlled by companies having manufacturing and/or headquarters in another country. Second, the need to adapt increasingly sophisticated products and systems to local conditions requires the localisation of R&D. Third, more and more companies are obtaining their knowledge resources from countries and regions where such resources can be more easily be obtained and the costs may be considerably lower.

These trends pose fundamental challenges for the national system of innovation, and it is possible to identify new approaches which reflect the ongoing transformation. One is the formation of a research policy for the European Union, as manifested in the R&D Framework Programme, of which the content and orientation of a fifth version is now being discussed. However, until recently its R&D policy has reflected a desire to support EU "champions" in key sectors where national governments did not successfully support their national champion. A similar ambition can clearly be seen in several of the EUREKA programmes and is obvious from the formation of the Joint European Sub-micron Silicon Initiative (JESSI) which aimed to recreate a basis for an independent capability in integrated circuit technology. It was surprising to see this initiative getting strong political support at a time when European companies were seeking global partners rather than partners within their own geographic area. The dichotomy between national and global initiatives is illustrated by Japanese approaches in recent years.

Global Technological Initiatives from Japan

In October 1980, the *Japan Economic Journal* (now the *Nikkei Weekly*) reported that Japan, the United States, Germany, Britain and France were jointly going to undertake research and development for making a practical fifth generation computer available in the 1990s, the Fifth Generation Computer Project (FGC). The ten-year project, which was given a budget of 65 000 million yen, was started in early 1982, and immediately founded the Institute for New Generation Computer Technology. The direct foreign participation never materialised, however, although the project triggered intensive activity at the EC Commission in Brussels, in London and in several other places. The outcome, rather than collaboration along the lines suggested by the Japanese, was a number of competing projects, including the Alvey Programme in the United Kingdom and, to a lesser extent, the ESPRIT programme which is part of the European R&D Framework Programme.

More recently Japan established the Real World Computing (RWC) programme that began functioning for a ten-tear period in 1992. Its origin can be found in a MITI report from the Research Committee of New Information Processing Technology, established in 1989. The committee assessed systems for new processing technologies and conducted feasibility studies to propose specific R&D plans. The RWC Programme closely co-operates with the Electrotechnical Laboratory of MITI, and has created a research network in Tsukuba Science City. However, the programme has only attracted foreign participation from the German National Research Centre for Computer Science, the Institute of Systems Science at the National University of Singapore, the Stichting Neurale Netwerken in the Netherlands, and the Swedish Institute of Computer Science (SICS). The United States maintains an interest in the project but apparently only in order to gain access to research results on optical computing and optical devices.

The Joint International Research Programs into an Intelligent Manufacturing System (IMS) is another proposal to provide a platform for a broad international programme to do research on some important technologies for the factories of tomorrow, in particular system technologies and interface protocols in order to make various devices operate in a seamless environment. The project is also scheduled to last ten years, like the two previous examples, and the planned budget is about $1.5 billion, to be borne by the public and private sectors in Japan, North America and Europe. An International Institute for the Promotion of IMS has been established at locations outside Japan. Within the institute there will be a joint international research centre which will manage specific research projects that are expected to have members from universities, research institutes and private industry. The research will be oriented towards five areas: configuration of production systems, information and telecommunications technology for IMS, production and control equipment, new materials for upgrading production equipment, and human factors in production.

The overall aims of IMS is to integrate and systematise production technology for common use around the world. The specific Japanese concern may be a desire to provide manufacturing environments that are attractive to young people, highly flexible and require little labour which is in short supply. The latter point may have alarmed the foreign partners as they are afraid that the project will give Japanese manufacturers a leading edge in robotics equipment and other automated production systems. Another related aspect is the fact that new standards in manufacturing technology will be established, at least on a de facto basis.

Regionalisation

Regionalisation covers a spectrum that ranges from simple customs unions to economic integration based on monetary union, common economic policies and the creation of a single integrated market. The majority of regional economic integration schemes are akin to the customs union and various forms of liberalisation of national markets. Today, the most advanced example of regional economic integration is the European Community, renamed the European Union in November 1993.

Major differences can be found among the existing examples of regionalisation, and no single example of a regional economic unit is fully comparable to others. In Asia, and particularly East and Southeast Asia, the movement towards regionalisation is characterised by a multiplicity of ad hoc forms of co-operation which are operating under multilateral organisations.

One of the contributors to the 1995 International Forum on Asian Perspectives, Min Tang, stated:

"In recent years, one of the most significant developments in the Asian economy has been the rapid growth of regional co-operation. Within a few years, a number of regional initiatives have been endorsed and various forms of co-operative ventures have been established. The results of these developments can be seen in the formation of the Asia-Pacific Economic Cooperation (APEC), the ASEAN Free Trade Area (AFTA) and the revival of the South Asian Association for Regional Cooperation (SAARC) as well as various innovative types of sub-regional co-operative ventures. This is in contrast to Asia's historical record on co-operation. For many years, the pace of regional co-operation was very slow compared with other regions of the world. The only exception is probably the Association of South East Asian Nations (ASEAN). However, the contribution of ASEAN has been primarily political rather than economic".[12]

Tang identified five major reasons for this new wave of regionalisation in Asia. First, the increase in trade protection in industrialised countries, the Single Market in Europe, and the North American Free Trade Agreement (NAFTA) have prompted the search for ways to hedge against a further weakening of the world trading system.

Second, the increase of intraregional trade among Asian countries has become an important driving force for economic co-operation. Third, the increased flows of intraregional investment in Asia have complemented the growth of intraregional trade, and reinforced the interdependence of Asian economies. Fourth, economic deregulation and liberalisation in Asian countries, including the opening up of centrally planned economies, has provided a stable foundation for the success of regional co-operation. Fifth, the opening up of the centrally planned economies in Asia has provided enormous business opportunities for regional co-operation.[13]

A European Perspective?

The European Union mentions in its most recent report on *Science and Technology Indicators* that "global collaborative R&D programmes have been an emerging phenomenon in recent years. Two schemes have emerged as a result of Japanese initiatives: the Intelligent Manufacturing Systems Project and the Human Frontier Science Programme".[14] The same report observes that in the future it is likely that there will have to be a substantial increase in the level of S&T co-operation between industrialised countries of the world. The reasons for this are: *(i)* the increasing costs of R&D, *(ii)* growing proliferation and specialisation in most fields of research and *(iii)* financing problems of both governments and private industry.

The expansion of strategic alliances erodes national or supranational control of innovations and has become a major policy issue. Thus the European Union is affected both by the rapid expansion of strategic alliances, where companies want to reduce their financial and technological risks, and by the emergence of initiatives for global science and technology programmes. These two ongoing changes should have a direct bearing on policies for science and technology as well as for industry. There are also serious implications for companies that have not yet fully recognised the changes that are occurring. As Lasserre and Schütte stress: "In a global partnership the first step is the creation of an awareness that there is something to learn from the other side. This is no easy undertaking for Western firms, which are successful in their own markets and proud of their past technological achievements." They further observe: "Organisational learning does not happen without substantial management guidance and without a positive attitude at top management level".

Strategic alliances raise other policy concerns as well. In the realm of competition policy, for example, the 1993 EU Commission White Paper on Growth, Competitiveness and Employment, noted:

> "The establishment of a coherent and concerted approach to strategic alliances, the uncontrolled development of which could result in the creation of oligopolistic situations prejudicial to competition at world level. The growing number of industrial and technological alliances will have an impact on all markets. These effects must consequently be assessed

simultaneously and in a concerted manner by the competent authorities pending the introduction of appropriate international rules, particularly in the competition field, so that the Community is not placed as a disadvantage by the strict rules it imposes on itself in this connection. In addition, Community firms must be able to rely on flexible instruments of co-operation, in legal and tax matters as well as in others, to allow them to enter into the alliances that are necessary to counterbalance the weight of some of their US and Japanese competitors".[15]

The form and cohesiveness of alliances can differ widely. On the one hand there are relatively loose alliances, which in reality are based on long-term contracts and provide great flexibility and almost complete autonomy for the partners. On the other hand, some partners prefer a much closer arrangement that justifies the establishment of a joint venture, with an equity stake by both partners. Strategic alliances have rapidly emerged as one of the major factors shaping the dynamics of competition in a wide array of industries.

Parent companies that continue to treat engineering and marketing in their home markets as core competencies may eventually defeat the very objective of an alliance. Separating customer responsibility between the parent company in the home market and the alliance in the foreign market, may cause co-ordination problems which will become increasingly serious as the foreign market served by the alliance is moving towards maturity.

The world has also increasingly come to understand that the burst of economic growth in Asia is not a fleeting development but a sustainable one. The economic and industrial policies in Europe, and in the European Union should therefore incorporate a global perspective in which it is understood that economic and industrial relations must increasingly be based on mutuality. Otherwise there is a great danger that Europe and its companies will lose many opportunities to enter into long-term and advantageous relations with partners in Asia.

The market for large commercial aircraft provides a further example. Supply today is dominated by Boeing in the United States and the Airbus consortium in Europe. However, the real market expansion is taking place in Asia, where domestic airlines will buy a large number of aircraft in order to meet the demands from their customers. The big US and European manufacturers in the past marketed their aircraft on the strength of their technological and industrial production capabilities at home. However, the technologically advanced countries of Asia are demanding joint development and joint manufacture of the aircraft they are purchasing. Chinese Taipei, Korea and China have aggressively pursued such possibilities, and the latter two countries have made attempts to form a consortium with one of the major aircraft manufacturers.

According to recent reports, China will establish a partnership with an EU consortium to build a new 100-seat commercial aircraft that is expected to cost about $2 billion to develop.[16] The letter of intent identifies the European Aero International

Regional (AIR) to become China's partner in creating a strong Asian presence in the aircraft industry that has hitherto been dominated by Western companies. The significance of the deal for Europe is that it promises an entry into Asia's aviation market which is expected to be about 50 per cent of the world market by 2015. China is expected to order some 200 aircraft over the coming decade alone. The AIR consortium would have a 30 per cent stake in the development project which is expected to generate a market for some 1000 aircraft.

Originally South Korea and China discussed a joint partnership with US and European aircraft manufacturers. The talks collapsed because of disagreement over shareholding and the site of the final assembly plant. It has been reported that China demanded the majority share in the consortium, demanded to become the project leader, and demanded that both assembly lines and the future joint company be established in China[17]. Samsung Aerospace Industries Co. and Aviation Industries of China are now pursuing partnerships on their own in order to obtain financial and technological resources to develop advanced civilian aircraft. The shifting balance of the market is evident from the fact that US and European makers were competing for a 20 per cent share of the project in order to strengthen their position in the Asian market.

The rapid expansion of Asian markets is evident in many other fields as well, and this is prompting European companies to reconsider their strategies. For example, SKF, the world's leading supplier of bearings, has recently decided to establish a major joint venture in China.[18] SKF is transferring key technologies and management skills and has a 51 per cent stake in the new venture that is expecting to capture 30 per cent of the large and rapidly increasing market for bearing boxes, which are essential for the modernisation of China's railways.

The telecommunications industry, characterised by a very rapid growth of strategic alliances, illustrates that notions of national and corporate sovereignty are being replaced by new structures that some observers refer to as virtual corporations. This change has been preceded by significant changes in national systems of regulation that have liberated companies from national straitjackets. An example is the recently established alliance between British Telecom and CSA Holdings (an information technology company) in Singapore. BT and CSA expect to capture a share of the booming Asian market for computer-related services. The information-technology market in Asia is estimated to have reached US$30 billion and is growing by more than 25 per cent a year. The alliance will initially focus on potential customers in Singapore, Malaysia and Indonesia before moving on to China and other large markets.[19]

These examples illustrate major changes in the relationships between European companies and their partners in the expanding markets. The chemical and pharmaceutical industries offer similar examples where the strength of European companies is attractive to Asian partners. Initially, many partnerships are based on combining European prowess in technological development and manufacturing skills

...... the local market access and acumen of the Asian partners, sustained by the steady expansion of Asian markets. In many instances, it can be expected that European and Japanese companies will join forces to exploit Asian markets.

This chapter has shown that the private sector is responding to major changes in competitive challenges, naturally in their home countries but increasingly in the global economy, where what are often referred to as the dynamic Asian economies (DAE) play an increasingly significant role. Aside from the DAE, there is enormous potential for catching up elsewhere in Asia. This potential constitutes a continuing competitive challenge to Europe which will induce closer relationships between the two regions. Strategic alliances will be at the heart of those relationships. They will initially be dominated by partnerships where European partners provide technology and management inputs while the Asian side provides other essential inputs for meeting market demands. There can be do doubt that in the longer term such alliances will develop into partnerships that encompass full mutuality. Unless this is fully realised, and unless such relationships are supported by governments and policy makers, Europe will lose out and become simply an onlooker with respect to the changes occurring in Asia.

Notes

1. The author was Professor of Research Policy and Director of the Research Policy Institute, Lund University; and is now at the European Institute of Japanese Studies, Stockholm School of Economics. He has greatly benefited from in-depth discussions with Charles Oman of the OECD Development Centre who offered many constructive suggestions for improving the logic and contents of this chapter. He also profited from discussion with Hellmutt Schütte.

2. Lasserre, P. and H. Schütte (1995), *Strategies for Asia Pacific,* Macmillan Business, Basingstoke.

3. Badaracco, Joseph L. Jr. (1991), *The Knowledge Link: How Firms Compete through Strategic Alliances*, Harvard Business School Press.

4. Toshiba press release, July 13, 1992.

5. Author's estimate.

6. *Toshiba Annual Report 1993*, p. 4.

7. Comments by M. Ohtsuki of Fujitsu Co.

8.   The observations in this paragraph are from Cyrus F. Friedheim, Jr., "The Trillion Dollar Enterprise", International *Economic Insights*, July-August 1993, pp. 29-31.

9.   Comments by Tsuyoshi Kawanishi, senior executive vice president of Toshiba.

10.   *Ibid.*

11.   Yoshino, F. F. (1993), "Challenges for the High-tech Industry, *Journal of Japanese Trade & Industry*, August, pp. 46-48. This listing was made by Yasuo Kato, executive vice president of NEC, who with reference to the fact that R&D costs have increased exponentially, particularly in recent years, said that ". . . it is difficult for a single corporation to shoulder the huge financial burden of R&D". The article was obtained from the Nikkei Telecom Database, http://www.nikkei.co.jp/enews/html.

12.   Tang , M. (1995) "Asian Economic Co-operation: Opportunities and Challenges", in Kiichiro Fukasaku (ed.), *Regional Co-operation and Integration in Asia*, OECD, Paris 1995, pp. 195-248.

13.   *Ibid.* pp. 205-6.

14.   *The European Report on Science and Technology Indicators 1994*, Executive Summary, Report EUR 15929, October 1994

15.   *Growth, Competitiveness, Employment - The Challenges and Ways Forward into the 21st Century*, White paper, European Commission 1993, pp. 61-62.

16.   "Political Winds Sweep Chinese Airplane Deal Into European Hangar - Beijing Signs Letter of Intent To Make EU Consortium Partner in $2 billion Project", *Wall Street Journal Europe*, 12 April 1996.

17.   "Korea and China Search for New Aircraft Partners", *International Herald Tribune*, 20 June 1996

18.   "SKF tar grepp om Kinamarknad" (SKF captures the China market), *Dagens Industri*, April 1996.

19.   "British Telecom Forms an Asian Alliance", *International Herald Tribune*, 20 June 1996

Natural Resources, Economic Structure, and Asian Infrastructure

Douglas H. Brooks and Elizabeth E. Leuterio[1]

The physical environment affects the growth patterns of nations by changes in the supply of natural resources, structural change of the economy, the dynamics of comparative advantage, and the interaction of the environment with infrastructure. A country's comparative advantage depends on the relationships between its resources, their relative prices and the technology that can be used for exploiting resources. Over time, a nation's economic structure and comparative advantage change as a result of capital accumulation, population growth, development of human resources and changes in stocks and quality of natural resources.

Physical infrastructure plays a key role as a source of demand for resources and by facilitating their development for other uses. This is quite obvious in urban areas, although some rural infrastructure such as large irrigation projects and energy generation schemes also underscore the interaction between natural resources, infrastructure and changing economic structure. Most economic analyses of infrastructure concentrate on public investment because of data limitations and the definition of infrastructure capital "that makes the most sense from an economics standpoint consists of large capital intensive natural monopolies such as highways, other transportation facilities, water and sewer lines, and communications systems" (Gramlich, 1994,). However, recent technological advances have increased the scope for private sector participation in the development and operation of infrastructure.

Macroeconomic studies have found that infrastructure, including transportation, water and sanitation, power, telecommunications and irrigation, accounts for one-third to one-half of public investment (3-6 per cent of gross domestic product) and, not surprisingly, that infrastructure capital has a positive and significant effect on economic output and growth (Kessides 1993). Recent data for selected economies in developing Asia seem to reflect these findings. The newly industrialising economies (NIEs) of Hong Kong, the Republic of Korea, Singapore, and Chinese Taipei have high per capita gross domestic products and levels of infrastructure compared to other countries in the region (Tables 1 and 2). Macroeconomic or industry-level studies of infrastructure suffer from weaknesses in determining the mechanisms by which contributions to economic output and growth are made, while microeconomic studies fail to capture fully the externalities by which infrastructure enhances labour and capital productivity.

Few Asian countries with abundant natural resources have developed them so that they can support vigorous, broad-based economic growth. By contrast, some of the most robust economies have very limited resource bases (Hong Kong and Singapore are the most obvious examples). This chapter will discuss some of the ways in which physical infrastructure can convert constraints of the natural environment into economic opportunities, examine the relationship between natural endowment, infrastructure and economic structure in the Asian context, and discuss Asia's needs and possible financing mechanisms for developing physical infrastructure.

The chapter's first two sections briefly describe the role of natural resources in the development process and the role of physical infrastructure in exploiting the potential of natural resources. A third section examines the relationship between economic structure and Asia's demand for infrastructure. This is followed by a discussion of infrastructure financing and the importance of pricing and regulation. Finally, areas for further action are identified for the public sector in host countries, for domestic and international investors, and for multilateral institutions.

The Role of the Natural Environment in Asian Development

The relationships between natural resources and labour, capital and technology reflect and influence the economic structure and comparative advantage. Table 3 presents data on the state of natural resources and economic structure in selected countries in developing Asia. The table provides a partial picture of the status of forests, land use and the availability and utilisation of fresh water. The data portray the major differences in resources and their uses among the countries in the region.

Even by the year 2010, slightly more than half of the economically active population in developing Asia is still expected to be engaged in agriculture, emphasizing the continuing importance of the natural environment in a changing economic structure. Yet Asia is already the region which has suffered the worst soil erosion. Asian forests, coastal and inland wetlands, coral reefs and other ecological systems are being degraded or destroyed at relatively high rates by historical standards. In the 1980s, the annual rate of tropical deforestation in Asia was 1.2 per cent, slightly higher than in sub-Saharan Africa where it was less than one per cent. Water shortages in the region are becoming more critical and more common. The well-known congestion and pollution of Asian urban centres such as Bangkok, Manila and Jakarta argue for policy changes with respect to infrastructure.

Table 1. Income, Growth and Infrastructure in Selected Economies (I)

Country	Average annual growth of real GDP (%)		GDP per capita ($)	Electricity Installed generating capacity (megawatts)	Electricity Average annual growth in consumption (%)	Electricity Consumption per capita (kWh)	Electricity Systems losses (% of total output)	Telecommunications Average annual growth in number of telephones (%)	Telecommunications Telephone mainlines (per 1 000 persons)	Telecommunications Faults (per 100 mainlines per year)
	1981-90	1991-95	1995	1992	1981-93	1993	1992	1981-91	1992	1992
Newly Industrialising Economies										
• Hong Kong	6.9	5.6	23 992	8 932	7.5	4 684	11	6.9	485	22
• Korea, Rep. of	12.7	7.5	10 029	24 120	9.3	2 616	5	18.8	357	13
• Singapore	6.5	8.4	29 212	4 553	8.2	5 973	5	5.7	415	11
• Chinese Taipei	8.0	6.7	12 335	19 247	8.0	4 756	n.a.	5.1	n.a.	n.a.
People's Republic of China	10.4	11.8	573	166 532	7.5	601	7	11.6	10	n.a.
Mongolia	5.4	-2.6	369	1 033	5.0^a	883	n.a.	4.6	30	43
Southeast Asia										
• Cambodia	n.a.	6.0	276	n.a.	n.a.	8	n.a.	n.a.	n.a.	n.a.
• Indonesia	6.0	7.7	1 006	10 874	14.7	206	17	16.0	8	49
• Lao PDR	n.a.	6.4	382	n.a.	9.3	59	n.a.	3.7	2	12
• Malaysia	5.2	8.6	4 235	6 504	9.5	1 466	9	13.3	112	78
• Myanmar	-0.1	5.9	1 778	880	7.4	47	35	5.8	2	n.a.
• Philippines	1.0	2.2	1 054	6 881	4.3	327	13	7.2	10	10
• Thailand	7.9	8.4	2 766	12 806	11.9	970	10	12.7	31	32
• Viet Nam	7.1	8.2	261	3 409	n.a.	58	24	n.a.	2	n.a.
South Asia										
• Bangladesh	4.3	4.1	261	2 690	11.8	51	32	10.8	2	n.a.
• Bhutan	7.5	5.2	416	n.a.	34.4^a	105	n.a.	5.2	n.a.	n.a.
• India	5.6	4.7	353	78 996	7.9	270	23	5.6	8	218
• Maldives	12.1	6.5	1 190	n.a.	21.7^a	121	n.a.	21.0	n.a.	n.a.
• Nepal	4.9	4.8	221	269	11.7	34	24	17.2	3	168
• Pakistan	6.1	4.8	452	9 369	10.2	297	17	12.0	10	120
• Sri Lanka	4.2	5.4	708	1 407	6.9	186	17	7.1	8	n.a.
Central Asian Republics										
• Kazakhstan	n.a.	-15.4	930	n.a.	n.a.	4 768	9	n.a.	88	n.a.
• Kyrgyz Republic	n.a.	-13.8	320	n.a.	n.a.	2 170	10	n.a.	75	30

Notes :   n.a. : data not available. a : average for 1981-91.

Sources :   ADB (1994b) ; ADB (1994d) ; ADB (1996a) ; ADB (1996b) ; World Bank (1994 & 1996).

157

Table 2. Income, Growth and Infrastructure in Selected Economies (II)

Economy	Average annual growth of real GDP (%)		GDP per capita ($)	Motor Vehicles			Roads in good condition (% of paved road)	Railways		Water	
				Average annual growth in number (%)	Number per 1 000 population	Road density (Km per million persons)		Rail traffic units (per thousand $ GDP)	Diesels in use (% of diesel inventory)	Population with access to safe water (% of total)	Losses (% of total water provision)
	1981-90	1991-95	1995	1981-91	1991	1992	1988	1992	1992	1991	1986
Newly Industrialising Economies											
• Hong Kong	6.9	5.6	23 992	3.3	63.3	268	n.a.	n.a.	n.a.	100	n.a.
• Korea, Rep. of	12.7	7.5	10 029	19.8	73.0	1 090	70	146	88	78	n.a.
• Singapore	6.5	8.4	29 212	5.8	145.0	993	n.a.	n.a.	n.a.	100	8
• Chinese Taipei	8.0	6.7	12 335	17.8	167.5	n.a.	n.a.	n.a.	n.a.	n.a.	n.a.
People's Republic of China	10.4	11.8	573	11.8	4.5	n.a.	n.a.	n.a.	82	71	n.a.
Mongolia	5.4	-2.6	369	n.a.	17.1	n.a.	n.a.	847	58	66	n.a.
Southeast Asia											
• Cambodia	n.a.	6.0	276	n.a.	n.a.	n.a.	n.a.	n.a.	n.a.	n.a.	n.a.
• Indonesia	6.0	7.7	1 006	11.4	18.5	160	30	27	75	42	29
• Lao PDR	n.a.	6.4	382	0.4	4.1	516	n.a.	n.a.	n.a.	28	n.a.
• Malaysia	5.2	8.6	4 235	9.1	123.1	n.a.	n.a.	30	76	78	29
• Myanmar	-0.1	5.9	1 778	1.0	2.7	210	n.a.	n.a.	75	33	n.a.
• Philippines	1.0	2.2	1 054	3.9	19.9	242	31	n.a.	n.a.	81	53
• Thailand	7.9	8.4	2 766	14.8	51.1	841	50	75	72	72	48
• Viet Nam	7.1	8.2	261	n.a.	n.a.	n.a.	n.a.	n.a.	60	50	n.a.
South Asia											
• Bangladesh	4.3	4.1	261	6.0	1.0	59	15	37	74	78	47
• Bhutan		7.5	5.2	416	9.4	2.7	n.a.	n.a.	n.a.	n.a.	34
• India		5.6	4.7	353	11.2	893	20	488	n.a.	90	75
• Maldives	12.1	6.5	1 190	n.a.	n.a.	n.a.	n.a.	n.a.	n.a.	n.a.	n.a.
• Nepal	4.9	4.8	221	6.5	2.0	139	40	n.a.	n.a.	37	45
• Pakistan	6.1	4.8	452	7.4	7.0	826	18	137	78	50	40
• Sri Lanka	4.2	5.4	708	7.0	23.6	536	10	65	n.a.	60	n.a.
Central Asian Republics											
• Kazakhstan	n.a.	-15.4	930	n.a.	n.a.	6 747	n.a.	n.a.	54	75-94	n.a.
• Kyrgyz Republic	n.a.	-13.8	320	n.a.	n.a.	n.a.	n.a.	n.a.	n.a.	75-94	n.a.

Notes and sources: see table 1.

Table 3. **Natural Resources and Economic Structure in Selected Asian Developing Economies**

	Forest Area		Land Use, 1993		Freshwater resources: annual withdrawal 1970-92[b] per capita (m³)				Share of GDP, 1995 (%)				
	Total area (thousand sq. km) 1990	Annual deforestation (per cent of total area) 1981-90[a]	Irrigated area (per cent of arable land)	Arable land (per cent of land area)	(per cent of total water resources)	Total	Domestic	Industrial and agricultural	Agri-culture	Industry	Services	Exports[c]	Invest-ment
Newly Industrialising economies													
• Hong Kong	0	-0.5	33.3	6.1	n.a.	n.a.	n.a.	n.a.	0.2	18.1	81.7	139	33.1
• Korea, Rep. of	65	0.1	71.1	19.0	41.7	625	116	509	6.7	30.5	62.8	28	36.6
• Singapore	0	0.9	n.a.	1.6	31.7	84	38	46	0.2	42.7	57.1	177	33.9
• Chinese Taipei	n.a.	n.a.	n.a.	24.3	n.a.	n.a.	n.a.	n.a.	3.1	38.9	58.0	38	24.5
People's Republic of China	1 247	0.7	53.8	9.9	16.4	462	28	434	18.9	53.0	28.1	26	39.5
Mongolia	139	0.9	5.7	0.9	2.2	273	30	243	23.1	42.1	34.8	56	23.7
Southeast Asia													
• Cambodia	n.a.	n.a.	3.9	13.3	n.a.	n.a.	n.a.	n.a.	44.6	18.7	36.7	20	21.5
• Indonesia	1 095	1.0	24.3	10.4	0.7	95	12	83	15.9	42.2	41.9	25	38.3
• Lao PDR	132	0.9	16.0	3.4	0.4	259	21	239	56.5	18.9	24.6	21	n.a.
• Malaysia	176	2.0	32.7	3.2	2.1	768	177	592	13.9	47.1	39.0	90	40.6
• Myanmar	289	1.3	11.1	14.6	n.a.	n.a.	n.a.	n.a.	46.1	15.3	38.6	2	13.0
• Philippines	78	3.3	28.6	18.5	9.1	686	123	562	21.5	35.5	43.0	35	22.3
• Thailand	127	3.3	25.0	34.4	17.8	606	24	582	10.9	42.2	46.9	39	40.0
• Viet Nam	83	1.5	33.8	16.9	7.7	416	54	362	33.9	27.7	38.4	23	27.6
South Asia													
• Bangladesh	8	3.9	32.8	72.6	1.0	212	6	206	32.8	19.6	47.6	12	14.8
• Bhutan	28	0.6	29.6	2.4	0.0	14	5	9	37.6	28.3	34.1	35	54.5
• India	517	0.6	28.9	55.9	18.2	612	18	594	27.8	31.1	41.2	12	24.0
• Maldives	n.a.	n.a.	n.a.	10.0	n.a.	n.a.	n.a.	n.a.	n.a.	n.a.	n.a.	n.a.	n.a.
• Nepal	50	1.0	36.6	17.0	1.6	148	6	142	41.9	19.3	38.8	18	20.2
• Pakistan	19	3.4	82.3	27.0	32.8	2 053	21	2 032	24.0	27.0	48.9	16	19.1
• Sri Lanka	17	1.4	59.1	14.4	14.6	503	10	493	19.8	31.3	48.9	34	25.7
Central Asian Republics													
• Kazakhstan	n.a.	n.a.	6.4	12.7	30.2	2 264	91	2 173	15.8	40.5	43.7	28	24.0[c]
• Kyrgyz Republic	n.a.	n.a.	64.3	7.1	24.0	2 663	80	2 583	45.9	25.9	28.2	34	30.0[c]

Notes: n.a.: data not available ; a : Negative values represent an increase in forest area ; b : Water withdrawal data refer to any year from 1970 to 1992 ; c : data refers to 1994.

Sources: ADB (1996b); World Bank (1994 and 1996).

Infrastructure and exploitable natural resources are basic to household activities and to economic life. This is evident when natural disasters or civil disturbances destroy or damage roads and transport facilities, communication links, water systems and power stations. Major disruption of infrastructure reduces the quality of life as well as productivity. Conversely, improved infrastructure enhances welfare and fosters economic growth.

Although data are limited, it is known that there has been considerable growth of infrastructure in recent decades. This can be measured in terms of inventory, production or services. It has been found that in low income economies in Asia, the greatest increase in availability of telecommunications, sanitation facilities and water supplies occurred between 1975 and 1990. In middle income economies, growth was mainly in the power and telecommunications sectors.

However, even in this latter group, a majority of the population still lack access to water and sanitation facilities, a significant number of people still lack access to clean water and a larger number lack adequate sanitation. Transport networks that are already inadequate are rapidly deteriorating in many countries. Over two billion people still do not have electricity, while unreliable power systems hamper production and constrain development in many countries.

Although there was substantial progress in providing safe drinking water in the region during the 1980s, by the early 1990s more than half of the urban population still lacked access to potable water. The situation was even worse in rural areas, with the exception of some countries which have managed to achieve high rates of access to water in rural areas such as Bangladesh, India, and the People's Republic of China (UN ESCAP, 1996).

Greater industrial production associated with economic growth has increased the demand for energy in the region (Table 4). In most developing countries, commercial energy satisfies only a fraction of total energy needs. Total energy consumption per capita in 1993 ranged from 19 kg of oil-equivalent (kgoe) in Cambodia (the same as in 1985) to 6 627 kgoe in Singapore. However, apart from the NIEs and Malaysia, per capita energy consumption in developing Asia remains well below the world average of roughly 1 600 kg of oil-equivalent.

The growth of Asia's population in recent decades and increased availability of passenger transportation has provided mobility for a large number of people seeking economic opportunities. This is especially evident in urban areas where the population has sometimes grown at twice the national rate, greatly increasing the demand for transportation facilities. However, urban mass transportation has been developed slowly. Among the most recent urban mass transit systems are those in Seoul, Singapore and Hong Kong. The region has over 100 000 km of railroad tracks, with over half in China and India. Air traffic has experienced dramatic growth over the last decade.

Table 4. **Energy Indicators in Selected Economies of Developing Asia**

	Per capita energy consumption (kgoe)		Energy intensity in GDP^a (toe/'000 1993 US$)		Net oil import dependency (%)^b	
	1985	1993	1985	1993	1985	1993
Newly Industrialising Economies						
• Hong Kong	1 251	2 184	0.10	0.11	42.4	100.0
• Korea, Rep. of	1 273	2 801	0.31	0.37	49.1	64.5
• Singapore	6 551	6 627	0.53	0.33	99.4	100.0
• Chinese Taipei	1 875	2 730	0.30	0.26	50.2	61.8
People's Republic of China^c	513	676	n.a.	n.a.	-0.9	-1.0
Mongolia	1 577	1 176^d	n.a.	n.a.	n.a.	n.a.
Southeast Asia						
• Cambodia	19	19	n.a.	n.a.	n.a.	n.a.
• Indonesia^c	226	330	0.43	0.39	-154.7	-50.4
• Lao PDR	23	26	n.a.	n.a.	n.a.	n.a.
• Malaysia^c	805	1 691	0.35	0.51	-103.1	44.0
• Myanmar	57	40	0.04	0.03	0.1	20.4
• Philippines	195	285	0.25	0.35	62.9	43.3
• Thailand	314	705	0.27	0.33	53.8	59.2
• Viet Nam^c	78	97	n.a.	0.54	36.0	-13.7
South Asia						
• Bangladesh	43	63	0.24	0.30	36.0	27.0
• Bhutan	17	35	n.a.	n.a.	n.a.	n.a.
• India	174	285	0.74	0.96	12.6	17.0
• Maldives	114	145^d	n.a.	n.a.	n.a.	n.a.
• Nepal	18	38	0.12	0.21	53.3	60.8
• Pakistan	210	261	0.65	0.67	31.0	30.9
• Sri Lanka	109	149	0.23	0.25	70.3	72.3
Central Asian Republics						
• Kazakhstan	133	117	n.a.	0.19	n.a.	n.a.
• Kyrgyz Republic	n.a.	1 240^d	n.a.	n.a.	n.a.	n.a.

Notes: n.a. : data not available; a: defined as total primary commercial energy consumed divided by GDP at constant prices; b: refers to the ratio of net oil imports (including bunkers) to total primary energy requirements; c : net oil exporting country; d: data refer to 1992.

Sources: ADB (1994b); ADB (1996a).

Infrastructure in many countries of South and Southeast Asia is inefficient, if not inadequate (Tables 1 and 2). Systems losses as a percentage of total electric power produced in 1991 ranged from 5 to 35 per cent, while paved roads in good condition are less than 50 per cent of total paved roads. In addition, water losses, generally due to leaks, are almost 48 per cent of total water provided. As already noted, less than 50 per cent of the population has access to safe water in a number of countries.

Natural resource endowments and technology can also have important implications for social goals such as equity, as illustrated by the availability of water in many developing countries. "Because public services are overextended and underfunded, the inadequate supply is pre-empted by wealthier and more influential groups. Paradoxically, large numbers of poor people in urban areas depend on water vendors, paying a much higher price than a middle-class person pays" (Feder and Le Moigne, 1994, p. 26).

Physical Infrastructure Converts Constraints to Opportunities

Imagine what Hong Kong would be like without its port facilities, without its airport(s), without communication links to the outside world, without road or rail links to China. What would the economies of Indonesia or Kazakstan be like without the infrastructure for developing oil and gas resources? On the other hand, imagine what Nepal or Lao PDR would be like with widespread satellite communications, sewage and sanitation facilities, ample well-maintained roads, health care facilities, and sufficient electrical power for export earnings that increase domestic living standards, as is occurring in Bhutan. In Singapore, a decision has been made to ensure that infrastructure to support modern technology will be in place to support changes in the city-state's evolving comparative advantage.

Infrastructure can increase the productivity of land (e.g. by irrigation), capital and labour. It can have important implications for the use of time allocation, especially by poor people, of whom there are more in Asia than any other region, including sub-Saharan Africa. Infrastructure can save considerable time regularly spent gathering fuel or water, or walking to distant markets, thus providing more time for activities that generate income or otherwise contribute to the quality of life. Infrastructure can also increase labour productivity by the better health from improved water supply and sanitation, reduced air pollution and fewer congestion-induced traffic accidents. Furthermore, public investment in infrastructure provides complementary services for private capital investment, while other public investment crowds out private investment, especially if the public investment is financed by bank borrowing.

Certain challenges relating to infrastructure must be addressed by Asia's developing countries to maintain the momentum of economic development. The main challenges are posed by the present imbalance between the supply of and demand for infrastructure and the continued rapid growth in demand expected in the future. In many countries, the demand for infrastructure has grown faster than GDP over the last decade. This has often constrained growth. Inability to transport goods and people efficiently due to the lack of transportation facilities or an inadequate power supply to operate machines leads to microeconomic as well as macroeconomic bottlenecks. Moreover, lags in the development of rural infrastructure, urban water systems or electrical power supply, for example, lead to adverse effects on the economy.

Inadequate or unreliable infrastructure has high costs. "A 1987 study . . . of power outages in Pakistan estimated that the direct costs of load shedding to industry during a year, coupled with the indirect multiplier effects on other sectors, implied a 1.8 per cent reduction in GDP and a 4.2 per cent reduction in the volume of manufactured exports. In India, a 1985 study concluded that power shortages were a major factor in low capacity utilisation in industry, and estimated the total production losses in 1983-84 at 1.5 per cent of GDP" (Kessides, 1993, p. 10). Inadequate infrastructure can also cost an economy unrealised potential gains from trade.

The demand for infrastructure in the region is expected to increase rapidly in coming decades. Growth in population in itself will create large additional demand, which will be compounded by the demand created by rapid economic growth. In addition, recent policy reforms introduced or being implemented could require further infrastructure. Although the expected rates of growth in demand for infrastructure in each country in the region vary depending on a number of factors, it is clear that there will be a substantial increase in demand for infrastructure in the coming years.

Infrastructure can be viewed as an application of technology to the environment, adapting it to human needs or for conquering physical distances. Technological (and policy) factors determine whether infrastructure involves economies of scale or large sunk costs, which in turn may determine whether the service should be treated as a natural monopoly or competitively. Consequently, changes in technology can affect the environment-infrastructure relationship and whether the service is provided as a monopoly or competitively, and publicly or privately.

Combined-cycle gas turbines are now efficient at lower output levels than older power generation technologies, weakening the economies-of-scale argument for a natural monopoly in that field. Similarly, communication technologies that rely on satellite, microwave or cellular radio signal transmission have reduced the natural monopoly argument in telecommunications based on the large sunk costs of a network of cables. New techniques in electronic monitoring of road use, while perhaps not affecting monopoly characteristics, influence the potential for cost recovery and consequently the scope for private operation. To the extent that the infrastructure's network characteristics can be separated from other services, greater competition can be introduced in providing those services, with equitable access to the network ensured by regulation.

Economic Structure and Asia's Demand for Infrastructure

A common view of the development process begins with a rural, agrarian society. Gradually, saving and investment rates rise, human and physical capital are accumulated, labour becomes more productive, specialised and concentrated in urban areas, and the share of manufactured goods in the national product rises while that of agriculture declines. The share of services is also likely to rise. In the past, this occurred at a later stage in the development process, although more recently, the shares of services and manufacturing have increased together at the expense of agriculture in a number of countries.

Consequently, it could be expected that the development of physical infrastructure would proceed from a relative concentration on the support of agricultural production and marketing (primarily irrigation and rural-urban or export-oriented transportation facilities, which in addition to supporting agriculture expand rural, nonfarm, employment opportunities) to a relative concentration on industrial infrastructure. The latter would include, in particular, energy or power-related projects, and communications infrastructure. "Data for 1990 indicate that, while total infrastructure stocks increase by 1 per cent with each 1 per cent increment in per capita GDP, household access to safe water increases by 0.3 per cent, paved roads increase by 0.8 per cent, power by 1.5 per cent, and telecommunications by 1.7 per cent" (World Bank, 1994, p. 15). In other words, power and telecommunications are income elastic, while water supply and roads are income inelastic.

Evidence from East Asia suggests that this shift in the composition of infrastructure investment has indeed been taking place in the more advanced Asian economies (ADB, 1994a). However, it is less well known that the GDP in South Asia grew at an annual average rate of 5.6 per cent during the 1980s, well above the rest of the developing world outside Asia, and this growth is continuing to contribute to the region's dynamism in the 1990s. It is reflected in the increasing interest of international investors in the power and communications sectors of the subcontinent.

In the Central Asian Republics and, to a lesser extent, in other transitional Asian economies, the type of economic structure forced on the economy by central planning led to difficulties or inefficiencies relating to infrastructure. Lack of operational and financial authority was common in management of service suppliers. Low input tariffs for electricity and transportation, low infrastructure tariffs for industry and indirect subsidies for households combined to distort resource allocation in the development of infrastructure. This was compounded by distortions in the planning and financial sectors. As a result, the services provided were inefficient, with relatively overbuilt irrigation systems, power supplies and railroads, and relatively neglected non-defense communications and roads. In these countries, the difficulties of adjusting existing infrastructure and related policies, regulations and institutions are often greater than when developing new infrastructure, particularly in a context of severe budget constraints.

Throughout the region infrastructure needs are evolving as the opportunities diminish for expanding extensive agriculture, even for sustainable irrigation systems, while population, industry and services grow. Likewise, rapid expansion of trade-related infrastructure has been required by the rapid growth of the region's international trade in recent decades. From 1975 to 1995, developing Asia's port capacity increased from 3 million to 62 million TEU, an average annual growth of over 15 per cent.

Airfreight shipments in the region increased roughly 14 per cent annually from less than 2 billion to more than 30 billion ton-kilometres during the same period. Staff estimates by the Asian Development Bank indicate that both port capacity and airfreight shipments can be expected to continue growing at about 8 per cent annually for the next decade.

Demand for urban infrastructure, communications and other infrastructure for information technology may be expected to grow with service sectors in more advanced regions or countries. In fact, the demand for transportation of information (such as telecommunications) can be expected to grow faster than the demand for transportation of goods and people. Similarly, as the density of economic activity increases with population and economic growth, and modern flexible manufacturing practices spread, moving production closer to consumers, there may be an increasing demand for short-haul transportation relative to long-haul transportation, at least in the domestic context. The quality and reliability of infrastructure services may also be expected to become more important, particularly as an economy increases its competition for international markets.

At higher income levels, environmental implications of infrastructure also become more important. Studies have shown that environmentally friendly production technology is generally more cost-effective than ecologically disruptive technology. Technology specifically aimed at mitigating environmental damage is already an industry valued at over $500 million per year and growing. Whether or not growth in East Asia is considered miraculous, "Among the developing regions, it [East Asia] has the highest rate of deforestation, the highest intensity of energy use per unit of GDP, and the highest emission rate of carbon dioxide per unit of GDP" (Stern, 1994, p. 20). Estimates of the annual investment required by the year 2000 to improve the state of the environment of the developing member countries of the ADB range from $12.9 billion under a scenario extrapolating from recent trends to over $70 billion in a scenario of accelerated progress (ADB, 1994c).

From 1965 to 1989, energy consumption in developing East Asia grew at more than twice the rate of the world's total energy consumption, and with a different structure of energy sources. This is largely due to China's heavy reliance on coal, because the energy it used has a low efficiency and because it accounted for 80 per cent of developing East Asia's energy consumption in 1990. Drysdale and Huang (1995) estimate that China's share of world energy demand will rise from 8.5 per cent in 1990 to 19 per cent in 2010, with coal's share gradually declining as oil, gas, and electricity consumption grows more rapidly (see Table 5).

Table 5. Projections of Energy Demand in the Developing East Asian Economies, 2010

	1990 Amount (MTOE)	Share (%)	2010 Amount (MTOE)	Share (%)	Annual Growth (%)
People's Republic of China					
• Total Demand	682	100.0	2 484	100.0	6.7
• Oil	113	16.6	447	18.0	7.1
• Solid fuels	498	73.0	1 689	68.0	6.3
• Gas	12	1.8	75	3.0	9.6
• Electricity	59	8.7	273	11.0	8.0
Other developing East Asia					
• Total demand	329	100.0	1 102	100.0	6.2
• Oil	179	54.4	529	48.0	5.6
• Solid fuels	88	26.7	331	30.0	6.8
• Gas	29	8.8	121	11.0	7.4
• Electricity	33	10.0	121	11.0	6.7
World					
• Total demand	8 059	100.0	12 990	100.0	2.4
• Oil	3 061	38.0	4 547	35.0	2.0
• Solid fuels	2 286	28.4	3 897	30.0	2.7
• Gas	1 678	20.8	2 728	21.0	2.5
• Electricity	1 034	12.8	1 818	14.0	2.9

Notes: MTOE is million tons of oil equivalent; projections for the world are taken from IEA (1993), adjusted by the projections for China and other developing economies in this study.
Source: Drysdale and Huang (1995).

World energy consumption barely expanded in the early 1990s, with almost zero growth from 1990 to 1992. However, this does not reflect significant regional changes, such as the fall in the energy demand in the former Soviet Union and countries of Central and Eastern Europe. Developing Asia accounted for 21 per cent of the world primary commercial energy demand in 1992 and maintained an annual growth of 3.6 per cent during the 1990-1992 period. About 85 per cent of the region's primary commercial energy demand was accounted for by the developing member countries (DMCs) of the Asian Development Bank. Annual growth in demand in these countries was 6.4 per cent (ADB, 1994b). Also, as shown in Table 4, per capita energy consumption grew in almost all countries of developing Asia from 1985 to 1993, but the figures varied widely within the region.

During the 1960s and 1970s, the power subsector integrated small and inefficient utilities into larger units for economies of scale and to accelerate growth of power output in most of the ADB's developing member countries. As a result, installed power generating capacity nearly doubled in each succeeding decade, and the electricity supply increased in most of the DMCs on a per capita basis and in terms of area serviced.

Installed generating capacity in the DMCs increased from 114 130 MW in 1980 to 251 277 MW in 1990, a growth of 8.2 per cent per annum. The capacity is expected to increase further to about 450 000 MW by the year 2000 at an annual 6 per cent growth rate. The capital requirements for power generating plants and the associated transmission and distribution facilities during the 1990s are estimated to be about $45 billion a year (ADB, 1995b).

Foreign participation in energy projects could transfer technology that promotes energy efficiency. The global environmental effects from China's use of high-sulphur coal may make it increasingly in the interests of more developed countries to transfer such technology. Acid rain already affects Korea and Japan, and China's contribution to greenhouse gases is rising rapidly. Furthermore it may also be in the interest of the OECD countries to participate in developing efficient energy infrastructure in Asia for international security reasons, since a growing share of the region's energy sources are imported and there is intense competition for the imports.

Financing the Development of Asia's Infrastructure

Studies at the Asian Development Bank indicate that there will be a demand for infrastructure in Asia (excluding Japan and the NIEs) amounting to about $1 trillion during the 1994-2000 period (ADB, 1994a). This includes $300-$350 billion of investment for the power sector alone to the year 2000, another $300-$350 billion for transportation, $150 billion for telecommunications, and $80-$100 billion for water supply and sanitation. The projected annual investment for infrastructure would amount to an additional 2 per cent of GNP, increasing the approximately 5 per cent of GNP currently devoted to annual infrastructure investments to 7 per cent.

The high rate of domestic saving in developing Asia permits a high rate of domestic investment without turning to foreign resources. For the region as a whole, gross domestic saving exceeded gross domestic investment in 1995 by 0.3 per cent of GDP. This conceals considerable differences among subregions, from a resource surplus of 2.8 per cent of GDP in the NIEs and 2.7 per cent in China to a resource gap equal to 4.5 per cent of GDP in Southeast Asia (excluding Singapore). Consequently, foreign investment in the region frequently originates from within the region. "Two-thirds of the private investment in East Asia are by investors within the region" (World Bank, 1994, p. i). It should be noted that China received roughly half of all foreign direct investment in developing Asia during 1989-1994, largely for infrastructure, technology, and capital-intensive projects, and in 1995 it was again the largest recipient.

Opportunities for, and examples of, public-private and foreign-domestic partnerships have been increasing throughout the region. While the public sector is likely to remain responsible for a large share of infrastructure investment, private investment in Asian infrastructure is already occurring in countries such as China, Indonesia, Malaysia, and Philippines, largely by investors from within the region.

While water development, rural roads and mass transit largely remain the province of public sector investments, private investment tends to favour sectors such as power, telecommunications and toll roads. Lessons have been learnt in early private sector infrastructure projects, improvements made, and private investment is expected to continue increasing. The attractiveness of private financing for funding infrastructure has grown in recent years, but the number of new projects which actually get financed and built has been increasing relatively slowly.

According to some estimates, the overall value of projects planned worldwide in 1994 rose by more than half compared with the previous year to over $300 billion. However, only about 7 per cent of the projects reached the stage of obtaining financing. Given the pressure on governments to secure the assistance of the private sector and the growing availability of private expertise, the gap between the planned and actual numbers of projects that are finally negotiated and implemented is significant.

Limited government participation (including in the form of subsidies) in a joint project with the private sector is becoming more widespread and acceptable. Often governments grant subsidies to ensure financial stability of projects. This can be justified by the externalities involved. For example, developing a transportation infrastructure project via a build-operate-transfer (BOT) arrangement will produce advantages, not only for the users of the project (i.e., immediate project beneficiaries) but also for other users of the free network, which will be less congested as a result of the new project, and even for non-users (expected reduction of pollution, improvement of environment, reduction in noise pollution and traffic jams) and for the country as a whole (in terms of reduction in oil consumption or oil imports).

The scale and range of private investment and public-private partnership in Asian infrastructure is growing. In particular, Singapore is developing industrial estates with partners in China, India, Indonesia, Myanmar, and Vietnam. Private companies from Singapore, Japan, and Korea have joined with the Economic Development Board of Singapore, other state agencies, and the Government of China to establish the China-Singapore Suzhou Industrial Park Development in Jiangsu Province to penetrate the Chinese market and transfer Singaporean technology in areas of public administration and private sector activities. As though to refute allegations that this can only be done between ethnic Chinese in Asia, the Government of Singapore is also involved in a partnership with India to set up a technology park in Bangalore. Manufacturing firms from Hong Kong, Japan, Korea and Chinese Taipei have located in technology parks and investment areas near Manila and the Subic Bay in the Philippines.

Successful private financing depends on two important factors, namely government flexibility and understanding of business requirements (need for return on capital and other relevant financial/business ratios) on the one hand, and ingenuity by private investors in structuring proposed projects and tapping different sources of finance on the other. Progress is being made on both of these factors. A third important influence on the market for privately financed infrastructure over the longer term is technology, as already noted.

Advances in technology are changing the potential ownership structure in some sectors from natural monopolies to competitive enterprises. The policy environment can either promote or hinder this restructuring. In many countries, reform of the pricing system is needed to improve investment and avoid cost overruns. If pricing and tariff structures are not set properly, they may affect the commercial viability of an enterprise or may require supplementary subsidies which may distort resource allocation. Moreover, subsidies (including foreign aid) may reward or encourage avoidance of policy reform. Technological advances and policy reform increase the potential for privatisation to improve efficiency, which also requires a supportive legal, policy and regulatory environment, but this is beyond the scope of the present chapter.

For many types of infrastructure, it is possible to charge user fees which can then be used for repaying initial investments (and returns), operation and maintenance costs, or financing new investments. There is now a considerable body of literature on the advantages of user fees, which deals with subjects such as revenue generation, expenditure allocation guidance, taxation by willingness to pay, internalising spillovers, encouraging conservation and easing congestion.[2]

A key element in financing infrastructure is risk, both commercial and sovereign. Risk limitation then becomes an important aspect of investment negotiations between governments and private investors, especially private foreign investors. Large foreign investors may have an advantage in risk pooling across a diversified portfolio in multiple countries, access to export credits, and access to non-recourse loans in developed country markets. The underdeveloped financial markets in most developing countries, and especially the limited availability of debt instruments with a term structure sufficiently long to match the extended payback period of most infrastructure projects, is one of the main constraints to infrastructure development in Asia.

Build-own-operate (BOO), build-operate-transfer (BOT) and build-own-operate-transfer (BOOT) projects are the more familiar mechanisms by which developing countries in Asia are tapping the expertise and efficiency of the private sector in constructing infrastructure. There are various forms of BOO and BOT schemes in the region such as those for toll roads in China, Malaysia and Thailand; telephone facilities in Indonesia, Sri Lanka and Thailand; power generation in China; and energy, transportation and water resources in the Philippines. A large share of the power sector in Indonesia is now in private hands as a result of using such financing schemes. BOT arrangements receive much of the credit for relieving Manila's frequent brownouts, while private operation of the city's urban water supply systems is expected to reduce sharply the estimated 50 per cent of water currently lost to leakage. BOT projects are estimated to account for about 53 per cent of total committed infrastructure investments in the Philippines for the 1994-98 period.

In recent years, a number of Asian investment funds have been created to mobilise international capital, particularly from institutional investors in industrialised countries, to help finance Asia's infrastructure needs. The Asian Infrastructure Fund (AIF), in which the Asian Development Bank was an initial investor, was the first infrastructure investment fund in the region. The AIF is expected to invest in utility, transportation and communications projects in the People's Republic of China, Indonesia, Malaysia, Philippines, Chinese Taipei and Thailand, mobilizing up to $15 billion of additional resources for the region's infrastructure. Since then, infrastructure investment funds, similar to international mutual funds, or unit trusts, have been growing more rapidly in Asia than proposed projects found to be worthy of their investments. As Asian economies continue to grow and evolve rapidly, relieving the constraints and exploiting the opportunities of their physical environment through infrastructure investment will remain a crucial challenge.

Areas for Action

The large inflows of foreign direct and portfolio investment in Asia, especially East Asia, are relatively recent phenomenan. Even so, some lessons have been learned and more are being identified. If the major agents involved in infrastructure investment concentrate on their own comparative advantage while maintaining a broader co-operative perspective, they can ease physical constraints to development and exploit investment opportunities in a manner beneficial for all concerned.

The public sector in countries receiving infrastructure investment can encourage private sector participation (including foreign investment) by clarifying and enforcing rules and regulations, simplifying approval procedures, sharing risk where it has a comparative advantage, ensuring that tariffs are set appropriately and assisting the development of local capital markets. Some relatively simple measures such as introducing water markets, may save or delay unnecessary new infrastructure that would tend to perpetuate inefficient production or distribution systems, thereby improving overall efficiency. The public sector must also play its role by limiting monopoly rents and ensuring access to essential services for all sections of society. In addition, governments must address bilateral and border-related issues. They can develop public-private sector projects and facilitate customs clearance and use of foreign experts and workers.

Now South Asia too has started to reform its investment and trade policies. Bangladesh, India, Pakistan and Sri Lanka have all undertaken reforms to dismantle restrictions on domestic and foreign private investment and remove quantitative trade restrictions. These steps have been well received by the rest of the world, and foreign direct investment in South Asia has increased significantly in the 1990s. However, the State Electricity Boards, which generate and distribute power in India still set tariffs, collect revenues, and lose money, partly due to the high level of power theft. Arbitrary procedures in contract bidding and allocation, and extremely high license fees have frustrated efforts to improve efficiency in telecommunications, while unionised labour activities discourage private investment in port development.

170

European investment in Asia has been growing rapidly. According to Eurostat, the EU-12 nations invested 2.8 billion ecus in Asia in 1994, up from just 600 000 ecus in 1993. Of this total, only 9 per cent went to Japan, while 43 per cent went to Malaysia, Philippines, and Thailand (Daily News Digest 1996). Asea Brown Boveri (ABB) Ltd. estimates it has over $1.5 billion invested in Malaysia alone (Asian Wall Street Journal, 1996).

These emerging opportunities for private investment in Asian infrastructure can be fostered by both the public and private sectors. Private foreign investors can bring financing and technical know-how to help develop local capital markets. They can also find domestic partners for assistance in understanding local regulations and procedures, securing approval or licenses, ensuring local public acceptance or support, and raising local financing. Domestic private investors can look beyond their borders to the international infrastructure funds and foreign financial institutions for new sources and mechanisms of financing, and for information on what might make a proposed project more acceptable to foreign investors (and probably also more attractive to domestic private investors).

Multilateral organisations can play an important role as catalysts. Dissemination and exchange of information in international forums is a small but important activity. Multilateral financial institutions can assist through direct financing, securing co-financing, and providing loan guarantees. In Asia, one priority activity is helping to develop local capital and financial markets, particularly bond markets, so that the high Asian domestic saving rates can be converted to long-term productive investment.

Which sectors are ripe for greater private investment in infrastructure? As noted, power, transportation and communications will require massive investment in the near future, and all can offer reasonable rates of return. Cost recovery is fairly straightforward in telecommunications, which will be essential for growth in financial and information services, and it can be negotiated for power generation and distribution, given a stable and transparent regulatory environment. In transportation, cost recovery may be more difficult, but technological advances in monitoring and collection are enhancing opportunities, and transport infrastructure is becoming increasingly important for international competitiveness. In many Asian cities, lack of basic water supply and sanitation facilities remain important impediments to the development of human resources and shifting from simple agricultural production to food processing with higher value added. Environmental services can be expected to become a booming industry in Asia as societies react against environmental degradation as incomes rise. Another likely area for rapid growth in private investment is in maintenance of existing infrastructure facilities. Thus opportunities are not lacking.

Notes

1. The opinions expressed in this chapter are those of the authors and do not necessarily reflect those of the Asian Development Bank. V.V. Desai, William Nicol, and Z. Xiaoqiang provided valuable comments on an earlier version of this chapter. Any errors or omissions are solely the authors' responsibility.

2. For a brief review of advantages of user fees, see Gramlich, 1994.

References

ASIAN DEVELOPMENT BANK (1994a), *Annual Report 1993*, Manila.

ASIAN DEVELOPMENT BANK (1994b), *Energy Indicators of Developing Member Countries of ADB*, Manila.

ASIAN DEVELOPMENT BANK (1994c), *Financing Environmentally Sound Development*, Manila.

ASIAN DEVELOPMENT BANK (1994d), *Building for Development: Infrastructure in the Region*, ADB Theme Paper 1, Manila.

ASIAN DEVELOPMENT BANK (1995a), *Key Indicators of Developing Asian and Pacific Countries 1995*, Manila.

ASIAN DEVELOPMENT BANK (1995b), "Bank Policy Paper for the Energy Sector," November.

ASIAN DEVELOPMENT BANK (1996a), *Key Indicators of Developing Asian and Pacific Countries 1996*, Manila.

ASIAN DEVELOPMENT BANK (1996b), *Asian Development Outloook 1996 and 1997*, Oxford University Press, Hong Kong.

ASIAN WALL STREET JOURNAL (1996), "As Some in Europe Hesitate, ABB Goes Full-Tilt in Asia", 29 February.

DAILY NEWS DIGEST (1996), Part II, 16 February.

DIRECTORATE-GENERAL OF THE BUDGET, ACCOUNTING AND STATISTICS (1995), *Statistical Yearbook 1995 of the Republic of China, Chinese Taipei.*

DRYSDALE, P. and Y. HUANG (1995), "Growth, Energy and the Environment: New Challenges for the Asian-Pacific Economy", *Asian-Pacific Economic Literature* 9(2), November, 1- 12.

FEDER, GERSHON, and G. LE MOIGNE (1994), "Managing Water in a Sustainable Manner", *Finance and Development*, June, 24-27.

FOOD AND AGRICULTURE ORGANIZATION (1995), *Production Yearbook 1994*, Vol. 48, Rome.

GRAMLICH, E.M. (1994), "Infrastructure Investment: A Review Essay", *Journal of Economic Literature*, Vol. XXXII, September, 1176-1196.

INTERNATIONAL ENERGY AGENCY (1993), *World Energy Outlook*.

KESSIDES, C. (1993), "The Contributions of Infrastructure to Economic Development: A Review of Experience and Policy Implications", World Bank Discussion Paper No. 213, Washington, D.C.

MUNNELL, A.H. (1992), "Infrastructure Investment and Economic Growth", *Journal of Economic Perspectives*, Fall 6(4), 189-98.

PRIVATISATION INTERNATIONAL (1995), *Infrastructure Yearbook 1995*, Rodney Lord, ed., Privatisation International Ltd., London.

STERN, E. (1994), "Developing Asia: A New Growth Pole Emerges", *Finance & Development*, June, 18-20.

UN ECONOMIC AND SOCIAL COMMISSION FOR ASIA AND THE PACIFIC (1995), *Quality of Life in the ESCAP Region*. New York.

UN ECONOMIC AND SOCIAL COMMISSION FOR ASIA AND THE PACIFIC (1996), *Economic and Social Survey of Asia and the Pacific 1996*, New York.

WORLD BANK (1994) *Infrastructure Development in East Asia and Pacific: Towards a New Public-Private Partnership*, Washington, D.C.

WORLD BANK (1996), *The World Bank Atlas 1996*, Washington, D.C.

WORLD BANK, various issues, *World Development Report*, Oxford University Press, New York.

The Institutional Environment for Investments in China and ASEAN: Current Situation and Trends

Jesus Estanislao

FDI Flows in the East Asian Region

More than any region in the world, East Asia has continuously attracted increasing amounts of foreign direct investments (FDI) since the latter half of the 1980s. The steady flow of investments can be attributed to the sustained and rapid growth of the East Asian economies, their increasing share of world trade and the relatively stable economic and political environment of the region. In the early 1990s, while the rest of the world experienced a slowdown in economic growth, East Asia was the only region able to maintain high growth.

From 1989 to 1994, FDI flows to the region grew by 31.25 per cent on an annual basis. Of the investments that have poured into the region, China and the ASEAN countries (Indonesia, Malaysia, Philippines, Singapore, Thailand and Vietnam) account for an average of 81 per cent of total investments with the rest divided among the more developed East Asian countries such as Hong Kong, Japan, Korea and Chinese Taipei. The average growth rate of FDI flows in China and ASEAN is three times greater than in the more developed East Asian countries (see Figures 1 and 2).

Focus: FDI Flows in China and ASEAN

Among China and the ASEAN countries, the biggest recipient of FDI flows from 1989 to 1994 was China, with half of the total. The second largest recipient of FDI was Singapore, with 21 per cent, followed by Malaysia with about 14 per cent. Indonesia and Thailand each received 6 per cent. The Philippines managed to attract only 2 per cent of total investments, while Viet Nam got less than 1 per cent.

Figure 1. **FDI Inflows to East Asia, 1989-1994 (in million US$)**

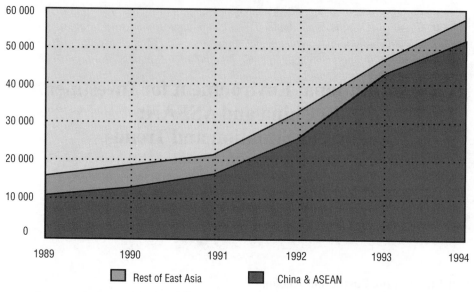

Source: 1995 UN *World Investment Report*.

Figure 2. **Share of China and ASEAN to East Asian FDI,
1989-1994 (in percent)**

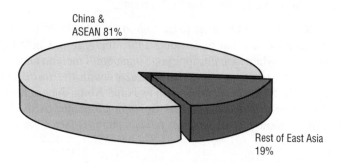

Source: 1995 UN *World Investment Report*.

Figure 3. **Distribution of FDI Flows to China and ASEAN, 1989-1994 (in percent)**

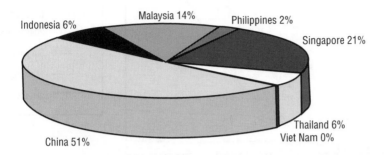

Source: 1995 UN *World Investment Report.*

Over this six-year period, foreign direct investments in China, Indonesia and Malaysia were steadily increasing. Singapore also displays this general trend. On the other hand, FDI flows to the Philippines and Thailand have fluctuated. In Vietnam, while investments may be the lowest among the group, they have managed to increase over the years (see Figure 4).

The attractiveness of the East Asian region as an investment site has been largely due to its sound macroeconomic policies and open investment climate. For their part, China and the ASEAN economies have been successful in capturing a large share of the investments because of their increasing outward orientation and openness. Since the early 1980s, these economies have implemented economic liberalisation measures which entailed a shift from import-substitution to export-promotion. Reforms were not only aimed at providing more incentives to investors but also at providing a more open institutional environment for investments. This means addressing foreign ownership issues, lowering tariff levels and phasing-out non-tariff barriers, as well as implementing clear-cut policies and fostering a general attitude of openness towards foreign investments.

In recent years, China and the ASEAN countries have stepped up the liberalisation of their foreign investment policies. Conditions for full foreign ownership have been relaxed and previously restricted sectors have been opened up. As competition for foreign investments becomes stiffer, these countries need to exert more effort to attract foreign direct investments. Thus, it can be expected that the trend will be towards greater openness and more liberal investment policies.

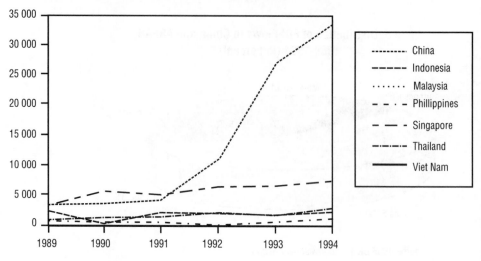

Figure 4. **FDI Flows to China and ASEAN (in million US$)**

Legend:
- China
- Indonesia
- Malaysia
- Phillippines
- Singapore
- Thailand
- Viet Nam

Source: 1995 UN *World Investment Report.*

Policies Towards Foreign Investments

Tables 1 to 18 provide information on various aspects of policy towards foreign investment, and how that policy may have changed in recent years, in China and each of the six main ASEAN countries: Indonesia, Malaysia, the Philippines, Singapore, Thailand and Viet Nam. The information is presented in a manner that facilitates cross-country comparisons.

Table 1 summarises general policy provisions, and notes the direction of policy change in each country. Table 2 focuses on policy restrictions on FDI, including limits on foreign equity, conditions for 100 per cent ownership (including trade-related investment measures, or TRIMS) and so-called negative lists, which preclude or restrict FDI in certain sectors. Table 3 provides information on policies toward FDI in special zones, and Table 4 does so for FDI in special industries or sectors.

Table 5 summarises the relevant information on tariff levels in each country, and Table 6 on non-tariff barriers to trade in goods.

Table 7 summarises the extent of the public sector's role in the economy, Table 8 looks at the privatisation of public assets, Table 9 at government procurement policies, and Table 10 at subsidies to particular sectors.

Table 11 focuses on each country's formal dispute-settlement mechanisms, Table 12 on the extent of regulation of the labour market, Table 13 on the extent of labour's influence on government policy toward business, and Table 14 on government policy toward labour unions.

Table 15 assesses the centres of power in national and local governments, Table 16 looks at bribery and corruption, Table 17 at the influence of special-interest groups, and Table 18 at the general attitude in each country towards foreigners and towards foreign investment.

Conclusion

The Asia-Pacific region is the new growth centre of the global economy, with China and the ASEAN economies as important players in this region. Given the worldwide trend of trade and investment liberalisation and the developments in the AFTA, APEC and WTO, one can expect China and ASEAN to be poised to seize the opportunities to be gained from liberalisation.

The region is aware of the benefits of foreign investments. The acquisition of foreign capital, technology, as well as organisational and managerial practices could greatly enhance the productivity and competitiveness of firms, contributing to the improvement of the overall economic performance of China and the ASEAN economies.

The general policy of openness towards foreign investments is proof of the region's recognition of the benefits to be derived from foreign investment flows. This openness is characterised by increased foreign participation in most sectors of the economy. While some restrictions are still present, there is a conscious move to ease or remove the remaining restrictions on ownership. A most recent case is the Philippines, which has lowered the minimum capital requirement for foreign investments. Negative lists which apply to foreign investments are being shortened, if not scrapped, to allow greater foreign participation in previously special or prohibited sectors. The practice of subsidising state enterprises is also gradually being removed, providing more room for foreign investment.

To enhance the investment climate, tariffs and other barriers to trade are being lowered under the region's commitment to the AFTA, APEC and the WTO. This will assure the flow of goods and services in the region.

Another positive factor that will increase the potential of the region is the notable increase in capital spending. Investments in vital infrastructure such as energy-supply networks, telecommunications, roads and ports have been made and more projects are underway, as are substantial investments in education, industrial training and promotion of research and development. These are necessary to provide a solid base for production in the region.

China and the ASEAN region must, however, accelerate their efforts. They must step up their privatisation programmes, as state enterprises will continue to pose unfair competition. In China and Vietnam, substantial parts of the economy remain under state-control. In Thailand, there is still some resistance towards privatisation by interest groups. Lessons can be learned from the privatisation experiences of Indonesia and the Philippines, where funds were used to promote competition and increase the efficiency of domestic enterprises. Caution, however, must also be exercised so that public monopolies do not become private ones, as has occurred in Indonesia.

The region's dispute-settlement mechanisms must also be improved. These procedures are highly developed only in Malaysia and Singapore, whereas they remain deficient in the other countries of the region, making it difficult to enforce decisions needed to assure long-term investments.

Dialogue and mutual consultation should replace confrontation with various groups in the economy, such as labour and other special interest groups. Stable policies and a stable environment are needed to reduce the risks faced by foreign investors. Moreover, if economic reforms are to succeed, they must be supported by the majority. A false sense of economic nationalism must also be set aside and tough decisions may need to be made in this respect.

Most trade flows through investment channels which must be kept open. If China and the ASEAN economies are to capture a larger share of both trade and investments, then they must provide an open institutional environment for investment. This will not only increase the benefits to be derived from the removal of protectionist barriers for the region, it will also have a beneficial effect for the rest of the world.

Table 1. General Provisions and Direction of Policy Toward Investments

Indonesia	Malaysia	Philippines	Singapore	Thailand	Viet Nam	China
• Promotes investments that increase non-oil exports, encourages processing of raw materials into finished goods, uses local products or components, transfers technology and skills and saves foreign exchange. • Investments are also encouraged in projects where local capital is limited or where advanced technology is needed. • Most investments are structured as joint ventures to foster the development of domestic industries.	• Prioritises investments in capital-intensive, value-adding and high-technology industries, particularly in the manufacturing sector. • Promotion of Investments Act of 1986 contains the principal incentives for investment in agriculture, manufacturing, tourism and other commercial undertakings. The government encourages joint ventures.	• Encourages investments in sectors that provide significant employment opportunities, increase the productivity of resources, improve technical skills and strengthen international competitiveness.	• Singapore is one of the most open countries in the region. Investments are encouraged and allowed in almost all sectors of the economy.	• Prefers investments in activities that are labour-intensive, export-oriented, raw material-intensive, and import substituting. • BOI's preferred Investment List includes construction & infrastructure, R&D services, and agro-industries.	• Beginning 1986, foreign investments are encouraged in high technology industries, labour-intensive production and infrastructure to strengthen the country's industrial development.	• The country's open-door policy is recognition of the need for foreign capital and technology. Foreign investments are promoted to generate foreign exchange. Areas promoted are agriculture, energy-development, electronics and manufactures. Generally, it promotes labour-intensive and high technology industries.

181

Table 2. **Restrictions and Trade-related Investment Measures**

Indonesia	Malaysia	Philippines	Singapore	Thailand	Viet Nam	China
Maximum Foreign Equity Allowed						
• Foreign ownership is limited to 80% for total investment of at least US$1M. Foreign ownership will be reduced to 49% or less within 20 years from commercial production. • Foreign investors who issued more than 20% of their equity through the capital markets were allowed to maintain up to 55% of shareholdings to qualify as a domestic market enterprise: this allows them to distribute goods at retail level & obtain credit from state banks. • In 1986, minimum sum for foreign investments was reduced to US$250 000. Liberalised ownership rules with longer divestment periods and equity requirements for some joint ventures have been relaxed.	• Domestic Investment Policy requires 60%–40% ownership in favour of local enterprises. • In industries where local expertise and capabilities are satisfactorily developed, government limits level of foreign equity. There are generally no restrictions in the manufacturing sector.	• Under the 1987 Omnibus Investments Code, a 60%–40% equity rule prevails in favour of local enterprises. • The Foreign Investment Act of 1991 allows 100% foreign equity in any business without incentives except those in the Negative List.	• Singapore has no limits on foreign investment except in public utilities and telecommunication.	• The Alien Business Law of 1972 allows foreign participation in certain enterprises provided that Thai ownership is more than 50%. • Thailand is presently revising the Alien Business Law to further liberalise trade and industry.	• The Law on Foreign Investment provides for 3 forms of foreign investment contractual business co-operation ventures, joint ventures and wholly owned foreign enterprises. In joint ventures foreign participation should be at least 30% of prescribed capital. In 1993, the government adopted the BOT scheme which allows 100% foreign capital or combined capital.	• Foreign investment can take place in the form of equity joint ventures, contractual joint ventures and wholly owned foreign enterprise.

Table 2. (continued.)

Indonesia	Malaysia	Philippines	Singapore	Thailand	Viet Nam	China
Conditions for 100% Ownership						
• Foreign ownership is granted for the following cases: (1) total paid-up capital is at least US$50M; (2) company is located outside Java, and (3) company is located in a bonded area and all its products are for export.	• No equity condition is imposed on manufacturing projects that export 80% or more of total production. For high-technology projects and other priority products for the domestic market, 100% foreign ownership may be allowed. For sales to the domestic market, maximum foreign equity is 60% is prescribed. • Foreign ownership is allowed if: (1) investment in fixed assets (excluding land) is at least RM50M or have at least 50% value added; (2) products do not compete with existing domestic products; (3) projects that involve extraction or mining and processing of mineral ores.	• Foreign ownership is allowed in domestic market and export enterprises not in the Negative List.	• No limits on foreign investment.	• Currently, any firm that exports all or at least 80% of its production may be completely foreign owned although full ownership may be negotiated on a case-by-case basis at lower export levels. • For projects in agriculture, fishery, mining and services, foreign investors may hold majority or all shares if capital investment is over 1M baht. However, Thai nationals must acquire at least 51% control within 5 years of operation. In manufacturing projects for the domestic market, maximum foreign participation is 49%. For export enterprises that sell 50% of total sales is exported, majority foreign ownership is allowed.		• In wholly owned foreign enterprises, the following conditions apply: it must utilise advanced technology & equipment; develop new products or improve existing ones, and must export more than 50% of output.

183

Table 2 (continued, end)

Indonesia	Malaysia	Philippines	Singapore	Thailand	Viet Nam	China
Negative Lists						
• Negative list defines areas restricted to foreign investments. This includes retailing and advertising. In 1989, a new list replaced the Investment Priority List. As a result, more than 300 sectors were opened to foreign investors and only nine sectors remained closed.	• Although investment is promoted in all areas, certain targeted sectors and activities are promoted by the government. Such areas include agriculture & agro-processing, forestry, manufacturing, hotel & tourism projects and the film industry.	• The foreign investment Negative List restricts foreign participation to a maximum of 40%. List A prohibits foreign equity in areas mandated by the Constitution such as mass media, engineering and accountancy.	• No negative list but foreign investment is limited in public utilities and telecommunications.	• Has a Negative List of areas closed to foreign investments.	• In mid-1991, foreign investors are prohibited from doing business in the following areas: exploitation of rare minerals, large-scale supply of power and water, communications, shipping and aviation tourism, and trade services.	• Restricted areas include public utilities, transport, real estate, trust and investment leasing.

Table 3. Special Zones for Foreign Investments

Indonesia	Malaysia	Philippines	Singapore	Thailand	Viet Nam	China
• Indonesia has 2 duty-free zones, Batam Island and Surabaya. Projects in free trade zones are allowed 95% foreign ownership.	• The Free Trade Zone Act of 1972 established free trade zones designed for establishments producing or assembling goods for export. Labuan Island is being promoted as an international offshore financial centre.	• RA 7916 or the Special Economic Zone act of 1995 created ecozones or selected areas which are found in highly developed regional growth centres with adequate infrastructure, industrial capacity for development and availability of labour. These zones have the potential to be developed into agro-industrial, industrial, tourist/recreational, commercial, banking, investment and financial centres. This includes the Subic Bay Freeport and Clark Special Economic Zone. In addition, there are three major EPZs with plans for expansion.	• Free trade zones have been in operation since 1969. These areas facilitate and promote the handling of transhipment cargo. The country has six free trade zones.	• The Thai government has divided the country into 3 zones for the purpose of decentralisation. Zone 3 or the Investment Promotion Zone allows full foreign ownership for manufacturing projects. In 1995, BOI relaxed equity condition for joint ventures selling to the domestic market located in Zone 3.	• Foreign-owned or joint ventures are allowed in EPZs. These are devoted to light manufacturing industries such as garments and textiles, leather, footwear, paper, packaging and printing products, food and beverage, home appliances, plastic products and electronics. • Among the services are banking, insurance, construction, auditing, fuel and gas supply and import/export related sectors.	• China's open door policy began in isolated areas or special economic zones (SEZ) with considerable autonomy for attracting foreign investments. The SEZs are designed to encourage foreign capital and technology by offering various incentives such as duty-free importation, lower taxes and administrative autonomy in order to boost the development of China.

Table 4. Policies Towards Foreign Investments in Special Sectors

Indonesia	Malaysia	Philippines	Singapore	Thailand	Viet Nam	China
• Since 1988, foreign investors have been allowed to set up joint ventures in banks, finance, insurance and securities companies. Foreign investors are also allowed to enter shipping, civil aviation, telecommunications, media and energy sectors. However, full ownership is normally not permitted. Retail and wholesale trading is reserved under the negative list.	• From 1994-1995, Malaysia further liberalised its financial services. It has increased entry of foreign banks, increased equity participation in insurance, and liberalised the shipping, telecommunications, and transport sectors. It has also opened 64 service sectors including computers, audio-visual, transport and business services.	• Recently liberalised its financial sector to promote more innovation in terms of products, services as well as technology. Since 1994, foreign banks have been allowed entry and further liberalisation of the sector is planned. Foreign banks are also allowed to establish subsidiaries and enter into joint ventures. The insurance, financing and securities industry is generally open to foreign firms. Recent policies are also being adopted to liberalise and deregulate the shipping, telecommunications, and energy sectors. • However, the media remains closed under the negative list. There is pending legislation to open up retail trade.	• The country is relatively open to foreign investment, especially in banking, and other related institutions, energy, services and trading firms. However, there are restrictions for the transport, telecommunications and media sectors.	• Thailand plans to transform its economy into a strong regional financial centre by the year 2000. The government has recently allowed more foreign banks to set up branches in the country. It is also set to liberalise the telecommunications, retail, constructions and transport services.	• The government has allowed the entry of foreign banks to modernise its financial system. BOT arrangements are encouraged for infrastructure and energy projects.	• In the SEZs, foreign banks are generally allowed entry and this is also extended to insurance and securities firms. • Limited foreign ownership is allowed in civil aviation industry including airport facilities. Joint ventures are allowed in energy and infrastructure projects.

Table 5. **Tariff Levels**

Indonesia	Malaysia	Philippines	Singapore	Thailand	Viet Nam	China
• Tariff levels have considerably fallen since 1985 when the government announced an across-the-board reduction in the range and level of import tariffs. At present, tariff levels range from 0-100% with an average rate of 20% compared with 37% before 1985.	• Import duties are relatively high ranging from 0% to 300% though most goods fall within the 15% to 25% range. • In implementing the Uruguay Round commitments in market access, Malaysia has unilaterally accelerated the tariff cuts on a number of items. In 1995, a total of 2 317 items were involved. An additional 1 047 items will be included in 1996.	• Executive Order (EO) 413 modified the rates of duty on 4 353 tariff lines. It reduced the range of tariffs from 10%-50% to 10%-30% and compressed tariff levels from a seven-tiered to a four-tiered band, creating a simpler and more uniform tariff structure.	• Tariff levels are the lowest compared to its ASEAN neighbours with 70% of its tariff lines set between 0-10%. • The government aims to reduce tariff bound rates for 2 480 tariff lines bound under the Uruguay Round standard of 10% to 6.5% and bind additional 291 tariff lines at a maximum rate of 6.5% thus extending UR tariff binding coverage from 70% to 75% of all tariff lines.	• After a period of heavy protectionism in the late 1980s when relatively high tariff rates were adopted, Thailand has recently embarked on a tariff reduction programme in compliance with its commitment under AFTA. Beginning 1995, Thailand has cut tariffs on 8 013 goods and an additional 3 908 tariff items have been reduced, affecting 11 product categories. Imported raw materials and essential production inputs are subject to relatively low tariff rates.	• Import duties are relatively high ranging from 3% to 100%. The lowest rates are levied on imports of raw materials and capital equipment, while the highest are levied on imports of luxury goods.	• China's tariff regime is characterised by a relatively high average tariff and a large number of tariff bands with wide dispersions. In 1993, the average unweighted stood at approximately 40%. Rates tend to be lowest for raw materials and higher for finished consumer goods. The structure of tariffs gives rise to very high rates of effective protection for some finished goods.

187

Table 5 (continued, end)

Indonesia	Malaysia	Philippines	Singapore	Thailand	Viet Nam	China
• In line with the government's efforts to promote an open economy, the reforms in the tariff structure have ensured that over half of the domestic output from import competing sectors have tariffs of 10% or less. Imports are grouped into two lists and highest rates of duties are imposed on the least essential items.		• In 1991, EO 470 provided for a more gradual approach to tariff reform. Tariffs were set at a minimum rate of 3% and a maximum of 30%. Tariffs were brought down to four layers: 3%, 10%, 20% and 30%. EO 470 covers 94.38% of all tariff lines. • Beginning 1996, the four-tiered tariff system was narrowed further to two tiers in preparation for a uniform tariff rate of 5% by 2004.		• Tariffs on fast-tract products will be cut from 25% to zero to 5% by 2000. Normal-track tariffs are subject to 30% taxation. In the case of the 3 908 items, which now attract taxes of up to 100%, tariffs will be cut to 30% or less.	• Upon its entry into ASEAN, Viet Nam has agreed to join the Common Effective Preferential Tariff (CEPT) Scheme for AFTA beginning January 1996 and complete implementation of the CEPT Agreement by the year 2006.	• Since the APEC Bogor Meeting in 1994, China has reduced the regulatory tariff on some products. In 1996, China promised to slash substantially the tariff on 4 994 tariff lines. The average tariff rate will be cut from an average 35.9% to 23%.

Table 6. Non-tariff Barriers to Trade in Goods

Indonesia	Malaysia	Philippines	Singapore	Thailand	Viet Nam	China
• Since 1986, the government has moved to dismantle the complex import system. It also set out to phase out NTBs and move towards an import regime based solely on tariffs. • The share of imports subject to NTBs fell from 43% in 1986 to 13% in June 1991, and the promotion of domestic production protected by NTBs has declined from 41% to 22%. Nevertheless, some important subsectors in manufacturing such as engineering goods, paper products and food processing and a significant proportion of agricultural goods remain subject to NTBs.	• The government enforces import controls through a system of import licensing. This is used to protect domestic producers from imports and ensure adherence to sanitary, safety, environmental and copyright requirements. • Imports are regulated through various Schedules of Customs Order, which in some cases prohibit the importation of certain goods for religious, moral, security, environmental protection or similar reasons.	• Generally, all merchandise imports are freely allowed. Between 1981-94, the government has implemented an import liberalisation programme where import restrictions on more than 2 700 products have been removed. • Imports into the Philippines are generally free from licensing requirements unless otherwise subject to prior approval by appropriate government agencies. However, the government prohibits the importation of some products for reasons of health, morality, balance of payments and national security. The Philippines likewise sets technical standards and regulations.	• The Singapore government initially introduced quotas to protect infant industries (e.g. textiles). In addition, import licensing has been used to regulate the trade of a limited range of goods for social or security reasons. Among those items which require licensing when imported into Singapore are films, publications, live animals, food, ornamental fish, fresh or frozen meat, arms and explosives, medicines and drugs.	• The Thai Government uses import licensing, largely to protect infant industries. While the coverage of import licensing has decreased since the late 1970s, the number of products currently under licensing is greater than in the early 1980s. Around 100 product categories are affected by import licensing. About one-fourth of these are composed of agricultural commodities such as rice and sugar. Industrial products covered by import licensing include certain textile products, machinery items, motor vehicles, motorcycles, paper products, chemicals, porcelain items, and building stones. • There are local content rules on dairy products, tea and motor vehicles as a way of aiding local producers. • The government also regulates imports to meet certain technical regulations and standards for health and safety reasons.	• The government regulates trade through the administration of quotas and the issuance of import and export licenses. Granting of trading licenses by the relevant ministry for trading activities are permitted under certain requirements. • To ensure the quality of goods moving in and out of the country, these are subject to quality inspections. Importers and exporters of such goods are required to pay a fee of 0.3% of the total value of all goods inspected.	• Several levers of state control over Chinese foreign trade activity have remained; such as export and import licensing; restrictions on foreign exchange retention and use; commodity inspection; customs regulation and protective duties; and state pricing of traded goods, especially imports. • Although the scope of state planning has been reduced, substantial portions of imports remain regulated by licensing and other forms of control. Import licensing has been used for a variety of purposes including implementing the state plan, protecting certain sectors, and containing overall imports for BOP purposes. In 1993, 53 product categories representing 30% of total imports were subject to licensing. State control is also exercised over the pricing of imports. State price controls are used to promote exports and restrict imports.

189

Table 6 (continued, end)

Indonesia	Malaysia	Philippines	Singapore	Thailand	Viet Nam	China
• However, goods equivalent to about 1/4 of domestic production are still subject to import licenses. The main product areas affected by licensing reforms have been engineering, tires, paper, glass, man-made fibres, textiles, iron and steel and plastics. The import-licensing system also permits the government to informally apply directives, quotas and prohibitions to many products. Only Indonesian nationals are authorised as importers, with some exceptions for foreign investors. • Formal or informal quotas or prohibitions are applied by State trading companies. The importation of restricted goods, such as strategic agricultural commodities like rice, sugar and soybeans, fresh fruits, milk products, batik goods, garlic, some steel items and strategic minerals like coal, are permitted only when there are shortfalls in domestic production. • Indonesia has an extensive system of sanitary and health regulations. The regulations are set by the Department of Health.	• Malaysia does not generally impose technical standard requirements, such as verification or testing procedures on imports. • Health certificates from the exporting country as proof of the acceptability of the health status of the imported goods are required in the cases of all imported foods and agricultural products.					• Beginning 30 June 1995, China removed quota, licensing and other non-tariff measures from 367 tariff lines. In 1996, China was planning to eliminate the quota, licensing and other import control measures on about another 170 tariff lines, accounting for over 30% of the commodities subject to import quota and licensing requirement.

Table 7. Extent of Public Sector's Role in the Economy

Indonesia	Malaysia	Philippines	Singapore	Thailand	Viet Nam	China
• Public expenditure averaged 18.3% of GDP between 1989-1994, up from 11.7% between 1986-90. Mostly channelled to development & debt servicing. Infrastructure & education get the highest share of public spending. Debt-service ratio was 32.4% in 1994.	• Has run large deficits at times (as high as 19% of GNP in 1982), caused by high levels of public investment, but has cut them sharply (to 5% since 1988) when they threatened economic growth.	• Budget deficit showed a rising trend in the 1982-92 period due to saving-investment gap. In the past, ever higher expenditures were heavily concentrated on personnel payments & public debt servicing, absorbing nearly 2/3 of tax revenues.	• Since 1987, the government has maintained policy of holding operating & development expenditure to within 20% of GDP and the number of government employees within its 1986 level.	• Public expenditure has been relatively stable, averaging 14% of GDP between 1986-94. Major spending areas were infrastructure & education. Roughly 80% of government spending is current expenditures, consisting of salaries & other inflexible items. Debt-service ratio was 11.2% in 1994 and 10.9% in 1995.	• In recent years, government spending has increased quite rapidly due to adjusted salaries for government employees & infrastructure spending. Public expenditures averaged 24.5% of GDP between 1989-1994, with most spending directed at infrastructure and education. Higher spending is expected as there is great demand for transport, energy and other physical infrastructure to support a rapidly growing economy.	• China's government consumption is considered very high due to the fact that the state owns most of the economy. In addition, difficulties between central & provincial governments in their fiscal relations result in an increasing proportion of government revenue (and spending) controlled at the provincial level.

191

Table 7. (continued)

Indonesia	Malaysia	Philippines	Singapore	Thailand	Viet Nam	China
• A balanced budget law serves as a check on irresponsible fiscal behaviour. Government reduced current outlays through a 3-year freeze on civil salaries (1986-88) and much slower growth in the civil service (though increasing again in 1994). • Roughly 2% of the population is on civil service employment. Set to expand due to programme of decentralisation begun in 1994.	• The highest in the survey, public expenditure averaged 25% of GDP between 1986-90, rising to 27.2% between 1989-1994. In mid-1980s, 40% of public spending was allocated to financial transactions, rather than current or development expenditure on real goods & services. Under present strategies, bulk of public investment will be focused on infrastructure, energy & education projects to "support the expansion of the economy".	• Public expenditure averaged 19% of GDP during 1989-94, an increase from 16.2% during 1986-90. Majority of spending goes to education and infrastructure such as energy, communications & transport. Debt-service ratio averages around 30%.	• From 1987-93, government expenditure averaged 17% of GDP. It was 13% of GDP in 1994-95 and about 15.6% in 1995-96, primarily in education, housing, transport & communications and security. Continuous budget surpluses (except for 73-74 & 87-88) were obtained by a buoyant tax structure, capital revenue from government land sales, a policy of restricting public expenditure & by limiting the growth of public sector employment.	• Had a budget deficit of nearly 5% of GDP in 1980, but through increases in tax revenue, reduction in expenditure & solid growth performance, situation moved to a surplus of 2.5% of GDP by 1992 and a surplus has continued since then. • A 1959 Budget Law limits budget deficits to 20% of total expenditure.	• About ¼ of the economy is state-controlled. Government maintains outright control over strategic sectors, including defence, energy, transport, infrastructure and forestry. It maintains at least a 51% controlling stake in mining, plantation, management, food wholesaling, paper processing, petrochemical industries, steel, cement, shipyards & fisheries.	• Public expenditure averaged 19.9% of GDP between 1989-1994, slightly up from 18% during 1986-90. Mostly on education & social services, construction & defence. Debt-service ratio is around 10% between 1994-95. • Employing over 100 million people, more than 100 000 state-owned firms have been touched little by economic reform. Including dependants, about 304 million people owe their livelihood to state firms. • Local governments control about 80% of state-owned firms.

Table 7. (continued, end)

Indonesia	Malaysia	Philippines	Singapore	Thailand	Viet Nam	China
• In mid-1980s, there were 214 centrally owned public enterprises (PES) plus many others at provincial & local levels. The central enterprises are in agriculture, manufacturing, trading, banking, public utilities & other services. PES comprise a large proportion of the production sector & enjoy monopolistic privileges but are largely inefficient.	• In 1983, public sector employment was frozen with a moratorium on civil service salary increases. • In 1992, public enterprises accounted for almost 1/3 of GDP, dominated by a few large firms like Petronas, the national oil company.	• Since 1994, the government has successfully reined in government spending through tax reforms, freezing civil service employment, decreasing allocations to local government units, cutting down public investment & significantly reducing outlays for interest payments and programme of privatisation. This has resulted in budget surplus. Public expenditure as % of GDP is forecast to average 12% per annum. • Under Marcos, the government took over several private corporations and set up its own firms with public funds. Government-owned & controlled corporations (GOCCs) numbered over a 1000 in 1990, ranging from the national oil company, steel, shipping, hotels, airlines, banking, etc.	• Government linked corporations (GLCs), together with statutory boards, provide almost 18% of total employment in 1990. While only accounting for 4.4% of the 500 largest firms in the country in 1990, GLCs accounted for 12.2% of sales, 19.5% of profits & 22.9% of the assets of the total. • There are several government-run monopolies and semi-monopolies, particularly in utilities such as telecom, electricity & water. GLCs also command a major slice of the banking & shipping industries.	• A 1976 Act limits the government's annual foreign borrowing to no more than 10% of the budgetary appropriations with the same ceiling being applied to government guarantees for borrowing by public agencies & state enterprises. • State enterprise system remains a prominent feature of the Thai business landscape. From more than 100 in 1975, there are 64 state enterprises by end 1994, with recorded assets of $35bn & contributing about 14.5% of GDP	• State sector's contribution to GDP grew from 23.7% in the mid-1980s to 29.4% in 1990 to 40.4% in 1994. • State firms control about 85% of fixed assets in industry, employing 90% of skilled workers or about 7% of country's workforce. Accounted for 49% of all tax receipts. • A 1995 survey indicated as much as 66% of state firms were in poor financial shape.	• Chinese authorities report that 40% of state-owned firms lost money in 1994, though an improvement over 60% in 1993. Returns on investment in SOEs dropped steadily from 11.9% in 1985 to about 1.9% in 1993. • Unpaid debts of these firms rose 74% in 1994, roughly equivalent to about 84% of GDP and 30% of industrial output. Bailing out SOEs accounted for about 60% of budget deficit.

Table 8. **Privatisation of Government Assets**

Indonesia	Malaysia	Philippines	Singapore	Thailand	Viet Nam	China
• Strategy is privatisation through international markets by listing of shares. Revenues from privatisation earmarked to support debt repayment.	• Began in 1983, the privatisation programme is aimed at (1) relieving the burden on government finance, (2) improving economic efficiency & promoting competition, (3) increasing ethnic participation in the local economy through equity offers. This takes the form of partial or total divestment of government companies, corporatisation of government departments, leasing, management buy-outs & BOT arrangements.	• Launched in 1986, privatisation policy aimed at increasing efficiency in economy and reducing drain on budget. • Focus on transfer of government-owned & controlled entities & non-performing assets to the private sector. Directed at state monopolies in power, transport, waterworks as well as banks, airlines, pulp & paper, hotels, shipping, telecom, mining, fertilizer, and steel sectors.	• In 1987, the government formulated a 10-year timetable for substantial reduction in government ownership. Privatisation programme aimed at (1) withdrawing from commercial activities; (2) adding breadth & depth to stock market by floatation of the shares of GLCs and statutory boards; (3) avoiding or reducing competition with the private sector.	• Privatisation policy was adopted as a means of mobilising financial & managerial resources from private sector to implement development plan. Had 61 state enterprises, especially in public utilities and infrastructure development. • Mixed approach to privatisation, retaining state involvement especially in infrastructure & basic utilities. Efforts since the 1980s have slowed down.	• Its privatisation policy is focused on restructuring, equitisation and liquidation. • The government is set to trim its roster of 7 000 state-owned firms to 300 so-called "strategic enterprises" divided into 15-20 economic groups. Direct state control of firms will be minimised in favour of forming general or economic groups able to compete internationally. Move to merge state firms in petroleum, cement, steel, garment and telecom sectors.	• Official policy decrees that state-owned firms will remain backbone of country's economy, with privatisation limited to smaller firms and joint stock options. • Reform of state-owned enterprises includes mergers, take-overs & re-organisations, & improved enterprise management.

Table 8. (continued, end)

Indonesia	Malaysia	Philippines	Singapore	Thailand	Viet Nam	China
• Privatisation focused on telecom, the state bank, electric utilities, steel and road projects. It was soon planned to add airlines, railway companies, plantation firms, chemicals and fertiliser companies, aerospace & shipbuilding, banks & finance houses, media firms, etc.	• In a decade, about 77 projects or firms have been either wholly or partially sold off to private sector. Directed at public utilities like electricity, postal service, telecom services & gateways. About $24 billion is saved yearly through privatisation measures as government steps up sale of public agencies to trim the bureaucracy and build infrastructure. In 1990, 246 government agencies and companies have been identified for privatisation, including utilities, energy, solid waste disposal, highways & ports. Another 77 projects have been identified for privatisation in 1995.	• Managed by the Asset Privatisation Trust, schemes include mergers, holding companies, consolidations, and leveraged buy-outs. Methods include selling of shares in stock market, bidding, negotiated sales and direct debt buy-outs. • Government earned $5 billion from sale of 424 government corporations & other assets as of June 1995, helping to produce a fiscal surplus. About 68% of total revenues from privatisation have been generated between 1992-95. • Around 130 government-owned and controlled corporations have yet to be privatised. Initiated BOT schemes.	• Since 1985, the government has divested its shareholdings in 58 government-owned companies (29 in full, 29 in part). • Since 1983, GLCs have started to be privatised to enhance the private sector's role in future growth. Two-thirds of GLCs are joint ventures. Twelve are publicly listed on stock exchange. • But since the statutory boards and GLCs are not a drain on the budget but are in fact net contributors, there is no budgetary pressure to privatise.	• Allow private sector to participate in provision of public utilities. Eventual privatisation of state enterprises in telephone & electricity planned.	• Full government withdrawal from active management of firms is planned in 2 years. Yet efforts hampered by equivocation & bureaucratic delay. • State firms have been reduced to 6 600 from a 1991 high of more than 12 000, a 48% decrease. Proposed reforms would allow state firms to mortgage assets, take on joint venture partners, & reinvest their own profits, with no state interference. They could also issue bonds & sell a fixed percentage of equity to foreign investors. Nearly all JVs are with state enterprises.	• Key aspect of China's public enterprise reform has been the delegation of managerial responsibility. Further reforms of SOEs expected to increase their independence from the state & make them fully responsible for their production, investment & employment decisions. • Government has pledged to keep only 1 000 of the most important companies and let the other large & medium-sized state-owned enterprises find their own way, but it has often bailed out losers for fear of creating massive unemployment.

Table 9. Government Procurement Policies

Indonesia	Malaysia	Philippines	Singapore	Thailand	Viet Nam	China
• PES and state projects are required to procure goods & services from domestic suppliers as much as possible.	• Policies are characterised by certain restrictive policies as indicated by the low foreign share in government purchases. Generally, Malaysia has practised an open-tender system in government procurement. However, for foreign equity ownership of companies or joint ventures, bidding for government tenders is limited to 30% to meet certain socio-economic objectives.	• Generally does not discriminate against foreign bidders. Technically, there are no restrictions for telecom industry which is open to the private sector. The same applies to power generation & distribution and construction equipment. • However, government favours local firms in public procurement for certain products. Policy lacks clarity especially for infrastructure projects, power facilities, general construction and telecom. Partly due to the on-going process of privatisation of government corporations.	• Procedures are based on open, competitive and transparent tendering which applies for all tenders exceeding S$5 000 for goods & services and S$30 000 for works, accounting for 85% of all tenders called. Selective tendering accounted for only a small percentage of government purchases.	N/A	N/A	N/A

Table 10. **Subsidies to Special Sectors**

Indonesia	Malaysia	Philippines	Singapore	Thailand	Viet Nam	China
• Subsidies extended to state-distributed products such as fertilizer, foodstuffs, gas & electricity, and especially agricultural products such as rice.	• Under its ten-year Industrial Master Plan, incentives are provided to promote reinvestments, industrial linkages, exports and training.	• Subsidies to inefficient state enterprises led to inefficient utilisation & ultimately drained government resources. Recent policy geared toward phase out of wasteful subsidies & ineffective incentives through deregulation and rational pricing policy. • Subsidies extended to food staples, oil, public utilities and social services. Also to agricultural sector, through farm support & credit, and export financing.	• Most public enterprises are self-financing and government avoids extending large subsidies to them. GLCs are required to remain viable without budgetary support. • Subsidies extended to research & development, housing development, human resources training and to help domestic industries to invest abroad as part of its regional strategy.	• Subsidies are extended to SOEs and to sectors such as agricultural areas.	• Almost all sectors rely on public subsidies, though subsidies to SOEs are being phased out. State-owned enterprises have privileged access to bank credit, at low interest rates.	• State companies receive preferential treatment from government, like tax breaks. Government absorbs most debt of state-owned enterprises. They have preferential access to subsidised credit & foreign exchange as well as lower priced production inputs. • Policy of subsidising urban consumers, farmers & loss-making state-owned enterprises is gradually being phased out.

Table 11. Formal Dispute Settlement Mechanisms

Indonesia	Malaysia	Philippines	Singapore	Thailand	Viet Nam	China
• A system of resolving commercial disputes is virtually non-existent. There is also a shortage of information on laws & regulations, which creates great uncertainty. Until recently, there was a confusing collection of laws governing different types of companies in different industries. • The World Bank recommends better training to promote commercial law competence and improve pay for judges to help speed up resolution.	• Based on British model, legal system is generally well developed. Company law follows British practice. Though judicial independence has some limits.	• While enjoying a well-established judicial system, irregularities are common. It has been said that most business contracts are dragged through the courts, as a means of preventing opponents from doing things. Though judiciary is fairly independent from political control, enforcement has much to be desired.	• Legal system is highly developed and efficient. Right to fair trial is respected.	• Although generally regarded as independent, the judiciary has a reputation for being susceptible to bribery. Enforcement is rather arbitrary and lax.	• Great gap between written law and its implementation. Lack of uniform commercial code to protect private sector against government seizure, to regulate business transaction and management of enterprises, to prohibit unfair competition from state enterprises. • There are attempts to create greater transparency in legal process. Though, political considerations routinely encroach on legal process.	• Law is vaguely written & inconsistently interpreted, while enforcement is lax. All too often, politics interferes with both interpretation & enforcement of the law. The increase in commercial disputes has been attributed to an imperfect legal system and ineffective government supervision. Many enterprises lack knowledge of international & domestic rules and regulations. • Process of legal reform is currently being undertaken to make system more professional and independent.

198

Table 12. **Extent of Regulation of Labour Market**

Indonesia	Malaysia	Philippines	Singapore	Thailand	Viet Nam	China
• Until 1990, strikes were illegal in Indonesia. Legally, a strike is allowed only if the Ministry of Manpower fails to resolve the dispute and permission is granted to strike. The government also sets the minimum wages, which are differentiated by area and reviewed periodically.	• Wages in the private sector are determined by mutual agreement between the employees and the employer and are governed by the provisions of the contracts of employment. • The Ministry of Human Resources fosters, facilitates and pursues new initiatives towards a wage reform aimed at introducing a flexible wage system through the Tripartite National Advisory Council.	• Since 1986, the government has veered away from the practice of mandating regular wage increases, stating that wages must be determined by market forces. The government has also tightened the regulations concerning formalities required before going on strike. • Under the present administration, wages are set by Regional Wage Boards after consultations with various labour groups concerned.	• In 1987, the shift towards a flexi-wage system was implemented on recommendation of the National Wage Council. More than three-quarters of unionised companies have adopted a formal flexi-wage system. • Recent years have also seen additional policy measures to increase the supply and quality of labour. In 1989, criteria for granting of resident status to foreigners were relaxed with a view to encouraging more skilled labour to move to Singapore, particularly from Hong Kong.	• The Labour Relations Act sets up a system of conciliation and arbitration and delineated the sectors of the economy in which strikes were permitted. Strikes are prohibited in public utilities, hospitals, public enterprises, and transportation facilities; and in such other enterprises as the Minister of the Interior deems essential to the economy or public order, or that will result in hardship to the public or endanger national security.	• The labour market is strictly regulated by the Vietnamese Communist Party (VCP), especially in state enterprises. To a large extent, the VCP represents management against labour, especially in the way state enterprises and agricultural co-operatives are run. The VCP arbitrates or mediates disputes between managers and workers, domestic & foreign business partners, landowners and newcomers. • Since 1989, however, more responsibility has been delegated to managers of SOEs such as decisions regarding laying off employees, forming joint ventures with foreigners, etc. Managers together with the party hierarchy and local administration have often moved to restructure the firm completely without waiting for equitisation.	• The Chinese government restricts the mobility of Chinese workers and keeps a lid on the wage differences among various enterprises. The restrictions also maintain the state's prerogative to be the final arbiter in labour management decisions. • In the mid-1980s, the Chinese government carried out wage and employment reforms that resulted in the first significant decentralisation of state sector wage and employment decisions in almost 30 years. State industrial enterprises adopted a wage system that linked the size of their wage bill to an index of performance, and they were given the power to determine their own internal wage structure. As a result of these reforms, the wage payment scale used in state industrial enterprises no longer corresponds with that used in government administrative units.

Table 13. **Extent of Labour Unions' and the Labour Sectors' Influence on Government Policy towards Business**

Indonesia	Malaysia	Philippines	Singapore	Thailand	Viet Nam	China
• The FBSI (All Indonesia Labour Federation), a major labour federation in Indonesia composed of 21 industrial unions, maintains close relations with the Suharto government.	• Malaysian labour movement has faced some handicaps that prevented it from exercising its influence because of racial divisions and strict government regulation. • The Malaysian Trade Union Congress (MTUC) remains the country's dominant labour federation with 300 000 members and 142 affiliated unions.	• The restoration of political democracy in 1986 allowed for more freedom of action for labour unions, but their influence on policy is limited as intense interunion rivalry hampers the movement. • It is estimated that there are about 2.4 million organised workers or 10.2% of the labour force. As of 1992, there were almost 4 000 registered local unions, double the number in 1985.	• The leading union body, the National Trade Union Congress (NTUC), enjoys a productive relationship with the ruling PAP (People's Action Party). From an economic standpoint, they share a common view of the broad policy framework needed for the country's development.	• The Thai union movement is weak and fragmented. Less than 5% of the work force is organised, divided into more than seven hundred unions, most of which are organised on an enterprise level. Private sector unions, remain very weak. The effects of rapid economic change have contributed to the fragmentation of the workforce.	(See above.)	• In reality, labour unions are politically subordinate to the Party and government. Union effectiveness, as far as official policy is concerned, takes the form of unions helping the government achieve economic growth and modernisation, as well as protecting workers' welfare, providing education facilities, and so on. Unions are expected to co-operate with management. Their role centres on "labour productivity, worker morale and welfare rather than the interpretation of national policy." (see above)

Table 13. (continued, end)

Indonesia	Malaysia	Philippines	Singapore	Thailand	Viet Nam	China
	• The MTUC is affiliated with the ruling UMNO party as part of the National Front. • The labour movement has been weakened by the growth of company unions. These unions, unaffiliated with the MTUC, had one-third of all union members in 1988.	• The largest labour federations are the Trade Union Congress of the Philippines (TUCP) and the May First Movement (KMU). The TUCP and the KMU represent opposite poles. • Unions have indirectly influenced policy through legislators and executive branch officials who are either union members or supported by the union during elections. Though national unions have had qualified success in national policies such as over wages and pricing, much of the strength of the labour movement is in local unions, many of which are not affiliated with national unions, particularly in large enterprises. • Generally, unions are fragmented and incapable of acting on a nation-wide scale. Moreover, the effectiveness of mass actions, especially strikes, is limited by laws which give employers opportunities to take precautionary actions and lessen the impact of strikes.	• Union density declined as the structure of the economy shifted towards services in the 1970s and 1980s, and now stands at less than 25% of the eligible labour force, with a concentration in manufacturing and construction. This structure is compatible with the enterprise-based flexibility that has been a priority of policy since 1986.	• State enterprise unions, on the other hand, made major gains in the political sphere, as evident in the campaign to halt the privatisation of state enterprises and in the government's decision to introduce social welfare legislation. State enterprise unions are at the forefront of more general struggles for basic rights, assisting the private sector unions in campaigns to force employers to abide by the law and protesting against unfair labour practices.		

201

Table 14. Government Policy towards Labour Unions

Indonesia	Malaysia	Philippines	Singapore	Thailand	Viet Nam	China
• Although the law allows the freedom to form unions, in practice the state controls worker organisations and strictly supervises the establishment of unions.	• The government maintained strong control over the conduct of collective bargaining, and the power of unions was kept within strict bounds. The basic legislation governing the system are the Industrial Relations Acts of 1977 and 1980. • In light of the government's desire to create an investment-friendly environment, it has prohibited union negotiation of such issues as promotion, transfer, new hiring, assignment of duties, dismissal, and reinstatement, and intervenes in the arbitration of disputes.	• The constitution guarantees the right to organise, collective bargaining and to strike. Though the law requires unions to register and allows the government to arbitrate in strikes. • In 1989, legislation was passed calling for a wider use of voluntary arbitration under a tripartite body. It legalised strikes in government and non-profit enterprises.	• Labour unions in Singapore have a close relationship with the People's Action Party (PAP). They tend to work in co-operation with government rather than against it.	• The Labour Relations Act of 1975 established the right of employees to organise and provided some protection of unions engaged in collective bargaining. • The government has encouraged labour-management co-operation at the enterprise level to supplement collective bargaining. • However, the government has imposed two important restrictions: (a) the Registrar has the power to register and dissolve unions and (b) outsiders cannot participate or become leaders of trade unions. Only employees of a given undertaking can apply for registration and be elected as a member of the administrative committee of the union.	(See above.)	• Enterprise unions are politically subordinate to the Party and government. Under the 1982 Constitution, workers do not have the right to strike. All unions are under the leadership of the national trade union federation, which is controlled by the Communist Party at both the provincial and the national level.

Table 15. **Power Centres in the National and Local Governments**

Indonesia	Malaysia	Philippines	Singapore	Thailand	Viet Nam	China
• In power since 1967, President Suharto and his GOLKAR party remains the focal point of Indonesian politics. • Old age and ill health, however, leaves questions about a post-Suharto scene. Political uncertainty over leadership succession could have grave consequences for the economy.	• Prime Minister Mahathir's rule of Malaysia's federated parliamentary democracy appears unchallenged. The hold of the National Front coalition, dominated by Mahathir's UMNO party, over the reigns of power remains virtually unassailable. The monarchy remains, largely having a symbolic role.	• Political power remains relatively diffused, institutionally (between the executive and legislature) and geographically (between the central and local governments). Though the position of the president remains a focal point of political dynamics. Fixed term limits ensure regular turnover of officials. Recent law has decentralised more authority and resources to local government units.	• The country remains a one-party state, dominated by the ruling People's Action Party (PAP), Patriarch Lee Kwan Yew, prime minister from 1959 to 1990, remains influential.	• Thai politics have been characterised by the constant shifting of factional alliances between the Thai elite and the military resulting in frequent changes in government. The country's monarch, King Bhumibol, plays a stabilising role during times of political crisis.	• Power resides in the Vietnamese Communist Party (VCP). Changes in party leadership and intra-party alignments have not drastically altered the party's hold over the country.	• The Chinese Communist Party (CPP) is the centre of political power and authority in the country. Paralleling the government, the party assumes the responsibility for political education, ideological guidance, and discipline, supervision of state enterprises. The post-Deng Xiaoping scene remains uncertain.

Table 16. **Improper Practices: Bribery and Corruption**

Indonesia	Malaysia	Philippines	Singapore	Thailand	Viet Nam	China
• Ranked in the top three most corrupt countries in Asia. It exists at almost all levels of government and administration and is made worse by the pitiful salaries paid to civil servants.	• Corruption exists, allowing well-connected local companies to obtain lucrative contracts under controversial circumstances. However, it is still possible for most foreign companies to operate in the country without getting involved in shady dealings.	• Corruption is rife and, typical of the country's political system, is decentralised. Even if one is prepared to pay a bribe, it does not necessarily guarantee a favourable outcome. One's opponents always have the option of bribing someone else to stop anything constructive being done.	• Singapore is well-known for its tough stance on graft. In the past, however, there have been a number of highly-publicised corruption cases. Once uncovered, however, tough legal action follows.	• Corruption is a serious problem in the country-less in daily dealings of private companies than in certain big-ticket infrastructure projects involving the public sector. The result is that many important projects are either delayed or inflated in costs.	• Many party and government officials use their privileged political positions to gain the inside track in new economic deals. The country's recent economic prosperity has offered ample opportunities for these practices.	• China ranked among the top three most corrupt countries in Asia. The entire system lacks transparency, leaving the door open for influence peddling and backroom deals. The problem is especially serious in the booming coastal cities in the South.

204

Table 17. **Influence of Special Interest Groups on Government Decisions**

Indonesia	Malaysia	Philippines	Singapore	Thailand	Viet Nam	China
• By far, the most influential group is the military which maintains representations in the parliament and on all advisory bodies, in all strategic offices of the civil government, and state enterprises. • Pressure group activity is not officially tolerated in Indonesia. But there have been cases where certain sectors were able to exert influence on government policies. This include religious fundamentalists and technocrats in business. The Chinese minority remains an important source of commercial influence.	• Ethnic rivalries persist in Malaysia. Malays make up 47% of the population. Ethnic Malays are given special privileges designed to raise their economic status. The Chinese though less numerous, predominate in business, industry, the technical fields, and professions such medicine. The rise of religious fundamentalism is also a constant concern in the country.	• The traditional elite, which is composed of the few powerful families that still dominate the agriculture, industry and banking sectors, are still very influential players in the Philippines political scene due to their economic and financial power, their personal and family connections to high-level officials and legislators, and their domination of the mass media. However, the open democratic system has allowed other groups to voice their sentiments. The Church can exert considerable influence in a country comprised of more than 80% Catholics.	• Chinese predominate in Singaporean society, though other ethnic groups are given ample representation. The business elite and the middle class can influence policy, in a somewhat limited way.	• The dominant force in Thailand since 1947 has been the military, which has benefited from the strength of its solid hierarchical structure and from the weakness of the civilian political parties. Rising prosperity of most Thais has produced a more assertive middle class especially in urban areas.	• The political reforms in Viet Nam have permitted greater social freedom, of which certain groups have taken advantage. These include private businessmen, farmers, the media, members of veteran organisations, religious groups, and environmentalists. However, the system clamps down hard on dissidents who wish to shake it up and push it in the direction of democracy.	• The government cracks down on dissent and limits the formation and activities of groups and individuals. However, rapid economic growth, especially in the coastal provinces have given rise to commercial and other entities that operate freely from the central government. The military, especially after the Tiananmen incident in 1989, remains an important and crucial supporter of the Party.

Table 18. General Attitude Towards Foreigners and Foreign Investments

Indonesia	Malaysia	Philippines	Singapore	Thailand	Viet Nam	China
• The increasing range of foreign influences is sometimes perceived as a threat to national identity. Protectionist lobbyists are strong. • Foreign Investment Law allows foreign investor to appoint own management, but must use Indonesian labour except in positions where suitable nationals are not available.	• Malaysian society is not generally anti-foreign. Though, outbursts of nationalism surfaces to serve political purposes. • Malaysia's New Economic Policy (NEP) extends preferential treatment to ethnic Malaysians and limits foreign control over the economy. • The government allows the employment of technical and skilled foreign personnel in areas where there is shortage of local talent. But it requires a training program to transfer skills to locals.	• The country is generally open, especially to Western influences. Its long relationship with the US and the widespread use of English make Filipinos more open to foreigners. However, there is a tendency for some protectionist sectors to put national pride and loyalty/nationalistic tendencies ahead of economic considerations. • The constitution limits foreign ownership of property and so-called strategic industries. Foreigners need to obtain work permits and are required to train local counterparts. Foreign nationals employed in supervisory, technical or advisory positions should not comprise more than 5% of total workforce. Foreigners may also retain top management positions if the majority of capital stock is foreign-owned.	• Singapore readily interacts with foreigners, encouraging multinationals and foreign capital to set up shop in the country. There is a large expatriate community in the country. The government is however on guard against foreign values it considers inimical to the interests of society. • The ethnically diverse country resorts to nationalist propaganda to promote national unity. • Foreigners are required to obtain work permits, limited in duration and restricted for certain categories.	• Relatively open society and does not vigorously oppose foreign influence. Thai nationalism exists in a more subtle form which foreign investors can easily learn to avoid. • Foreign employment is subject to the Alien Occupation Law. It requires all aliens to obtain work permits. However, special treatment may be given under the Investment Promotion Law.	• In its desire to catch up, locals are open to enter foreign partnerships to assimilate product, market, management and technological knowledge. It periodically assures investors of assistance and co-operation of government. Though, some sectors remain suspicious of foreign influence especially in the military. • The state guarantees ownership of invested capital and provides favourable conditions and simple procedures for foreign investments. • Priority for locals, but foreign employment is permitted if specified in feasibility study. Foreign firms should provide training programmes for locals.	• Since the adoption of open-door policies, China has become more receptive to foreign business. However, some segments of the society remain suspicious. A resurgence of nationalism may be a problem during the transition to a post-Deng era. • The government is, however, opposed to certain foreign cultural influences and strictly regulates the flow of information.

Economic Environment in Asia for Investment

Naomi Chakwin and Naved Hamid[1]

In recent years there has been an acceleration in the restructuring of the world economy from nationally based production and division of labour towards a system based on global markets and relative endowments. The acceleration has been variously ascribed to the dramatic advances in technology, particularly in electronics, information processing and telecommunications; global political changes since the collapse of the former Soviet Union; and new perceptions of the opportunities for international trade following the successful completion of the Uruguay Round and the establishment of the World Trade Organization (WTO). However that may be, the primary instrument of this accelerated restructuring and relocation of world production is likely to be foreign direct investment (FDI), and its major beneficiary the developing world. This process is evident from the rapid growth in FDI flows to developing countries since 1990, as shown in Table 1.

In the developing world, Asia has a comparative advantage over other regions for attracting the industry being relocated and the associated investment flows. Asia is attractive to foreign investors because of its record of high growth, its huge potential market and its complementarity with the OECD countries in terms of endowments. Developing Asia is also likely to attract large amounts of direct investment in infrastructure because economic growth in the region is generating massive infrastructure investment requirements which are beyond the resources of most countries and are likely to provide profitable investment opportunities for foreign investors. At the same time, the required infrastructure is largely in place in OECD countries, where governments are removing controls from public utility firms which will be seeking to expand outside their national boundaries.

In view of these developments this chapter discusses the economic environment for investment in Asia. In the next section, we attempt to answer the question "What factors are important to the firm in its choice of the host country for investment?" The factors identified constitute the relevant subset of the "economic environment for investment" in a country for the purposes of this chapter. These factors will obviously depend on the type of FDI. We identify three possible types, i.e. natural resource-seeking, market-seeking and export-oriented FDI, but the discussion focuses on the latter two. In the section after that the existing "economic environment for investment" in Asia is described. The discussion is organised by country groups, based on factors such as size, present stage of economic development and similarities in the investment environment. Finally, in the last section expected developments in the medium term in the investment environment in developing Asia are discussed by region. Also estimates of the FDI flows to Asia and their sectoral composition are presented by region for the year 2001.

Table 1. **Capital Flows to Developing Countries and Asia, 1990-95**
($ billion)

Category	1990	1991	1992	1993	1994	1995
All Developing Countries						
Net Resource Flows	**101.9**	**127.0**	**155.3**	**207.3**	**207.4**	**231.4**
Investment	28.8	42.5	60.7	113.9	115.0	112.3
Foreign Direct Investment (net)	25.0	35.0	46.6	68.3	80.1	90.3
Porfolio Equity Flows	3.7	7.6	14.1	45.6	34.9	22.0
Debt	43.8	47.0	62.7	64.1	59.9	86.2
Official Creditors	28.5	28.0	23.1	23.6	16.1	31.4
Private	15.3	19.0	39.6	40.4	43.8	54.8
Grants	29.4	37.5	31.9	29.4	32.5	32.9
FDI as % of Net Resource Flows	24.5	27.5	30.0	32.9	38.6	39.0
Developing Asia						
Net Resource Flows	**38.2**	**45.5**	**62.7**	**83.3**	**99.1**	**120.8**
Investment	13.8	15.4	27.8	58.8	63.1	69.4
FDI (net)	11.4	14.3	22.3	38.7	44.3	55.7
FDI Asia excluding P.R.C.	7.9	10.0	11.1	11.2	10.5	17.7
Portfolio Equity Flows	2.4	1.1	5.5	20.1	18.8	13.7
Debt	19.7	24.5	30.0	19.9	30.5	45.6
Official Creditors	10.7	11.6	10.3	11.2	8.9	10.9
Private	9.0	12.9	19.8	8.7	21.6	34.7
Grants	4.8	5.5	4.9	4.5	5.5	5.8

Source: World Bank (1996*c*).

What Investors Look for in a Host Country

Decisions to invest abroad usually have two sets of components. One depends upon firm/industry-specific factors and the other on the host-country factors. The former are largely responsible for the decision to undertake the investment and the latter influence the destination of the investment. This section is mostly concerned with factors that influence a firm's choice of country/region after it has made a decision to invest. Firms invest outside their home country for one of three reasons: to exploit a natural resource available in the host country, to get access to the host country's protected market[2], or to maintain international competitiveness in the face of rising cost of labour and other non-tradeables in the home country. We refer to these three types of investments as natural-resource seeking, market-seeking and export-oriented FDI. Natural resource-seeking FDI, which consists of investment in areas such as mining, oil and gas extraction, etc., is probably the earliest type of foreign investment. However, since natural endowment and not economic environment is the primary determinant of such investments, in this chapter we focus on the other two types.

Market-seeking FDI has changed significantly in recent years. Since World War II it had been largely confined to the manufacturing sector[3], but due to the recent trends in most developing countries towards greater openness of the economy and privatisation of infrastructure, sectors such as power, telecommunications and financial services are attracting increasing amounts of foreign investment. Also because of the import-substitution industrialisation policies formerly followed by most developing countries, until recently FDI in the manufacturing sector generally served to leapfrog tariff barriers, with very little, or even negative, value added in the host country. However, import liberalisation and the electronics revolution, and the consequent development of machinery and processes which make smaller production runs possible without incurring significant cost penalties, have given rise to a more efficient FDI in industries catering primarily to the host country's market.

Export-oriented FDI is of relatively recent origin. The "product life cycle" theory of FDI, which postulates that as economic growth leads to higher wages in a country, labour-intensive industries will relocate to countries at a lower level of economic development, is most applicable to export-oriented FDI. However, the mere availability of cheap labour is insufficient to attract such investments. Factors such as location, infrastructure endowment and the policy environment are equally important. Export-oriented FDI is believed to be a major factor in developing Asia's economic success, and, thus it is the type of investment that developing countries most want.

There is a general agreement that macroeconomic and political stability, competitive exchange rates, relatively low-cost labour and good infrastructure are important in attracting FDI. However, opinions vary greatly on investment incentives. Guisinger and McNulty (1996) surveyed executives of a number of US transnational corporations (TNCs) to discover what were some of the key factors effecting a firm's decision to invest in a particular country. They found that currency transferability and convertibility, which are good proxies for openness and sound macroeconomic fundamentals, were the most important, followed by political stability. Some of the other factors, in order of importance, were national treatment of foreigners, macroeconomic stability and a large domestic market. From this survey, at least, it appears that investment incentive schemes do not have a significant influence on the choice of the host country.

However, most governments still believe that they need to provide incentives to attract FDI of the type they want. The package of incentives and policies used to attract and direct investment may be referred to as the country's investment regime. In Asia two types of investment regimes are emerging. The most familiar is the export-incentive regime. In this, incentives are geared primarily towards attracting export-oriented investment. Such regimes are generally limited to smaller countries where domestic market considerations are less important. However, when the host country has a large population like China, India or Indonesia, both investor and host country strategies change. In such cases, the investment regime is a combination of incentives and conditions that encourage the development of export industries as well as import-substitution industries which the host country considers to be important. We call this the mixed incentive regime. The strategy is to achieve rapid growth in output and employment through export-oriented industries, which generate foreign exchange and are usually low skilled and labour intensive, and at the same time acquire technologically sophisticated industries and expertise so as to reduce the country's dependence on foreign investment for sustaining future growth. This strategy is based on the recognition that independent technological development requires financial and skilled human resource investments beyond the developing country's resources and therefore imports and transfers of foreign technology have to serve as substitutes for local development. Mixed incentive regimes use access to their domestic markets as a bargaining chip for pushing foreign firms towards greater value added in the host country and transfer of technology. This can be a powerful tool in the case of countries such as China, India and Indonesia.

Table 2 explores the impact of government interventions to promote and direct industrial investment. The first round impact of interventions are divided into effects of trade, exchange rate and price policies, investment incentives and other industrial policy instruments on export-oriented and import-substitution industry. In the past, trade and exchange rate policies were widely used by developing countries to promote import-substitution industries (ISIs). While protection (tariffs and non-tariff barriers) may encourage ISIs, it leads to an overvalued currency and since the output of one industry is often the input of another, the overall impact on export-oriented industry (EOI) is negative, as shown in Table 2. Governments can compensate for that by export subsidies, duty exemptions for imported inputs and restrictions on export of raw materials. The first method is not permissible under WTO rules and the last approach would have adverse implications for the raw material producing sectors of the economy. In view of the shortcomings of import-substitution industrialisation strategies, developing Asian countries are moving away from using trade and exchange rate policies to promote industry, instead liberalising import policies and maintaining realistic exchange rates. To the extent that some protection for ISIs is provided by tariffs, attempts are made to insulate EOIs through import duty exemptions or schemes such as bonded factory warehouses and free trade zones.

210

Table 2. Impact of Government Interventions on Investment

	First Round Impact on	
	Export-Oriented industry	Import industry
I.A. Trade/Price Interventions (through outputs)		
A.Trade Policy		
1. Tariffs/NTBs (on Competing Imports)	+	+
2. Subsidies (on Exports)	+	n.a.
B. Exchange Rate Policy		
3. Overvalued Currency Price Policy	-	-
C. Price Policy		
4. Price Ceilings/Controls on Output	n.a.	-
I.B.Trade/Price Interventions (through inputs)		
A. Trade Policy		
1. Tariffs/NTBs (on Imported Inputs)	-	-
2. Taxes/Restrictions (on Exports of Inputs)	+	+
3. Import Duty Exemptions/Drawbacks	+	+
B. Exchange Rate Policy		
4. Overvalued Currency	0	+
C. Price Policy		
5a. Price Ceilings/Controls on inputs	+	+
5b. Subsidised Public Unity Inputs	+	+
5c. Minimum Wages	-	-
II. Incentives Targeted at Investment Cost		
1. Land/Buildings		
a. Subsidy on Price/Rent	+	+
b. Exemption/Rebate from Land Tax	+	+
2. Capital		
a. Income Tax Holiday/Reduction and Accelerated Depreciation Allowances	+	+
b. Interest Rates Subsidies	+	+
III. Other Industrial Policy Instruments		
1. Free Trade Zones/Export Processing Zone	+	+
2. Industrial Estates	+	+
3. Grants for R & D	+	+
4. Labour Training Grants/Subsidies	+	+
5. Government Procurement Preferences	n.a.	+
6. Guarantees against Domestic Competition	n.a.	+
7. Countertrade/Foreign Exchange Balancing/Minimum Export Requirements	n.a.	-
8. Limits on Royalties	-	-
9. Limits on Ownership	-	-
10. Domestic Content Requirements	-	-
11. Restrictions on use of Expatriates	-	-

Key: -: Negative impact, +: Positive impact, 0: No impact, n.a.: Not applicable
Source: Authors' estimates.

Another popular set of measures has been the use of tax holidays, subsidies on factory buildings and land development, low interest rates, etc., to reduce investment costs. However, most Asian countries are replacing such measures for a general lowering of income tax rates and providing better infrastructure because of a need for fiscal discipline, growing evidence that tax incentives have little impact on investment decisions and an ongoing process towards financial liberalisation.

Among the remaining industrial policy instruments, many have objectives other than investment promotion. For example, in Table 2, items III.7 and 8 are measures to reduce the pressure on the balance of payments[4] and II.9 to 11 are to promote local entrepreneurs, industrial linkages, managerial and technical skills and transfer of technology. Thus sectoral policy instruments available to governments to attract FDI, particularly the export-oriented variety, are now quite limited and consist largely of measures to compensate for distortions arising from government policies, e.g., import duty drawback schemes and FTZs/EPZs (I.B.3 and III.1), and market failures, e.g. grants and subsidies for research and development and skill development (III.3 and 4). Therefore, ensuring political and macroeconomic stability and the availability of infrastructure are increasingly seen as the key contributions of the government in attracting FDI. Other industrial policy measures mostly serve to channel FDI to maximise its contribution to a broad based industrial development of the country.

To sum up, the factors that affect the host country's decisions for attracting investment are political and macroeconomic stability, availability of infrastructure, natural resource endowment, economic policies relating to industry, trade and finance, wage costs, the investment incentive regime and the institutional framework such as the legal system, labour laws, etc. Investment flows are also influenced by factors like size (for example, China and India will attract substantial FDI just because they have a huge potential domestic market) and location (e.g. East and Southeast Asia have profited from their regional location because firms in Japan and the NIEs have found it easy to move their light, labour-intensive production to Malaysia, Thailand, Indonesia and the coastal provinces of China). Since political and macroeconomic stability, availability of infrastructure and natural resource endowment are outside the scope of this chapter, the discussion of the economic environment for investment in Asia in the next section will focus on the remaining factors listed above.

Investment Environment in Asia

The Asian region is often discussed as a single entity or block, probably because of its sustained rapid growth since the mid-1960s, the many common characteristics of its fast growing economies, such as export-oriented policies, high savings and investment rates, relative price stability and, since the mid-1980s, large inflows of FDI, and the continuous growth, beginning with Japan in the 1950s, spreading to the NIEs (i.e., Hong Kong, Korea, Singapore and Chinese Taipei) in the 1960s, to China, Indonesia, Malaysia, and Thailand in the 1980s, and to the Philippines, Viet Nam and

India in the 1990s. This expanding circle has given rise to "flying geese" as a metaphor for the pattern of Asian development in which, as one group of countries moves up the ladder of industrial development another group replaces it at the bottom. In economic literature, this process is referred to as the "product cycle" theory of development in which, as economic growth results in higher wages and other costs of production in one country, industries which are no longer competitive move to a country at a lower level of development and are replaced by more sophisticated industries moving from a country higher on the ladder. For example, industries such as textiles, garments, footwear, and simple consumer electronics moved from Japan to the NIEs, and then as the level of development in the NIEs increased, in turn, these industries moved from the NIEs to Malaysia, Thailand, Indonesia and China, while the next set of industries such as semiconductors, automobiles, metals, and chemicals moved from Japan (and other developed countries) to the NIEs.

However, this view of Asia is a gross simplification, as Asia is composed of a large number of countries with great differences in size and endowments, approaches to development and economic record. While it is true that in recent years there has been some convergence of economic performance and policies, significant differences in income levels, growth performance and economic environments still remain (see Table 3). Therefore, it is more appropriate to describe the different environments for investment in Asia. Consequently, we have divided developing Asia into three groups. Group I consists of Indonesia, Malaysia and Thailand, which fit the Asian development model well, and much of the discussion about this group is applicable to future developments in other Southeast Asian countries such as the Philippines and Viet Nam. China, which merits a separate discussion in view of its size and importance as a FDI recipient, is referred to as Group II. Finally, Asia's other giant, India, also because of its size and economic potential is Group III[5].

These three groups also reflect to a large extent the various stages of development in Asia. Bradford (1987) identified Malaysia, Thailand and Indonesia as the "next tier NIEs" almost 10 years ago and they have continued to fulfill these expectations. However, there are some important differences between the three countries. Malaysia is the most advanced and is classified as an "upper middle income" country by the World Bank. Labour shortages and increasing wage rates have reduced Malaysia's attractiveness for labour-intensive industries, but better infrastructure and more highly skilled workers have encouraged the entry of technologically sophisticated and capital intensive industries. Thailand is in transition from a simple, labour-intensive export-oriented industrial base to a more complex one, but better infrastructure, particularly in the transport sector, will be needed if it is to emulate Malaysia's success. Indonesia is different, in that it is a big country spread out over an archipelago with a large and diverse population. Also, it is at an earlier stage of industrial development than both Malaysia and Thailand, and to attract substantial FDI in the appropriate industries, Indonesia must improve its international competitiveness by increasing domestic competition, investment in physical infrastructure and the quality of its education system, while maintaining macroeconomic stability.

Table 3. **Selected Economic Indicators for Developing Asia**

	Size[a]		Income			Trade	
	Population (millions)	GNP[b] ($ billion)	Per Capita Nominal[c] ($)	PPP[c] ($)	GDP Growth Rate (%)[d]	Growth Rate in Exports (%)[d]	Openness[e] (XGS plus MGS)/GNP (%)[b]
	1994	1994	1994	1994	(1990-95)	(1990-95)	1994
A. Southeast Asia							
Malaysia	20	67	3 520	8 610	8.8	19.5	202
Thailand	59	142	2 210	6 870	8.9	18.8	90
Indonesia	191	168	880	3 690	7.9	11.8	61
Philippines	69	66	960	2 800	2.3	14.4	79
Viet Nam	73	16	190		7.2	26.1	72
B. People's Republic of China	1 192	521	530	2 510	10.5	19.9	47
C. South Asia							
India	901	289	310	1 290	4.8	11.8	29
Pakistan	127	52	440	2 210	4.8	10.9	43
Bangladesh	115	26	230	1 350	4.5	15.4	35
Total (A+B+C)	**2 744**	**1 347**					**59**
Total (A+B+C) % of world	49	5					

a.   ADB (1995).
b.   World Bank (1996c).
c.   ADB (1996a).
d.   World Bank (1996b).
e.   XGS = Exports of goods and services; MGS = Imports of goods and services

China has almost caught up with the Group I countries after 25 years of rapid economic growth, however, as a "transition" economy, its economic environment is significantly different from theirs. Because of its weak financial and tax system, China has had difficulty in maintaining a balance between growth and price stability, resulting in a stop-go cycle of growth. Some of the issues China will have to address if it is to sustain its rapid transformation are: reform of the large loss-making state enterprises, development of a legal system and a regulatory framework for private enterprise, the growing disparity between the coastal provinces and rest of the country, a huge floating population of workers, and financing its massive infrastructure investment requirements.

In terms of economic indicators such as investment, savings, economic growth, trade share and employment generation, India is significantly behind the countries in the other two groups. In 1991, India began a reform programme that includes trade liberalisation and opening up the economy for FDI, especially for private infrastructure development. However, the economic environment is quite different from the rest of Asia, for the legal, financial and other institutions pertaining to private enterprise are more developed than in most of the region, while the trade and investment regimes are still more restrictive than in other regional countries. The major challenges facing India are further deregulation and trade liberalisation, reduction of the fiscal imbalance and subsidies, and mobilisation of resources for improving its grossly inadequate infrastructure.

Tables 4 to 6 provide a comparative summary of some of the elements that define the economic environment for investment in the countries in the three groups. There are considerable differences in effective tax rates and wages. While the nominal corporate tax rate is more or less the same in all countries except India, the effective tax rates are the lowest in China and Malaysia, and the highest in India (Table 4). Tax holidays reduce the effective tax rates for eligible enterprises substantially in India and Thailand. Wages are the lowest in China and Indonesia (comparative data for India was not available), and surprisingly, despite its much lower per capita income, higher in Thailand than Malaysia (Table 5). There are no major differences in other costs, except that construction costs are significantly higher in Indonesia. While on paper there are many measures to promote FDI and export-oriented industries, the actual differences between countries are not very great (Table 6). Most countries have some income tax concessions (except Indonesia); reduction or exemption from import duties for exporters; few if any restrictions on repatriation of profits and dividends; bonded, export processing or free trade zones to attract export oriented FDI; and provisions for up to 100 per cent foreign ownership (with some restrictions in all countries). However, there may be significant differences in the investment environment because promotion measures and economic policies are implemented with varying degrees of effectiveness. Other important elements in the investment environment are the size of the market, quality of the labour force, availability of infrastructure, degree of openness of the economy, and institutional arrangements. Some of these issues are discussed next.

Indonesia, Malaysia, and Thailand

Malaysia has the smallest population and the highest per capita income of the countries in this region. It was one of the first in developing Asia to pursue a dynamic policy for attracting FDI, including promotion activities in developed countries and establishment of free trade zones (FTZs) for foreign investors, which provided good infrastructure, minimum government interference, tax holidays and duty-free imports of raw materials and machinery. Malaysia has also been able to maintain political

215

Table 4. **Income Tax Rates in Selected Countries**
(percentages)

Countries	Corporate Tax Rate	Effective Rate without Tax Holidays		Effective Rate with Tax Holidays	
		Manufacturing	Services	Manufacturing	Services
China	33	12.9	20.8	n.a.	16.1
India	55*	52.8	46.6	20.7	21.1
Indonesia	30	n.a.	n.a.	n.a.	n.a.
Malaysia	32	18.3	14.7	n.a.	11.5
Thailand	30	28.5	28.9	8.6	8.2

*   46 per cent for domestic companies.
Source: Pirnia (1995)

Table 5. **Labour and Other Costs**

	Average Wage 1994 (US$/day)		Port Costs (US$ per TEU)	Power (US cents/KWH)	Factory Constructioin Cost (US$/m²)
	Skilled	Unskilled	(1992)	(1994)	(1994)
Indonesia	6	2-3	109	4-8	200-300
Malaysia	13	5-8	114	3-6	125-170
Thailand	16	9	107	4-12	95-200
China	4-10	2-5	n.d.	5	180

Source: Lall and Rao (forthcoming)

and macroeconomic stability and currency convertibility. It is not surprising, therefore, that Malaysia, with a population of about 20 million, has been the largest recipient of FDI in developing Asia after China, with inflows averaging just under $5 billion per annum in the last five years (see Table 7). Since the early 1990s Malaysia has become increasingly selective in the FDI which it encourages. Tax holidays and other fiscal incentives have been greatly reduced and are only available for high technology industries and less developed areas of the country. FDI in labour-intensive industries is being actively discouraged, and the government is promoting subregional co-operation (in the form of growth triangles) and outward investment as a means of relocating such industries to neighbouring countries. Malaysia is now concentrating on attracting FDI in technology-intensive and more sophisticated industries, promoting Kuala Lumpur as a financial centre and establishing the country as a regional centre of excellence in education by getting reputable foreign universities to set up "offshore" campuses or joint venture universities in the country. Also massive investments in upgrading of infrastructure are being undertaken and the national goal is to achieve developed country status by the year 2020.

Malaysia is probably the closest to what is thought to be the Asian development model: an open economy, export-driven industrialisation largely based on FDI, close co-operation between the private sector and the government, and sound macroeconomic policies resulting in price stability and a high savings rate. Malaysia's present economic environment represents what other Southeast Asian economies

Table 6: **Promoting FDI and Export Oriented Industries**

	China	India	Indonesia	Malaysia	Thailand
Contact Agency	• Ministry of Foreign Economic Relations and Trade (MOFERT)	• Foreign Investment Promotion Board (FIPB)	• Capital Investment Co-ordinating Board (BKPM)	• Malaysian Industrial Development Authority (MIDA)	• Board of Investment (BOI)
Tax Holiday/ Concessions	• 2 years plus 50 % reduction for 3 years. • Reduced income tax rate of 15 per cent in SEZ,ETDZ. • Local income tax reduced to 10% for activities in SEZ. For export-oriented production a 50 % reduction in income tax each year exported >70 per cent of output. • For technology enterprises a 50% reduction in income tax for a three year period • duty free imports of inputs for export industries. • duty free import of investment goods in SEZs.	• 5 years for export oriented unit and infrastructure project companies. • Reduced income tax for economic development areas. • Refund of income taxes paid on export earnings. • Eight year, 30% tax exemption for 100% export firms. • Tariff reduction to 15% on import of capital goods used in export production. • Access to tax free capital goods for 100% export firms • Duty drawback scheme which allows direct and indirect exporters access to raw materials and intermediate goods free of import duties.	• None • Trade zones with privileges that include exemption from import duty, import surcharge, excise, income tax. • Drawback of import duty and VAT for export manufacturers. • Exemption from import duties on capital goods and raw materials for two years production.	• 5 years for 85 % of income for pioneer industries. • Potential pioneer status (income tax is paid on only 30 per cent of income for 5 years). • Full exemption from import duty on raw materials or components used for export production. Or if produced in a promoted zones for domestic or export market. • Partial import duty relief for goods produced for the domestic market. • Full drawback of import duty and sales tax is allowed on parts, components or packaging materials used in the manufacture of goods exported.	• 3-8 years depending upon zone. • Exemption or 50 per cent reduction of import duties and business taxes on imported machinery. • Reduction of import duties and business taxes of up to 90 per cent on imported raw materials and components.

217

Table 6 (continued, end)

	China	India	Indonesia	Malaysia	Thailand
Profits Repatriation	• Foreign exchange retention for exporters.	• Foreign Exchange retention for exporters	• No restrictions.	• No restrictions.	• No restrictions.
Guarantees/ Protection/ Legal System	• Unclear legal procedures. • Political authority and enforcement of regulations not fully tested. • Intellectual/design and patent protection lack formal legal guarantees.	• Internationally recognised legal system provides investor protection for contract, land rights, dispute arbitration, etc.	• Unclear legal rights, weak judicial system. • Bilateral agreements with a number of countries plus MIGA signatory protecting investments against political risks.	• Established legal system provides investors protection and fair arbitration disputes. • Bilateral protection against nationalisation, expropriation: free transfer of profits and capital.	
Promotional activities	• Special economic zones (SEZ)/ Open coastal areas, etc. • Economic and technological development zones (ETDZ), in 14 coastal cities-old urban districts.	• Export Processing Zones • Automatic approval of foreign ownership to 51% of equity in 34 priority areas. • Fast approval for investments entailing 100% foreign ownership of firms committed to 100% exports.	• Bonded zones. • Production activities located in tax free zones are given additional incentives.	• Free trade zones. • Pioneer status given to priority investment areas. • MIDA active and effective.	• Industrial estates. • Additional incentives for investment in outlying areas. • Additional incentives for export firms. • BOI active and effective.
Foreign Ownership	• Can be up to 100% in non-restricted areas.	• Can be up to 100%, but very restricted.	• Can be 100% for 15 years.	• Can be 100%.	• Can be 100%, up to 5 years.

Source: China - Price Waterhouse (1993) Interim Provisions on Guiding the Direction of Foreign Investment (promulgated jointly by the State Planning Commission, the State Economic and Trade Commission and the Ministry of Foreign Trade and Economic Co-operation on June 27, 1995) unofficial translation, Clifford Chance, World Bank (1993), (1995), *Business China* (various issues) India - World Bank (1993), *Business China* (various). Indonesia - Lall and Rao (forthcoming), Government of Indonesia (1994), World Bank (1993). Malaysia - MIDA (1993, 1992), Lall (1994), UNCTAD (1995a). Thailand - UNCTAD (1995b), Yan and Shilling (1995).

may look like in the future. However, Malaysia is also relatively small, and larger countries such as Indonesia, with their much bigger domestic markets, are likely to have more diverse and complex investment regimes

Table 7. **Net FDI in Selected Countries, 1990-95**

(FDI in $ billions, GDP in per cent)

	1990		1991		1992		1993		1994		1995	
	FDI	GDP	FDI	GDP	FDI	GDP	FDI	GDP	FDI	GDP	FDI	GDP
China	3.5	0.9	4.4	1.2	11.1	2.7	27.5	6.4	33.8	6.5	38.0	5.7
India	0.2		0.1		0.2		0.3	0.1	0.6	0.2	1.3	0.4
Indonesia	1.1	1.0	1.5	1.2	1.8	1.3	2.0	1.3	2.1	1.3	4.5	2.4
Malaysia	2.3	5.7	4.0	9.0	5.1	9.4	5.0	8.3	4.3	6.5	5.8	7.9
Thailand	2.4	2.9	2.0	2.1	2.1	1.9	1.7	1.4	0.6	0.5	2.3	1.5

Source: World Bank (1996c).

Thailand's economy has also performed remarkably well, the growth having been export led with manufacturing as the leading sector. Thailand was one of the primary beneficiaries of the industrial restructuring that took place in Asia following the major currency realignments in the mid-1980s, when the loss of competitiveness in labour-intensive industry in Japan and the NIEs resulted in massive relocation of industries such as textiles, garments, footwear and consumer electronics to other countries in the region.

To promote foreign investment, the government set up a Board of Investment, removed subsidies and marketing restrictions on a wide range of products, simplified investment procedures, reduced tariffs on imports and virtually eliminated exchange controls. To reduce concentration of industry in Bangkok, the country was divided into three zones with little or no incentives being provided to investors establishing industries in Zone 1, i.e., Bangkok and its immediate environs. Incentives, such as reductions in import duties on machinery and raw materials and corporate income tax were provided for industries locating in Zones 2 and 3. However, the outer areas, especially Zone 3, do not have adequate infrastructure to be attractive to foreign investors.

Thailand today has an open economy with few restrictions or government interventions. The investment regime is transparent and the procedures and incentives administered by the Board of Investment are simple and straightforward. In 1993 and 1994 FDI inflows showed a downward trend, largely because of congestion in Bangkok, delays in implementation of some large infrastructure projects, and declining attraction as a location for labour-intensive industries. However, while FDI in traditional areas such as textiles, garments and footwear declined, inflows into technologically more advanced areas such as automobiles and electronics continued to increase. The reversal in the downward trend in FDI in 1995 may indicate that increases in more sophisticated production are finally outpacing the slowdown in lower skilled, labour-intensive industries. Also, with its rapidly growing internal market, central location in Asia and liberal trade and exchange regimes, Thailand is fast emerging as a production centre for the Japanese and US automobile industry. It is possible that, just as Malaysia emerged as a regional export base for the electronics and electrical industry in the first half of the 1990s, Thailand could develop into the regional base for automobiles and components industry in the second half of the decade.

The third country in Group I is Indonesia, which is the fourth most populous country in the world and one of the most richly endowed in natural resources. Indonesia is considered to be another example of the "Asian development model," and is included, along with Malaysia and Thailand, in the category of the new NIEs. However, Indonesia's economy is not as open as Malaysia's or Thailand's. While substantive import liberalisation has taken place and the average tariff is now down to about 14 per cent, a significant proportion of manufacturing production remains protected. In the domestic market, barriers to competition, such as investment licensing and complicated procedures for importing capital goods, bringing in expatriate personnel, and permits are necessary for businesses, acquiring land and other matters. Competition is also restricted by cartels, price controls, entry and exit controls, public sector dominance and ad hoc interventions by the government in favour of specific firms or industries. The sectors in which such restrictions are common include cement, glass, plywood, paper, automobiles, steel, fertilizer, sugar, and flour and rice milling. The domestic economy is also dominated by about 200 conglomerates which control an estimated 40 per cent of GDP. Moreover, there is a high degree of concentration within the conglomerates, with about 14 groups accounting for more than half of the conglomerates' sales.

Nonetheless, Indonesia has been an important recipient of FDI in the region and FDI inflows more than doubled in 1995 to $4.5 billion and FDI approvals increased to a record $4 billion. However, because of the factors mentioned, the pattern of FDI in Indonesia is quite different from that in Malaysia and Thailand. About two-thirds of the FDI is in industry, with mining, tourism, real estate development and infrastructure making up the balance. Investment in manufacturing is mainly concentrated in large capital-intensive projects in chemical, including petroleum, paper and basic metals and metal goods industries, which accounted for almost three-fourths of the total cumulative FDI in the manufacturing sector as of December 1995.[6] Investment in export-oriented, labour-intensive industries such as textiles, garments, footwear, and consumer electronics accounted for about 15 per cent of the cumulative investment, with textiles making up the bulk of the total. In recent years, the share of labour- intensive, export industries has fallen, with FDI approvals for textiles declining from about 14 per cent of the total in 1991 to less than 2 per cent in 1995.

China

China is the largest country in the world in terms of both population and area. Net FDI flows in 1995 are estimated at $38 billion, which is almost one-quarter of the total FDI to the developing world. With real growth averaging over 10 per cent a year for the last decade and a half, the economy has grown fivefold since 1980 and seems likely to continue on a strong growth path into the next century. China clearly dominates developing Asia in terms of FDI, however, if FDI is seen as a percentage of GDP rather than an absolute number, the proportion in Malaysia is much higher (Table 7). This highlights an important point, that is, although current investment flows into China are large, given its size they are not excessive and China can continue to absorb such flows for a long time.

Unlike the countries in Group I, China is evolving from a command economy to a market economy. The pace and sequencing of economic liberalisation has made the transition successful so far. Agricultural reforms started the process in the late 1970s and the reform process continued with the establishment of four special economic zones (SEZs) in 1980 (Shenzen, Zhuhai, Xiamen and Shantou). The areas were chosen in the provinces of Guandong and Fujian because of their proximity to Hong Kong, Chinese Taipei and Macao. All enterprises, i.e. both foreign-funded and domestic, in SEZs were taxed at a concessional rate of 15 per cent and allowed to import building materials, office and production equipment, vehicles, etc. free of import duties. In addition, imports of inputs for production of exports were permitted free of import duties and licensing restrictions.

Hong Kong and Chinese Taipei consequently became the major investors in China and a key to the success of the SEZs. By the late 1980s more than half of China's exports to the rest of the world were handled by Hong Kong, and 70 per cent of the cumulative value of $100 billion in FDI commitments to China between 1985 and 1994 were from Hong Kong, being directed toward export-oriented joint ventures largely in Guandong (World Bank 1994, *Global Finance*, November 1995). Guandong today accounts for about 40 per cent of China's exports and 10 per cent of its GDP (*Business China* 1996).

The dominance of Hong Kong in China's FDI and trade is due to several factors:

1. A significant amount of the investment from Hong Kong to China is actually from China itself, referred to as "roundtripping" in the literature, and it is estimated that it could account for as much as 25 per cent of the total FDI flows into China;

2. Although direct foreign investment has been permitted since 1980 in the SEZs, factors such as language, culture, and the need to identify joint venture partners have made Hong Kong the logical base for foreigners interested in investing in China; and

3.   China's major focus has been on strengthening economic relationships with, as well as encouraging investment by, overseas Chinese and most of them, including those from Chinese Taipei, have found Hong Kong to be a convenient base.

In the mid-1980s about 70 cities and counties were declared open coastal areas (OCAs) where FDI was encouraged by offering foreign enterprises basically the same concessions as available in the SEZs, except that the reduced corporate income tax was somewhat higher at 24 per cent. In 1992, the concessions available in OCAs were extended to 23 open border cities, cities on the Yangtze River and inland provincial capitals. These measures have helped to disperse FDI more widely, e.g., between 1979 and 1985 the SEZs accounted for over 90 per cent of the $4 billion invested in China but by 1993 the SEZs and 14 open cities accounted for less than half of all foreign equity projects. (*China Statistical Yearbook,* 1987-1994). Until 1992, FDI was concentrated in power and real estate development, i.e., hotels, tourism related activities and office buildings, but since then investment in the manufacturing sector has increased substantially.

There have been liberal and rapid approvals in the promoted areas because of weak central control, but China's FDI policy regime is complex and the rules and regulations lack transparency. China is much more restrictive than most countries in terms of sectors closed to foreign investment, and in investment screening, performance, local content and trade balancing requirements, Also, weak legal protection against expropriation and inadequate dispute settlement in China is an impediment to FDI.

Infrastructure bottlenecks in China, as in all of developing Asia (with the possible exception of Malaysia), are both a major disincentive and an opportunity for FDI. However, FDI in infrastructure development is constrained because of the lack of a comprehensive, realistic and transparent investment framework. For example, China received substantial private investment in the power sector until the government decided in early 1995 to reduce the fixed rate of return to 12 per cent a year, subsequently increased to 15 per cent, and since then no large power projects have been initiated.

India

The New Industrial Policy was initiated in July 1991 and a gradual process of economic reform covering investment deregulation, promotion of the private sector and trade liberalisation, has continued since then. The sectors in which only public investment was formerly permitted which have been opened to private investment include: mining, coal, hydrocarbons, power, air transport, ports, roads, telecommunications and banking. In addition, automobiles and textile production are no longer subject to licensing, the ready-to-wear garment industry, previously reserved for the small-scale sector, has been opened to large enterprises, and automatic approval of foreign majority ownership is allowed in a number of industries, while for the rest the approval process has been liberalised. As a result, the Foreign Investment Promotion Board's rejection rate fell from 40 to 50 per cent prior to 1991 to under 10 per cent in 1993, while about 30 per cent of approvals were through the automatic route.

The telecommunications sector has been opened up for the private provision of basic services, as well as value added services, and concessions for a number of regions in the country have been awarded to private operators, mostly joint ventures. The government is promoting foreign investment in the power sector by providing sovereign guarantees, a guaranteed rate of return on equity, and a five-year tax exemption for power projects in backward areas. Several power projects involving multinational corporations and joint ventures sponsored by non-resident Indians are underway or planned. It seems probable that most of the additional investment in power generation will come from the private sector.

Trade reforms since 1991 have considerably eased import licensing requirements and, as a result, the proportion of the manufacturing sector protected by import restrictions has been reduced from 90 per cent to 50 per cent. Import tariffs have also been gradually lowered, with the maximum tariff rate being reduced to 50 per cent from 400 per cent in the pre-reform period. As a result, the trade-weighted average tariff has declined to 27 per cent from 87 per cent in 1990. The rupee has been made convertible on the trade account and the real effective exchange rate has depreciated by 30 per cent since 1990, making exports much more attractive then before. However, India remains a relatively protected market and, as a result, there is a need for the government to screen and restrict investment aimed at the domestic market, which unfortunately neutralises India's most important attraction for FDI. The government has provided a number of concessions to export-oriented FDI, but labour market rigidities, relatively high wages in the organised sector, and inadequate and poor quality infrastructure have prevented any significant inflows into the export sector.

Although moving cautiously with its market liberalisation, India is committed to the process, and the reforms have begun to generate increasing FDI flows. FDI has more or less doubled every year since 1992 to an estimated $1.3 billion in 1995. However, investment is largely concentrated in infrastructure, particularly power and telecommunications; and petroleum refining, petrochemicals and automobiles in the manufacturing sector.

Future Trends in the Investment Environment and FDI in Asia

The key external factors likely to affect the investment environment and FDI flows in Asian countries are the trend in global FDI, the pace of trade liberalisation at home and China's impact on the "product cycle" pattern of Asian industrialisation. There can be different estimates of these developments, and our view is presented here. First, FDI flows to developing countries will continue to increase for the rest of the 1990s, and Asia will maintain its position as the major recipient of FDI. Second, tariff and non-tariff barriers will recede fairly quickly in developing Asian countries over the next decade and the main uncertainty is the pace of liberalisation in the more highly protected countries such as China and India. The primary concern in these countries is that if they open up their internal markets too quickly their inefficient industries, especially the state enterprises, will be overwhelmed. However, we assume that significant import liberalisation will take place in these countries as well. Third, we believe there is an unfounded fear that China, with its large potential market, high growth rate, huge demand for investment funds and seemingly inexhaustible supply of cheap labour, may crowd out FDI from other countries in the region and overwhelm labour-intensive exports of countries that are just beginning the process of outward oriented growth. The reasons for this view are: *(i)* investors will prefer to disperse FDI among as many countries as possible to reduce risk; *(ii)* out of the three types of FDI discussed earlier, export-oriented FDI is the only one where labour costs are important in the choice of the host country, and export-oriented FDI is likely to be only a small proportion of the total FDI coming into Asia; and *(iii)* in any case, the labour costs in China are likely to rise fairly quickly as the market-oriented reforms reduce, and ultimately eliminate, implicit subsidies in public housing, education and health care. It is against this background that we discuss in this section the likely trends in the economic environment and FDI flows in different countries/regions.

Southeast Asia

Southeast Asian countries, except Indonesia, are likely to continue to follow the "flying geese" or "product cycle" pattern of development with Malaysia and Thailand in the forefront, the Philippines and Vietnam in the middle and Cambodia, Laos and Myanmar bringing up the rear. While the economic environment for investment in Malaysia and Thailand should become even more open and neutral over time, their environment today is a good example of what it will be like in the future for other countries in this group.

FDI flows are likely to stabilize at the present high levels in Malaysia, grow slowly in Thailand, and increase rapidly in the Philippines and Viet Nam. Malaysia does not lack capital for its infrastructure investments and is fast becoming an important source of FDI in the region. Malaysia's FDI is primarily in the areas of its strengths, such as agribusiness, particularly palm oil, tourism (hotels, resorts, etc.) and infrastructure. However, Malaysia also remains a very attractive destination for FDI, particularly in electronics, and should easily maintain the current levels of inflow. In 1995, Thailand saw a dramatic reversal in the stagnating/declining trend of FDI observed during the past five years, and its emergence as a regional centre for the automobile industry, and possibly other high value engineering industries, should result in a steady increase in inflows from the level reached in 1995. Political and macroeconomic stability, trade liberalisation, deregulation, and the elimination of the power shortages in recent years have put the Philippines on a high growth path fuelled by FDI. Growth and FDI flows are likely to accelerate for the rest of the decade, as the Philippines catches up with its neighbours and begins to achieve its real economic potential. Viet Nam, under its market-oriented economic reforms, has liberalised trade, provided protection for property and ownership rights and incentives for FDI, which have resulted in an explosive growth in GDP, exports and FDI since 1992. This trend is likely to continue at least for the rest of the 1990s. Myanmar has the potential for following the same path as Viet Nam, but any significant economic developments there must await the resolution of its long-standing political problems.

The pattern of development in Indonesia, however, is likely to differ from the rest of Southeast Asia. The reason is that its size, and the potentially huge internal market associated with it, encourages the pursuit of what we described as a balanced growth strategy. Thus, there is a strong possibility of continuing separation between enterprises producing primarily for export and those producing for the domestic market, with the economic environment for the former moving towards that in other Southeast Asian countries, while for the latter, continuing to be restrictive, non-competitive and high cost. However, the resulting dual industrial structure is likely to make it difficult to sustain the high growth rates observed in the past, and that could generate pressures to reduce and ultimately eliminate barriers separating the export and the domestic markets. Until that happens, FDI in Indonesia will continue to be concentrated in infrastructure, chemicals (including petroleum), real estate development, particularly tourism-related, and natural resource based sectors. FDI in the manufacturing sector, while less than what it could be, will be substantial. It will be divided about equally, with half going to export-oriented industries, both labour-intensive ones in FTZs and capital-intensive, natural resource based sectors elsewhere, while the other half will be oriented towards consumer durables, consumer electronics, automobiles, food processing, and petrochemicals for the domestic market. Given Indonesia's rich natural resource endowment, abundant labour, large domestic market and huge infrastructure requirements, there is considerable scope for continued growth of FDI over the medium term.

China

The most important issue for China in the near future is how well Hong Kong will be assimilated into the Chinese economy after its handover in June 1997. Currently, Hong Kong is probably the most open economy in the world, the bulk of FDI into China is either from Hong Kong or channelled through it, and Hong Kong is the conduit for a major portion of China's trade. Thus a smooth and successful transition could lead to a further opening up of China and the resulting synergy would help sustain its current high rates of growth in GDP, exports and FDI. Since the start of the economic reforms in 1979, China has had a pragmatic approach towards economic issues, with the highest priority being attached to economic development, and there is every reason to expect that this will continue in the future. Therefore, our projections are based on the assumption that the return of Hong Kong to China will have a positive impact on both economies.

While FDI in the export sector will continue to expand due to the abundance of low wage labour in China and marketing capabilities and connections of the trading houses in Hong Kong, the majority of the investment in China will be for infrastructure and production for the domestic market. China not only has a huge and rapidly growing domestic market, but also a well-developed engineering industry and a large, well-educated and skilled labour force. As incomes rise, the domestic market for consumer durables should grow explosively and a substantial part of FDI will be targeted at this market. As fiscal incentives to foreign investors are reduced, access to the domestic market will be the main bargaining chip for China to achieve its goals of promoting certain industries, acquiring sophisticated technology and developing regions which thus far have been left out of the industrialisation process. While the investment environment for export-oriented industries may become more open, transparent and similar to other countries in Asia, FDI targeted at the domestic market will be faced with a complex and difficult environment, where the conditions of access will be largely a matter of negotiation.

The other area that is likely to receive huge amounts of FDI in China is infrastructure, particularly power and telecommunications. China has immense needs for investment in infrastructure to remain internationally competitive, and it will be seeking FDI for a major portion of this investment. The one thing that is retarding FDI in infrastructure in China is the absence of a comprehensive and transparent policy framework for private investment. While the lack of a framework has not, thus far, adversely affect investment in manufacturing and real estate development, the risks and size of investments involved in infrastructure projects give critical importance to the policy framework. It is assumed that such a framework will be in place soon, and investment in infrastructure will accelerate.

South Asia

Infrastructure, particularly power, hydrocarbons and telecommunications are likely to be the area of concentration for FDI in India. Private sector participation in these areas has been given the highest priority by the government. Power generation and distribution are open to private sector investment, but a lack of a comprehensive policy, and decisions on issues such as tariffs, subsidies and payment of dues by state authorities, are inhibiting investment despite widespread interest. Incentives for oil and gas exploration, along with the move towards privatisation, should make the hydrocarbon sector extremely attractive to foreign investors. Guidelines, regulations and modalities for private investment in telecommunications, ports, railways and roads are being developed. Most major TNCs in telecommunications have shown great interest in investing in India, and a number of projects are already underway in this sector. While these areas should absorb the bulk of the FDI in India in the next decade, there is considerable potential for FDI in the tourism sector, such as hotels, resorts, etc., but this sector is still virtually closed to foreign investment. However, this could change because growth in tourism has the potential of providing India with large foreign exchange earnings, and balance of payments considerations may be an inducement to opening the sector to FDI.

In manufacturing, the potentially important industries for FDI are automobiles and components, white goods and components, consumer electronics, chemicals, and food processing. Some of these could also emerge as major export industries, however, because of a significant anti-export bias in the trade regime and labour market rigidities, initially FDI in the manufacturing sector will be largely restricted to production for the domestic market.

Over the longer term the composition of FDI in manufacturing will depend upon the pace of market liberalisation. Although India has abundant labour, wages in the organised sector are relatively high because of its labour laws and powerful unions. However, India has some unique advantages, besides its size, which could help attract FDI to the manufacturing sector. These include: *(i)* English is a working language, which can involve considerable saving of time and money for foreign investors since neither written or oral instructions, have to be translated, technical materials can be easily adapted and used, and managers from the parent company can quickly begin to work locally; *(ii)* The legal system, although slow, is well established with a tradition for fairness; *(iii)* There is a strong engineering base, and although machinery and equipment may be obsolete, the basic engineering infrastructure to adapt and use new technologies already exists; and *(iv)* There is a large reservoir of educated, skilled human resources, and since labour laws and unions do not extend to professionals, salaries of engineers, managers and technical staff are relatively low.

Perhaps some of these factors have enabled India to carve out a market niche in the software industry[7], despite the country's inward orientation and poor infrastructure. India's software industry has been growing at over 40 per cent a year. Export earnings from software exceeded a billion dollars in 1995, despite the fact that most firms have had to construct their own export infrastructure, such as dedicated satellite links.

Given their size, comparisons between China and India are inevitable. When China began its "open door" policy in 1980, FDI responded slowly at first (less than 1 per cent of GDP in 1990) and then rapidly to today's high levels. A similar pattern seems likely to occur in India. Since 1991, when India initiated a process of liberalisation, FDI has grown from an insignificant amount to 0.4 per cent of GDP in 1995. This trend is expected to continue, with the ratio of FDI to GDP approaching 1 per cent in 1996 and 3 per cent to 4 per cent of GDP by the end of the decade.

Pakistan has many of the same advantages as India, i.e., the widespread use of English, an established Western-based legal system, a potentially large internal market, an outmoded but substantial engineering industry and abundant labour with good mechanical and industrial skills. It also has similar drawbacks, such as a highly protective trade regime, a large fiscal imbalance, inadequate and low quality infrastructure, poor enforcement of intellectual property rights, etc. Thus, most of the conclusions for India are also valid for Pakistan.

Pakistan opened its economy to FDI almost completely in 1991, and has been successful in attracting substantial inflows, particularly in infrastructure. It is also pursuing an ambitious programme of privatisation of public utilities, and that too has attracted considerable FDI. Investment flows to Pakistan are estimated to be about 1.2 per cent of GDP in 1995. The country's infrastructure investment needs are immense, and given its aggressive privatisation policy and a well thought out policy framework for FDI in the power sector, it should be able to attract large amounts in this sector. The major uncertainty for FDI will be Pakistan's poor record of political and macroeconomic stability.

Estimated FDI in 2001

To put the discussion in a perspective, it would be extremely useful to have some estimates of future FDI flows to Asia. Therefore, a simple exercise is undertaken to get an idea of the magnitudes involved. The two variables we used are GDP growth rates and projected FDI/GDP ratios. For the former, forecasts of the Asian Development Bank (1996 a and b), the World Bank (1996) and Project Link (United Nations, 1996) were used to derive the baseline GDP growth rate estimates for the period 1996 to 2001 (see Table 8). The high scenario assumes 1 percentage point higher growth rate for all the regions. Estimating the FDI/GDP ratio five years hence is much more difficult. We used the change in the ratio between 1990 and 1995 and the preceding discussion in this section on the likely developments in the investment environment in the different regions to make an estimate of the baseline FDI/GDP ratio in 2001. Some of the key underlying assumptions are: *(i)* a 20 per cent reduction in the FDI/ GDP ratio for China because of the elimination of "roundtripping" after the takeover of Hong Kong in 1997; *(ii)* FDI flows to India will closely follow the Chinese experience of the 1990 to 1995 period; *(iii)* while investment in Malaysia and Thailand will be more or less stable, FDI flows to Indonesia, Philippines and Viet Nam will increase rapidly for the next five years, and the increase in the FDI/GDP ratio for Southeast Asia will be about half that in the 1990 to 1995 period. The high scenario assumes that the FDI/GDP ratio would be 1 percentage point higher than the baseline ratio.

Based on the above assumptions, it is estimated that FDI flows to Asia in the year 2001 will be $101 to $134 billion (Table 9). This represents about a doubling of FDI in five years, which seems rather low compared to the fivefold increase between 1990 and 1995. However, the huge increase in the last five years was partly because of explosive growth in China, which cannot be sustained. For Asia excluding China, FDI in 2001 will be three to four times the 1995 level, which is substantially more than the increase of 2.25 times in the 1990 to 1995 period. The most rapid growth will take place in South Asia, where FDI will increase from the current level of about $2 billion to about $25 billion in 2001.

We also attempted to distribute the investment into three categories, i.e., export-oriented industry, domestic-market-oriented industry and infrastructure. Since such a distribution for current inflows is not available, these numbers are merely educated guesses, based on the discussion of regional trends earlier in this section. Our conclusion is that in South Asia, infrastructure will be the most important sector for FDI, accounting for 60 per cent of the total, and export-oriented FDI will make up a relatively small proportion, about 10 per cent of the total (see Table 10). Southeast Asia will be the only region in which export-oriented investment will dominate, but even there infrastructure and domestic-market-oriented industry will account for half of the total FDI. In China, the distribution between the three categories is likely to be more or less the same, with export-oriented FDI being concentrated in the coastal provinces. An interesting conclusion emerging from this exercise is that less than a third of the FDI flows to Asia in 2001 are likely to go into export industries, i.e. contrary to popular fears, FDI flows from the OECD countries to Asia are likely to generate substantially greater opportunities for exports from OECD countries to Asia than competition from Asian exports in OECD countries.

Table 8. **Estimated GDP Growth Rate, 1996-2001**

(average annual percentage growth)

Country/Region	Various Forecasts	Assumed Baseline Growth Rate	Assumed High Growth Rate
China		8.5	9.5
ADB[1]	9.0		
Project Link[2]	8.3		
IBRD[3]	8.0-9.0		
South Asia		6.0	7.0
ADB[1]	6.0		
IBRD[3]	5.4		
India			
ADB[4]	6.6		
Project Link[2]	6.6		
Southeast Asia		7.5	8.5
ADB[1]	7.7		
Indonesia			
ADB[1]	8.0		
Project Link[2]	7.5		
Malaysia			
ADB[1]	8.0		
Project Link[2]	8.2		
Thailand			
ADB[1]	8.2		
Project Link[2]	8.0		
Asia		7.2	8.2
ADB[1]	7.2		
IBRD[3]	7.2		

[1] 1996-98   [2] 1996-2000   [3] 1996-2005   [4] 1996-2001

Sources: ADB (1996a) ; ADB (1996b) ; World Bank (1996a) ; United Nations (joint project of University of Pennsylvania, United Nations, and University of Toronto).

229

Table 9. Estimating FDI in Developing Asia in the Year 2001

Country/Region	FDI	FDI/GDP (%)		GDP Growth Rate (%) 1990 to 1995	Growth Rate 1996 to 2001		FDI/GDP Ratio in 2001		FDI in 2001 ($ billion)	
		1990	1995		Low	High	Low	High	Low	High
China	38.0	1.0	5.7	10.5	8.5	9.5	4.5	5.5	49	63
Southeast Asia	15.5	1.4	2.7a	7.5b	7.5	8.5	3.5	4.5	31	42
South Asia	2.2	0.1	0.4	4.8c	6.0	7.0	3.0	4.0	21	29
Developing Asia	55.7	0.9	3.3	7.9	7.2	8.2	4.2	5.4	101	134

a. FDI to Indonesia, Malaysia and Thailand was $12.6 billion or 2.9 per cent of the GDP.
b. Growth was 8.4 per cent if Philippines is excluded.
c. Growth was 5.4 per cent in the year 1991 is excluded for India.

Source: World Bank (1996c)

Table 10. **Distribution of FDI by Sector in the Year 2001**

| Country/Region | Export Market | | Domestic Market | | | |
| | | | Infrastructure | | Others | |
	%	$ billion	%	$ billion	%	$ billion
China	30	15-19	40	20-25	30	15-19
Southeast Asia	50	16-21	30	9-13	20	6-8
South Asia	10	2-3	60	13-17	30	6-10
Developing Asia	32	33-43	41	42-55	27	27-37

Source: Authors' estimates.

Notes

1. The opinions expressed in this chapter are those of the authors and do not necessarily reflect those of the Asian Development Bank.

2. It could also be to get access to a protected market in a third country to which the host country has preferential access by not being subject to textile quotas or having membership in a trade bloc.

3. In the 19th and early 20th centuries, foreign investment in infrastructure, particularly railroads and canals, was important.

4. As countries move towards realistic exchange rates the popularity of such measures is also declining.

5. Most of the conclusions for India are also applicable to South Asia in general and Pakistan in particular.

6. Approvals for the four capital-intensive industries increased from 66 per cent of the total FDI approved in 1991 to 89 per cent in 1995. The bulk of these approvals were for petroleum refining, petrochemicals and paper, which undoubtedly generate exports but are a part of "natural resource seeking" FDI.

7. Indian schools turn out over 20 000 computer science engineers a year and it is estimated that the cost of an Indian software engineer is about one-fifth of an American equivalent.

231

References

AMSDEN, A.H. (1993), "Structural Macroeconomic Underpinnings of Effective Industrial Policy: Fast Growth in the 1980s in Five Asian Countries", *Paper No. 57*, MIT and New School for Social Research, New York.

ASIAN DEVELOPMENT BANK (1991), *Studies of Asian and Pacific Economic Issues*, vol. 9, No. 1, Manila.

ASIAN DEVELOPMENT BANK (1993), *Studies of Asian and Pacific Economic Issues*, vol. 11, No. 1, Manila.

ASIAN DEVELOPMENT BANK (1995), *Key Indicators of Developing Asian and Pacific Countries*, Oxford University Press (China) Ltd, Hong Kong.

ASIAN DEVELOPMENT BANK (1996a), *Asian Development Outlook 1996 and 1997*, Oxford University Press (China) Ltd, Hong Kong.

ASIAN DEVELOPMENT BANK (1996b), *Country Economic Reports, Various Countries*, Manila.

BACHMANN, H.B. (1991), *Industrialized Countries' Policies Affecting Foreign Direct Investment in Developing Countries*, World Bank, vol. 1: Main Report, Washington, D.C.

BALASUBRAMANYAN, V.N. and D. SAPSFORD (1994), *The Economics of International Investment*, Edward Elgar Publishing Ltd., Aldershot.

BANK FOR INTERNATIONAL SETTLEMENTS (1995), *International Banking and Financial Market Developments*, Washington, D.C.

BORA, B. and M. PANGESTU (eds.) (1996), *Priority Issues in Trade and Investment Liberalisation: Implications for the Asia Pacific Region*, Pacific Economic Cooperation Council, Singapore.

BRADFORD, C.I., Jr. (1987), "NICs and the Next-Tier NICs as Transitional Economies", *in* Bradford and Branson (eds.).

BRADFORD, C.I., Jr. and W.H. BRANSON (eds.) (1987), *Trade and Structural Change in Pacific Asia*, University of Chicago Press, Chicago.

BRADFORD, C.I., Jr. (1993), "The East Asian Development Experience", document prepared for the *Handbook of Economic Development*.

CAVANAGH, J., D. WYSHAM and M. ARRUDA (1994), *Beyond Bretton Woods: Alternative to the Global Economic Order*, Pluto Press, Colorado.

and Technology Ltd, Beijing.

DREYER, J.S. *et al.* (1991), *Industrialized Countries' Policies Affecting Foreign Direct Investment in Developing Countries*, World Bank, vol. 2: Country Studies, Washington, D.C.

DUNNING, J. (1996), "The Nature of Transnational Corporations and their Activities", *Transnational Corporations and World Development*, United Nations, New York.

ECONOMIST INTELLIGENCE UNIT (1995*a*), *Country Report, 3rd Quarter 1995: India and Nepal*, The Economist, London.

ECONOMIST INTELLIGENCE UNIT (1995*b*), *Country Report, 4th Quarter 1995: China and Mongolia*, The Economist, London.

ECONOMIST INTELLIGENCE UNIT (1995*c*), *Country Report, 4th Quarter 1995: Indonesia*, The Economist, London.

ECONOMIST INTELLIGENCE UNIT (1995*d*), *Country Report, 4th Quarter 1995: Malaysia and Brunei*, The Economist, London.

ECONOMIST INTELLIGENCE UNIT (1995*e*), *Country Report, 4th Quarter 1995: Thailand*, The Economist, London.

ECONOMIST INTELLIGENCE UNIT (1995 and 1996), *Business China* (various issues), The Economist, London.

ESCAP (1995*a*), *Foreign Investment Guidelines: Malaysia*, United Nations, New York.

ESCAP (1995*b*), *Foreign Investment Guidelines: Thailand*, United Nations, New York.

GLOBAL FINANCE (1995), Vol. 9, No. 11, November.

GOVERNMENT OF INDONESIA (1994), *Indonesia: A Brief Guide for Investors* (BPKM).

GUISINGER, S.E. (1985), *Investment Incentives and Performance Requirements*, Praeger Publishers, New York.

GUISINGER, S.E. and D. MCNULTY (1996), "Private Sector Responses to Investment Rules: Evidence on U.S. Investors in the APEC Region", *in* Bora and Pengestu (eds.).

HAQUE, I. (1991), "International Competitiveness: Interaction of the Public and the Private Sectors", *EDI Policy Seminar*, Seoul, 18-21 April 1990.

INSTITUTE OF SOUTHEAST ASIAN STUDIES (1995), *The New Wave of Foreign Direct Investment in Asia*, Singapore.

INTERNATIONAL FINANCE CORPORATION (1993*a*), *A Comparative Assessment of India's Foreign Investment Environment*, Part I: Synthesis, The World Bank, Washington, D.C.

INTERNATIONAL FINANCE CORPORATION (1993*b*), *A Comparative Assessment of India's Foreign Investment Environment*, Part II: Background Information, The World Bank, Washington, D.C.

INTERNATIONAL MONETARY FUND (1995), *Annual Report 1995*, Washington, D.C.

LALL, S. (1994), *Malaysia's Export Performance and its Sustainability*, Asian Development Bank Staff Study, Asian Development Bank, Manila.

LALL, S. and K. RAO (forthcoming), *Indonesia: Sustaining Manufactured Export Growth*, vol. 1, Main report, Asian Development Bank Staff Study, Asian Development Bank, Manila.

MALAYSIAN INDUSTRIAL DEVELOPMENT AUTHORITY (1992 and 1993), *Malaysia: Investment in the Manufacturing Sector*, Percetakan Mega Sdn. Bhd, Malaysia.

OECD (1993*a*), *Promoting Foreign Direct Investment in Developing Countries*, Paris.

OECD (1993*b*), *Foreign Direct Investment Relations between the OECD and the Dynamic Asian Economies*, Paris.

OECD (1994*a*), *Statistics on International Direct Investment of Dynamic Non-Member Economies in Asia and Latin America*, vol. 2, Paris.

OECD (1994*b*), *International Direct Investment Statistics Yearbook — 1994*, Paris.

OECD (*1995a*), *Foreign Direct Investment: OECD Countries and Dynamic Economies of Asia and Latin America*, Paris.

OECD (1995*b*), *Linkages: OECD and Major Developing Economies*, OECD Development Centre, Paris.

OECD (1995*c*), *Geographical Distribution of Financial Flows*, Paris.

PANGESTU, M. (1995), "Evolution of Liberalization Policies Affecting Investment Flows in the Asia Pacific", papers prepared for the *FIAS High-Level Roundtable on Competition for Foreign Direct Investment-Implications for Asia and the Pacific*, Bangkok, 14-15 December.

PIRNIA, N. (1995), *The Role of Investment Incentives in Influencing Investors' Location Choices*, Foreign Investment Advisory Service (FIAS), The World Bank, Washington D.C.

PORTER, M. (1990), *The Competitive Advantage of Nations*, The Free Press, New York.

RANA, P. and N. HAMID (1995*)*, *From Centrally Planned to Market Economies: The Asian Approach*, vol. 1: An Overview, Oxford University Press, Inc, New York.

SHAH, A. (1995), *Fiscal Incentives for Investment and Innovation*, Oxford University Press, Inc, New York.

UNCTAD, Commision on International Investment and Transnational Corporations (1995a), *An Investment Guide for Malaysia*, United Nations, NewYork.

UNCTAD, Commision on International Investment and Transnational Corporations (1995b), *An Investment Guide for Thailand*, United Nations, NewYork.

UNITED NATIONS CONFERENCE ON TRADE AND DEVELOPMENT (1996*)*, *Transnational Corporations and World Development*, International Thomson Business Publishing, Inc, Boston.

UNITED NATIONS (1996), *Project Link, World Outlook*, Department of Economic and Social Information and Policy Analysis, New York.

WORLD BANK (1993), *A Comparative Assessment of India's Foreign Investment Environment,* Part I -Synthesis, Part II -Background Information, Washington, D.C.

WORLD BANK (1994*a*), *China: Foreign Trade Reform,* The International Bank for Reconstruction and Development, Washington, D.C.

WORLD BANK (1994*b*), *East Asia's Trade and Investment,* Washington, D.C.

WORLD BANK (1995), *China: Tax Policy Toward Foreign Direct Investment,* Washington, D.C.

WORLD BANK (1996*a*), *Global Economic Prospects and the Developing Countries,* Washington, D.C.

WORLD BANK (1996*b*), *The World Bank Atlas,* Washington, D.C.

WORLD BANK (1996*c*), *World Debt Tables,* Washington, D.C.

YAN, W. and J. SHILLING (1995), *Managing Capital Flows in East Asia,* The World Bank, Washington, D.C.

Second International Forum on Asian Perspectives

Programme

Second International Forum on Asian Perspectives

Experts Seminar

Monday, 3 June 1996

Co-Chairmen

Jean Bonvin, President,
OECD Development Centre

Pierre Uhel, Vice President,
Asian Development Bank

Opening Session

Welcoming Remarks
and Introduction

Jean Bonvin, President,
OECD Development Centre

Pierre Uhel, Vice-President,
Asian Development Bank

Co-Chairmen for
the Seminar

Vishvanath V. Desai, Director and Chief Economist,
Asian Development Bank

Ulrich Hiemenz, Director for Co-ordination,
OECD Development Centre

Session II: The Economic Environment for Investment in Asia

Naved Hamid and Naomi Chakwin,
(presented by Naved Hamid)
Asian Development Bank

Lead discussants:

Vincent Cable, Chief Economist,
Shell International UK

Ippei Yamazawa, Professor of Economics,
Hitotsubashi University, formerly Japan's
representative to APEC's Eminent Persons Group

Session III: Systems of Corporate Governance

Jean-Pierre Lehmann, Director,
European Institute of Japanese Studies

Lead discussants:

Supachai Panitchpakdi, Member of Parliament and
formerly Deputy Prime Minister and Finance
Minister, Thailand

Olivier Bouin, OECD Development Centre

Open discussion on Session II and III

Session IV: The Institutional Environment for Investments in China and ASEAN: Current Situation and Trends

Jesus Estanislao, President,
University of Asia and the Pacific, The Philippines
(presented by Ulrich Hiemenz)

Lead discussants:

Pierre Defraigne, Director, North-South Relations,
DGIB, European Commission

Tran Xuan Gia, First Vice Minister
of Planning and Investment, Vietnam

Session V: Natural Resources, Economic Structure, and Asian Infrastructure

Douglas H. Brooks and Elizabeth E. Leuterio
(Presented by Douglas H. Brooks)
Asian Development Bank

Lead discussants:

William Nicol, OECD Directorate for
Development Co-operation

Zhang Xiaoqiang, Director,
Department of Foreign Investment Utilisation,
State Planning Commission, China

*Update on negotiations towards a Multilateral
Agreement on Investment*

Rainer Geiger, Deputy Director, OECD Directorate
for Financial, Fiscal and Enterprise Affairs

Open discussion on Sessions IV and V

Session VI: Euro-Asian Corporate Alliances

Jon Sigurdson, Professor of Research Policy
and Director of the Research Policy Institute,
Lund University

Lead discussants:

N. Vaghul, Chairman of the Industrial Credit and
Investment Corporation of India, Ltd.

Charles Oman, OECD Development Centre

Open discussion and conclusions

Conference

Tuesday, 4 June 1996

Welcoming Remarks

Jean Bonvin, President,
OECD Development Centre

Pierre Uhel, Vice President,
Asian Development Bank

Inauguration

Jean Lemierre, Directeur du Trésor, France

Panel followed by
open discussion

Supachai Panitchpakdi, Member of Parliament
formerly Deputy Prime Minister and Finance
Minister, Thailand

Willy de Clercq, President of the External
Economic Affairs Commission of the European
Parliament and formerly Commissioner of the
European Commission

Tran Xuan Gia, First Vice Minister of Planning and
Investment, Vietnam

Xavier Musca, Deputy Director, Direction du
Trésor, in charge of Bilateral Affairs, France

Zhang Xiaoqiang, Director, Department of Foreign
Investment Utilisation, State Planning
Commission, China

Nicolas Imboden, Delegate of the Government of
Switzerland for Trade Agreements, Federal
Department of Public Economy

Open discussion

Panel followed by
open discussion

Pierre Defraigne, Director, North-South Relations,
DG IB, European Commission

Ippei Yamazawa, Professor of Economics,
Hitotsubashi University, formerly Japan's
representative to APEC's Eminent Persons Group

Hugh P. Barras, Director of International Affairs and Chief Executive Officer of Alcatel Standard A.G., France

Narayanan Vaghul, Chairman, Industrial Credit and Investment Corporation of India

William Witherell, Director, OECD Directorate for Financial, Fiscal and Enterprise Affairs

Makoto Taniguchi, Deputy Secretary General, OECD

Open discussion

End of Conference

LIST OF PARTICIPANTS

| Co-Chairmen | Jean Bonvin, President, OECD Development Centre |
| | Pierre Uhel, Vice President, Asian Development Bank |

High-Level Panel 4 June 1996

Hugh P. Barras	Chief Executive Officer and Director of International Affairs, Alcatel Standard A. G. France
Willy de Clercq	Member of the European Parliament, President of the External Economic Affairs Commission, Strasbourg, France
Nicolas Imboden	Délégué du Conseil fédéral, Office fédéral des Affaires économiques extérieures, Département fédéral de l'Économie publique, Switzerland
Jean Lemierre	Directeur du Trésor, Ministère de l'Économie et des Finances, France
Xavier Musca	Sous-directeur, Direction du Trésor en charge des Affaires bilatérales, France
Supachai Panitchpakdi	Member of Parliament, Thailand
Makoto Taniguchi	Deputy Secretary General, OECD
Tran Xuan Gia	First Vice Minister of Planning and Investment, Vietnam
Narayanan Vaghul	Chairman, Industrial Credit and Investment Corporation of India
William Witherell	Director OECD Directorate for Financial, Fiscal and Enterprise Affairs
Ippei Yamazawa	Professor of Economics, Hitotsubashi University, Japan
Zhang Xiaoqiang	Director, State Planning Commission, Department of Foreign Investment Utilisation, China

Authors and Expert Discussants - Experts' Seminar 3 June 1996

Olivier Bouin — Economist, OECD Development Centre

Douglas Brooks — Economist, Economics and Development Resource Center Asian Development Bank

Vincent Cable — Chief Economist, Shell International UK

Pierre Defraigne — Director, DG IB, Commission of the European Communities

Vishvanath V. Desai — Director and Chief Economist, Asian Development Bank

Rainer Geiger — Deputy Director, OECD Directorate for Financial, Fiscal and Enterprise Affairs

Naved Hamid — Senior Economist, Programs Department, East Division 2, Asian Development Bank

Ulrich Hiemenz — Director for Co-ordination, OECD Development Centre

Jean-Pierre Lehmann — Director, The European Institute of Japanese Studies, Stockholm School of Economics

William Nicol — Head of Division, OECD Development Co-operation Directorate

Charles Oman — Senior Economist, OECD Development Centre

Jon Sigurdson — Research Director, Research Policy Institute, University of Lund, Sweden

Ippei Yamazawa — Professor of Economics, Hitotsubashi University, Japan

Asian Development Bank
(in addition to those mentioned in the programme)

Mr. Barun Roy	Information Officer
Ms. Dorte Kabell	Strategy and Policy Officer

OECD Development Centre
(in addition to those mentioned in the programme)

Giulio Fossi	Head of External Co-operation Programme
Catherine Duport	Principal Administrator
Kiichiro Fukasaku	Principal Administrator
Isabelle Cornelis	Head of Library
Colm Foy	Head of Publications and Information
Henny Helmich	Administrator External Co-operation Programme
Byung-Hwa Lee	Visiting Fellow
Jianling Gai	Consultant
Jody Kaylor	Conference Secretariat
Sandra Lloyd	Conference Secretariat

MAIN SALES OUTLETS OF OECD PUBLICATIONS
PRINCIPAUX POINTS DE VENTE DES PUBLICATIONS DE L'OCDE

AUSTRALIA – AUSTRALIE
D.A. Information Services
648 Whitehorse Road, P.O.B 163
Mitcham, Victoria 3132   Tel. (03) 9210.7777
Fax: (03) 9210.7788

AUSTRIA – AUTRICHE
Gerold & Co.
Graben 31
Wien I   Tel. (0222) 533.50.14
Fax: (0222) 512.47.31.29

BELGIUM – BELGIQUE
Jean De Lannoy
Avenue du Roi, Koningslaan 202
B-1060 Bruxelles Tel. (02) 538.51.69/538.08.41
Fax: (02) 538.08.41

CANADA
Renouf Publishing Company Ltd.
5369 Canotek Road
Unit 1
Ottawa, Ont. K1J 9J3   Tel. (613) 745.2665
Fax: (613) 745.7660

Stores:
71 1/2 Sparks Street
Ottawa, Ont. K1P 5R1   Tel. (613) 238.8985
Fax: (613) 238.6041

12 Adelaide Street West
Toronto, QN M5H 1L6   Tel. (416) 363.3171
Fax: (416) 363.5963

Les Éditions La Liberté Inc.
3020 Chemin Sainte-Foy
Sainte-Foy, PQ G1X 3V6 Tel. (418) 658.3763
Fax: (418) 658.3763

Federal Publications Inc.
165 University Avenue, Suite 701
Toronto, ON M5H 3B8   Tel. (416) 860.1611
Fax: (416) 860.1608

Les Publications Fédérales
1185 Université
Montréal, QC H3B 3A7   Tel. (514) 954.1633
Fax: (514) 954.1635

CHINA – CHINE
Book Dept., China Natinal Publiations
Import and Export Corporation (CNPIEC)
16 Gongti E. Road, Chaoyang District
Beijing 100020 Tel. (10) 6506-6688 Ext. 8402
(10) 6506-3101

CHINESE TAIPEI – TAIPEI CHINOIS
Good Faith Worldwide Int'l. Co. Ltd.
9th Floor, No. 118, Sec. 2
Chung Hsiao E. Road
Taipei   Tel. (02) 391.7396/391.7397
Fax: (02) 394.9176

CZECH REPUBLIC –
RÉPUBLIQUE TCHÈQUE
National Information Centre
NIS – prodejna
Konviktská 5
Praha 1 – 113 57   Tel. (02) 24.23.09.07
Fax: (02) 24.22.94.33
E-mail: nkposp@dec.niz.cz
Internet: http://www.nis.cz

DENMARK – DANEMARK
Munksgaard Book and Subscription Service
35, Nørre Søgade, P.O. Box 2148
DK-1016 København K   Tel. (33) 12.85.70
Fax: (33) 12.93.87

J. H. Schultz Information A/S,
Herstedvang 12,
DK – 2620 Albertslung   Tel. 43 63 23 00
Fax: 43 63 19 69
Internet: s-info@inet.uni-c.dk

EGYPT – ÉGYPTE
The Middle East Observer
41 Sherif Street
Cairo   Tel. (2) 392.6919
Fax: (2) 360.6804

FINLAND – FINLANDE
Akateeminen Kirjakauppa
Keskuskatu 1, P.O. Box 128
00100 Helsinki

Subscription Services/Agence d'abonnements :
P.O. Box 23
00100 Helsinki   Tel. (358) 9.121.4403
Fax: (358) 9.121.4450

*FRANCE
OECD/OCDE
Mail Orders/Commandes par correspondance :
2, rue André-Pascal
75775 Paris Cedex 16 Tel. 33 (0)1.45.24.82.00
Fax: 33 (0)1.49.10.42.76
Telex: 640048 OCDE
Internet: Compte.PUBSINQ@oecd.org

Orders via Minitel, France only/
Commandes par Minitel, France
exclusivement : 36 15 OCDE

OECD Bookshop/Librairie de l'OCDE :
33, rue Octave-Feuillet
75016 Paris   Tel. 33 (0)1.45.24.81.81
33 (0)1.45.24.81.67

Dawson
B.P. 40
91121 Palaiseau Cedex   Tel. 01.89.10.47.00
Fax: 01.64.54.83.26

Documentation Française
29, quai Voltaire
75007 Paris   Tel. 01.40.15.70.00

Economica
49, rue Héricart
75015 Paris   Tel. 01.45.78.12.92
Fax: 01.45.75.05.67

Gibert Jeune (Droit-Économie)
6, place Saint-Michel
75006 Paris   Tel. 01.43.25.91.19

Librairie du Commerce International
10, avenue d'Iéna
75016 Paris   Tel. 01.40.73.34.60

Librairie Dunod
Université Paris-Dauphine
Place du Maréchal-de-Lattre-de-Tassigny
75016 Paris   Tel. 01.44.05.40.13

Librairie Lavoisier
11, rue Lavoisier
75008 Paris   Tel. 01.42.65.39.95

Librairie des Sciences Politiques
30, rue Saint-Guillaume
75007 Paris   Tel. 01.45.48.36.02

P.U.F.
49, boulevard Saint-Michel
75005 Paris   Tel. 01.43.25.83.40

Librairie de l'Université
12a, rue Nazareth
13100 Aix-en-Provence   Tel. 04.42.26.18.08

Documentation Française
165, rue Garibaldi
69003 Lyon   Tel. 04.78.63.32.23

Librairie Decitre
29, place Bellecour
69002 Lyon   Tel. 04.72.40.54.54

Librairie Sauramps
Le Triangle
34967 Montpellier Cedex 2 Tel. 04.67.58.85.15
Fax: 04.67.58.27.36

A la Sorbonne Actual
23, rue de l'Hôtel-des-Postes
06000 Nice   Tel. 04.93.13.77.75
Fax: 04.93.80.75.69

GERMANY – ALLEMAGNE
OECD Bonn Centre
August-Bebel-Allee 6
D-53175 Bonn   Tel. (0228) 959.120
Fax: (0228) 959.12.17

GREECE – GRÈCE
Librairie Kauffmann
Stadiou 28
10564 Athens   Tel. (01) 32.55.321
Fax: (01) 32.30.320

HONG-KONG
Swindon Book Co. Ltd.
Astoria Bldg. 3F
34 Ashley Road, Tsimshatsui
Kowloon, Hong Kong   Tel. 2376.2062
Fax: 2376.0685

HUNGARY – HONGRIE
Euro Info Service
Margitsziget, Európa Ház
1138 Budapest   Tel. (1) 111.60.61
Fax: (1) 302.50.35
E-mail: euroinfo@mail.matav.hu
Internet: http://www.euroinfo.hu//index.html

ICELAND – ISLANDE
Mál og Menning
Laugavegi 18, Pósthólf 392
121 Reykjavik   Tel. (1) 552.4240
Fax: (1) 562.3523

INDIA – INDE
Oxford Book and Stationery Co.
Scindia House
New Delhi 110001   Tel. (11) 331.5896/5308
Fax: (11) 332.2639
E-mail: oxford.publ@axcess.net.in

17 Park Street
Calcutta 700016   Tel. 240832

INDONESIA – INDONÉSIE
Pdii-Lipi
P.O. Box 4298
Jakarta 12042   Tel. (21) 573.34.67
Fax: (21) 573.34.67

IRELAND – IRLANDE
Government Supplies Agency
Publications Section
4/5 Harcourt Road
Dublin 2   Tel. 661.31.11
Fax: 475.27.60

ISRAEL – ISRAËL
Praedicta
5 Shatner Street
P.O. Box 34030
Jerusalem 91430   Tel. (2) 652.84.90/1/2
Fax: (2) 652.84.93

R.O.Y. International
P.O. Box 13056
Tel Aviv 61130   Tel. (3) 546 1423
Fax: (3) 546 1442
E-mail: royil@netvision.net.il

Palestinian Authority/Middle East:
INDEX Information Services
P.O.B. 19502
Jerusalem   Tel. (2) 627.16.34
Fax: (2) 627.12.19

ITALY – ITALIE
Libreria Commissionaria Sansoni
Via Duca di Calabria, 1/1
50125 Firenze   Tel. (055) 64.54.15
Fax: (055) 64.12.57
E-mail: licosa@ftbcc.it

Via Bartolini 29
20155 Milano   Tel. (02) 36.50.83

Editrice e Libreria Herder
Piazza Montecitorio 120
00186 Roma   Tel. 679.46.28
Fax: 678.47.51

Libreria Hoepli
Via Hoepli 5
20121 Milano   Tel. (02) 86.54.46
                      Fax: (02) 805.28.86
Libreria Scientifica
Dott. Lucio de Biasio 'Aeiou'
Via Coronelli, 6
20146 Milano   Tel. (02) 48.95.45.52
                      Fax: (02) 48.95.45.48

JAPAN – JAPON
OECD Tokyo Centre
Landic Akasaka Building
2-3-4 Akasaka, Minato-ku
Tokyo 107   Tel. (81.3) 3586.2016
                      Fax: (81.3) 3584.7929

KOREA – CORÉE
Kyobo Book Centre Co. Ltd.
P.O. Box 1658, Kwang Hwa Moon
Seoul   Tel. 730.78.91
                      Fax: 735.00.30

MALAYSIA – MALAISIE
University of Malaya Bookshop
University of Malaya
P.O. Box 1127, Jalan Pantai Baru
59700 Kuala Lumpur
Malaysia   Tel. 756.5000/756.5425
                      Fax: 756.3246

MEXICO – MEXIQUE
OECD Mexico Centre
Edificio INFOTEC
Av. San Fernando no. 37
Col. Toriello Guerra
Tlalpan C.P. 14050
Mexico D.F.   Tel. (525) 528.10.38
                      Fax: (525) 606.13.07
E-mail: ocde@rtn.net.mx

NETHERLANDS – PAYS-BAS
SDU Uitgeverij Plantijnstraat
Externe Fondsen
Postbus 20014
2500 EA's-Gravenhage Tel. (070) 37.89.880
Voor bestellingen: Fax: (070) 34.75.778

Subscription Agency/Agence d'abonnements :
SWETS & ZEITLINGER BV
Heereweg 347B
P.O. Box 830
2160 SZ Lisse   Tel. 252.435.111
                      Fax: 252.415.888

**NEW ZEALAND –
NOUVELLE-ZÉLANDE**
GPLegislation Services
P.O. Box 12418
Thorndon, Wellington Tel. (04) 496.5655
                      Fax: (04) 496.5698

NORWAY – NORVÈGE
NIC INFO A/S
Ostensjoveien 18
P.O. Box 6512 Etterstad
0606 Oslo   Tel. (22) 97.45.00
                      Fax: (22) 97.45.45

PAKISTAN
Mirza Book Agency
65 Shahrah Quaid-E-Azam
Lahore 54000   Tel. (42) 735.36.01
                      Fax: (42) 576.37.14

PHILIPPINE – PHILIPPINES
International Booksource Center Inc.
Rm 179/920 Cityland 10 Condo Tower 2
HV dela Costa Ext cor Valero St.
Makati Metro Manila   Tel. (632) 817 9676
                      Fax: (632) 817 1741

POLAND – POLOGNE
Ars Polona
00-950 Warszawa
Krakowskie Prezdmiescie 7 Tel. (22) 264760
                      Fax: (22) 265334

PORTUGAL
Livraria Portugal
Rua do Carmo 70-74
Apart. 2681
1200 Lisboa   Tel. (01) 347.49.82/5
                      Fax: (01) 347.02.64

SINGAPORE – SINGAPOUR
Ashgate Publishing
Asia Pacific Pte. Ltd
Golden Wheel Building, 04-03
41, Kallang Pudding Road
Singapore 349316   Tel. 741.5166
                      Fax: 742.9356

SPAIN – ESPAGNE
Mundi-Prensa Libros S.A.
Castelló 37, Apartado 1223
Madrid 28001   Tel. (91) 431.33.99
                      Fax: (91) 575.39.98
E-mail: mundiprensa@tsai.es
Internet: http://www.mundiprensa.es

Mundi-Prensa Barcelona
Consell de Cent No. 391
08009 – Barcelona   Tel. (93) 488.34.92
                      Fax: (93) 487.76.59

Libreria de la Generalitat
Palau Moja
Rambla dels Estudis, 118
08002 – Barcelona
        (Suscripciones) Tel. (93) 318.80.12
        (Publicaciones) Tel. (93) 302.67.23
                      Fax: (93) 412.18.54

SRI LANKA
Centre for Policy Research
c/o Colombo Agencies Ltd.
No. 300-304, Galle Road
Colombo 3   Tel. (1) 574240, 573551-2
                      Fax: (1) 575394, 510711

SWEDEN – SUÈDE
CE Fritzes AB
S–106 47 Stockholm   Tel. (08) 690.90.90
                      Fax: (08) 20.50.21

For electronic publications only/
Publications électroniques seulement
STATISTICS SWEDEN
Informationsservice
S-115 81 Stockholm   Tel. 8 783 5066
                      Fax: 8 783 4045

Subscription Agency/Agence d'abonnements :
Wennergren-Williams Info AB
P.O. Box 1305
171 25 Solna   Tel. (08) 705.97.50
                      Fax: (08) 27.00.71

Liber distribution
Internatinal organizations
Fagerstagatan 21
S-163 52 Spanga

SWITZERLAND – SUISSE
Maditec S.A. (Books and Periodicals/Livres
et périodiques)
Chemin des Palettes 4
Case postale 266
1020 Renens VD 1   Tel. (021) 635.08.65
                      Fax: (021) 635.07.80

Librairie Payot S.A.
4, place Pépinet
CP 3212
1002 Lausanne   Tel. (021) 320.25.11
                      Fax: (021) 320.25.14

Librairie Unilivres
6, rue de Candolle
1205 Genève   Tel. (022) 320.26.23
                      Fax: (022) 329.73.18

Subscription Agency/Agence d'abonnements :
Dynapresse Marketing S.A.
38, avenue Vibert
1227 Carouge   Tel. (022) 308.08.70
                      Fax: (022) 308.07.99
See also – Voir aussi :
OECD Bonn Centre
August-Bebel-Allee 6
D-53175 Bonn (Germany) Tel. (0228) 959.120
                      Fax: (0228) 959.12.17

THAILAND – THAÏLANDE
Suksit Siam Co. Ltd.
113, 115 Fuang Nakhon Rd.
Opp. Wat Rajbopith
Bangkok 10200   Tel. (662) 225.9531/2
                      Fax: (662) 222.5188

**TRINIDAD & TOBAGO, CARIBBEAN
TRINITÉ-ET-TOBAGO, CARAÏBES**
Systematics Studies Limited
9 Watts Street
Curepe
Trinidad & Tobago, W.I. Tel. (1809) 645.3475
                      Fax: (1809) 662.5654
E-mail: tobe@trinidad.net

TUNISIA – TUNISIE
Grande Librairie Spécialisée
Fendri Ali
Avenue Haffouz Imm El-Intilaka
Bloc B 1 Sfax 3000   Tel. (216-4) 296 855
                      Fax: (216-4) 298.270

TURKEY – TURQUIE
Kültür Yayinlari Is-Türk Ltd.
Atatürk Bulvari No. 191/Kat 13
06684 Kavaklidere/Ankara
                      Tel. (312) 428.11.40 Ext. 2458
                      Fax : (312) 417.24.90

Dolmabahce Cad. No. 29
Besiktas/Istanbul   Tel. (212) 260 7188

UNITED KINGDOM – ROYAUME-UNI
The Stationery Office Ltd.
Postal orders only:
P.O. Box 276, London SW8 5DT
Gen. enquiries   Tel. (171) 873 0011
                      Fax: (171) 873 8463

The Stationery Office Ltd.
Postal orders only:
49 High Holborn, London WC1V 6HB
Branches at: Belfast, Birmingham, Bristol,
Edinburgh, Manchester

UNITED STATES – ÉTATS-UNIS
OECD Washington Center
2001 L Street N.W., Suite 650
Washington, D.C. 20036-4922
                      Tel. (202) 785.6323
                      Fax: (202) 785.0350
Internet: washcont@oecd.org

Subscriptions to OECD periodicals may also
be placed through main subscription agencies.

Les abonnements aux publications périodiques
de l'OCDE peuvent être souscrits auprès des
principales agences d'abonnement.

Orders and inquiries from countries where Distributors have not yet been appointed should be
sent to: OECD Publications, 2, rue André-Pascal, 75775 Paris Cedex 16, France.

Les commandes provenant de pays où l'OCDE
n'a pas encore désigné de distributeur peuvent
être adressées aux Éditions de l'OCDE, 2, rue
André-Pascal, 75775 Paris Cedex 16, France.

12-1996

OECD PUBLICATIONS, 2, rue André-Pascal, 75775 PARIS CEDEX 16
PRINTED IN FRANCE
(41 97 01 1) ISBN 92-64-15408-6 – No. 49235 1997